THE HO

BARANKO

COLORS: DAVE STEWART & CHARLIE KIRCHOFF

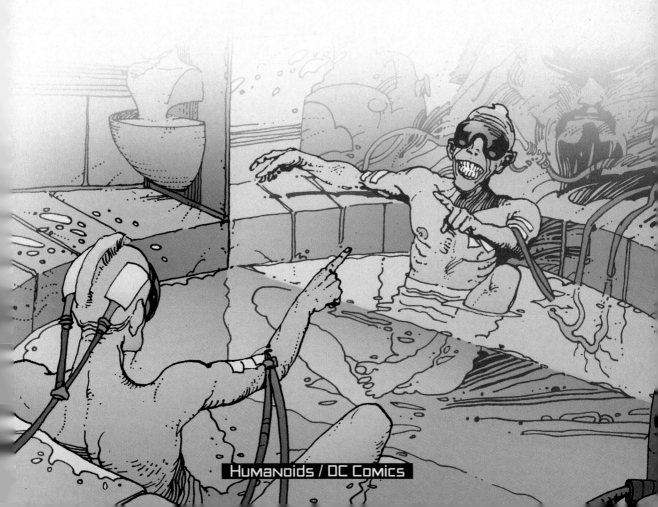

Humanoids / DC Comics

BARANKO
Writer/Artist
DAVE STEWART
Colors p. 3-48
CHARLIE KIRCHOFF
Colors p. 49-140
PAT MCGREAL with BARANKO
Translation

THIERRY FRISSEN
Book Designer
PAUL BENJAMIN & FABRICE GIGER
Editors, Original Edition
SUSAN M. GARRETT
Assistant Editor, Collected Edition

THE HORDE, Humanoids Publishing. PO Box 931658, Hollywood, CA 90094.
This is a publication of DC Comics, 1700 Broadway, New York, NY 10019.

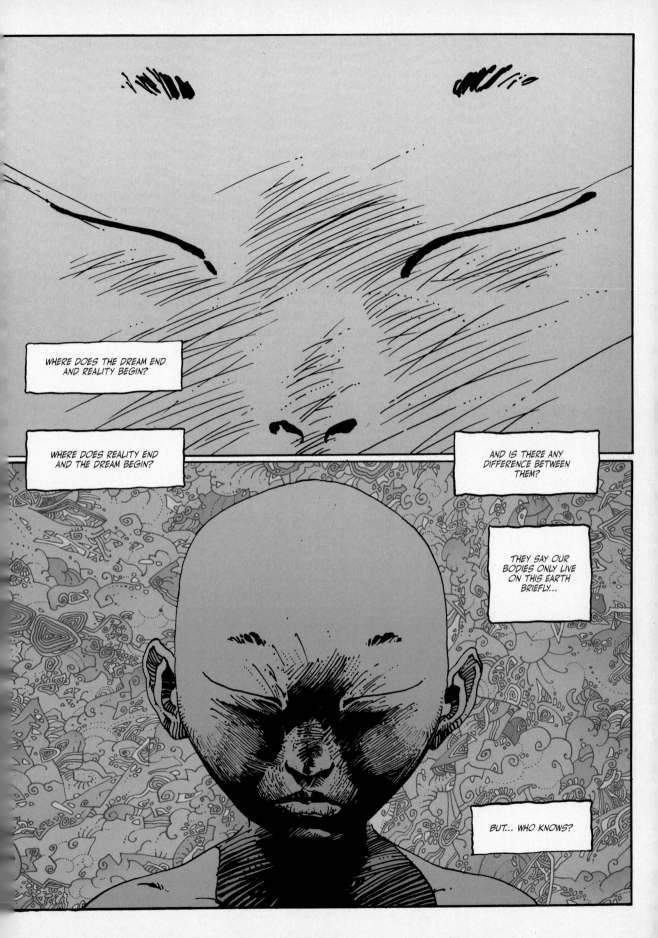

WHERE DOES THE DREAM END AND REALITY BEGIN?

WHERE DOES REALITY END AND THE DREAM BEGIN?

AND IS THERE ANY DIFFERENCE BETWEEN THEM?

THEY SAY OUR BODIES ONLY LIVE ON THIS EARTH BRIEFLY...

BUT... WHO KNOWS?

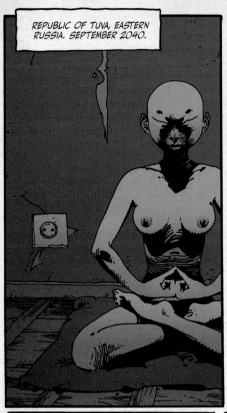

REPUBLIC OF TUVA, EASTERN RUSSIA. SEPTEMBER 2040.

RAIN.

IT'S *ALWAYS* RAINING IN KYZYL.

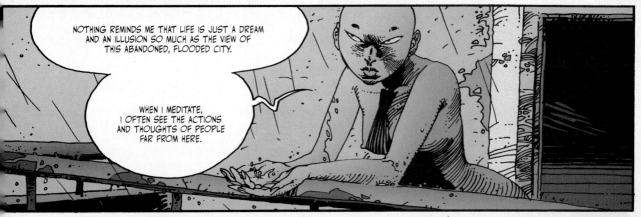

NOTHING REMINDS ME THAT LIFE IS JUST A DREAM AND AN ILLUSION SO MUCH AS THE VIEW OF THIS ABANDONED, FLOODED CITY.

WHEN I MEDITATE, I OFTEN SEE THE ACTIONS AND THOUGHTS OF PEOPLE FAR FROM HERE.

THEY FILL THEIR CONSCIOUSNESSES WITH PASSION AND DESIRE...

AND COMPASSION FOR THEM FILLS MY HEART.

BECAUSE DESIRE LEADS TO DISSATISFACTION, DISSATISFACTION LEADS TO FRUSTRATION, FRUSTRATION LEADS TO HATRED.

OM MANI PADME HUM...

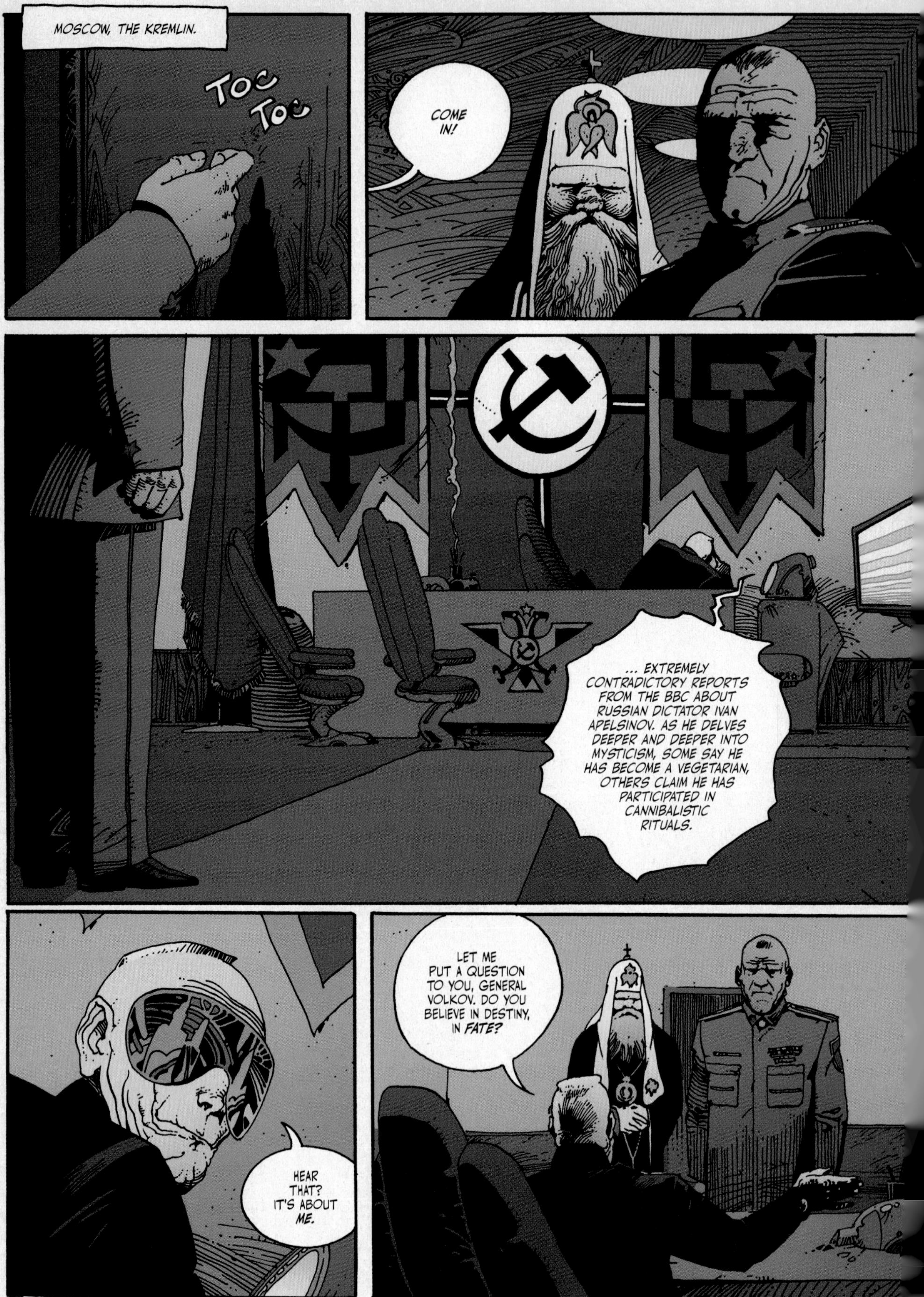
MOSCOW, THE KREMLIN.
TOC TOC
COME IN!
... EXTREMELY CONTRADICTORY REPORTS FROM THE BBC ABOUT RUSSIAN DICTATOR IVAN APELSINOV. AS HE DELVES DEEPER AND DEEPER INTO MYSTICISM, SOME SAY HE HAS BECOME A VEGETARIAN, OTHERS CLAIM HE HAS PARTICIPATED IN CANNIBALISTIC RITUALS.
HEAR THAT? IT'S ABOUT *ME.*
LET ME PUT A QUESTION TO YOU, GENERAL VOLKOV. DO YOU BELIEVE IN DESTINY, IN *FATE?*

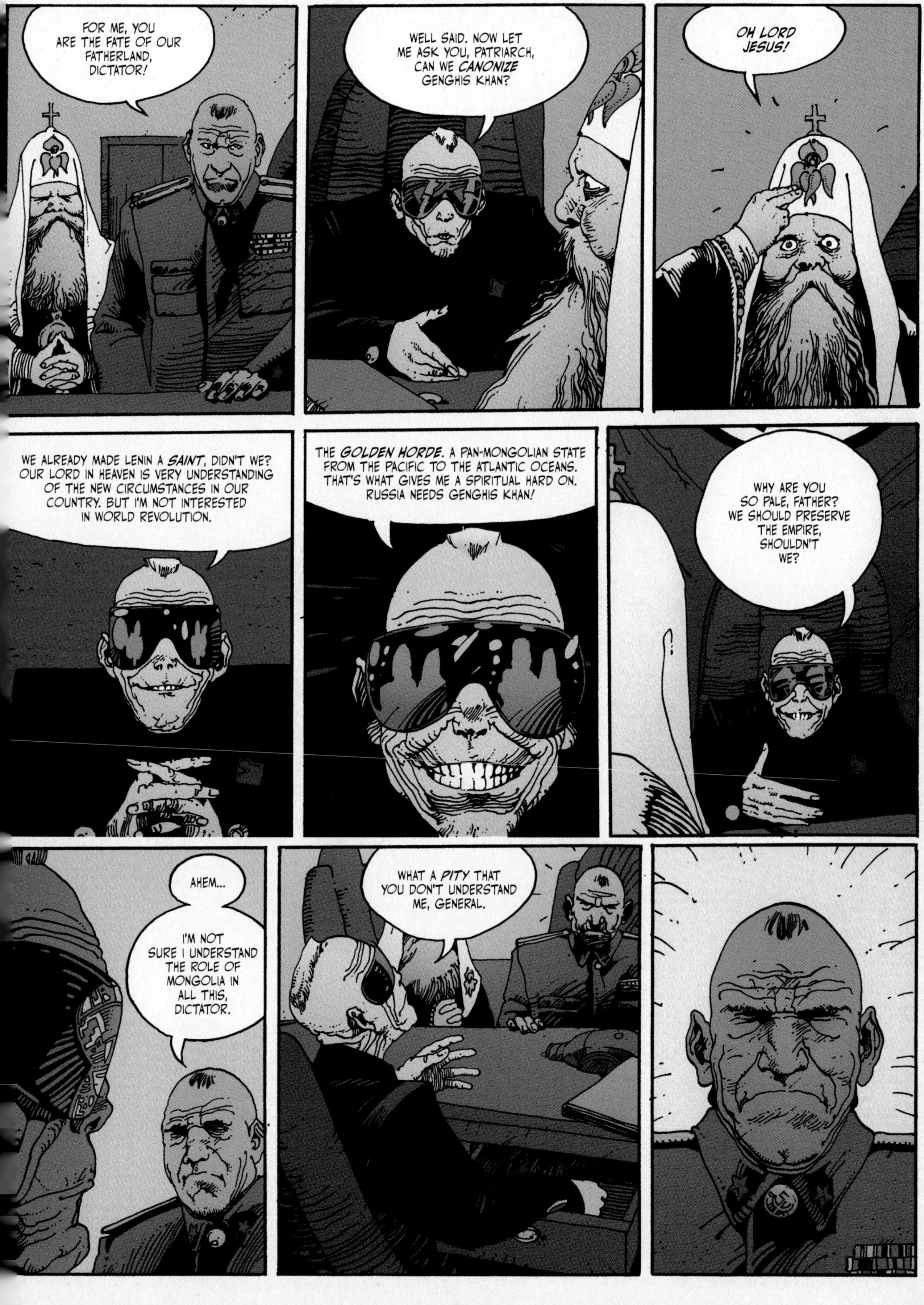
FOR ME, YOU ARE THE FATE OF OUR FATHERLAND, DICTATOR!
WELL SAID. NOW LET ME ASK YOU, PATRIARCH, CAN WE CANONIZE GENGHIS KHAN?
OH LORD JESUS!
WE ALREADY MADE LENIN A SAINT, DIDN'T WE? OUR LORD IN HEAVEN IS VERY UNDERSTANDING OF THE NEW CIRCUMSTANCES IN OUR COUNTRY. BUT I'M NOT INTERESTED IN WORLD REVOLUTION.
THE GOLDEN HORDE. A PAN-MONGOLIAN STATE FROM THE PACIFIC TO THE ATLANTIC OCEANS. THAT'S WHAT GIVES ME A SPIRITUAL HARD ON. RUSSIA NEEDS GENGHIS KHAN!
WHY ARE YOU SO PALE, FATHER? WE SHOULD PRESERVE THE EMPIRE, SHOULDN'T WE?
AHEM...
I'M NOT SURE I UNDERSTAND THE ROLE OF MONGOLIA IN ALL THIS, DICTATOR.
WHAT A PITY THAT YOU DON'T UNDERSTAND ME, GENERAL.

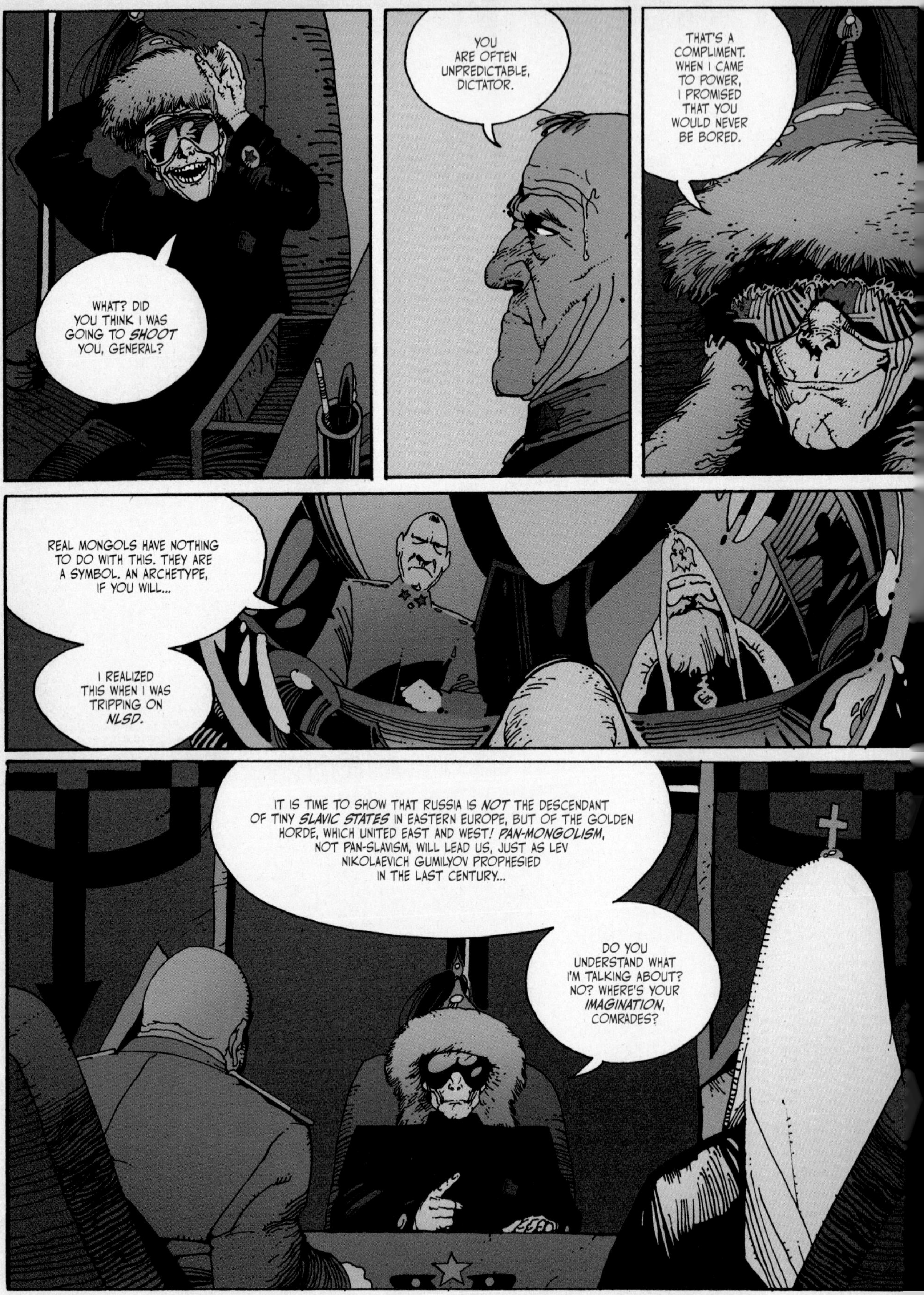

WHAT? DID YOU THINK I WAS GOING TO *SHOOT* YOU, GENERAL?
YOU ARE OFTEN UNPREDICTABLE, DICTATOR.
THAT'S A COMPLIMENT. WHEN I CAME TO POWER, I PROMISED THAT YOU WOULD NEVER BE BORED.
REAL MONGOLS HAVE NOTHING TO DO WITH THIS. THEY ARE A SYMBOL. AN ARCHETYPE, IF YOU WILL...
I REALIZED THIS WHEN I WAS TRIPPING ON *NLSD.*
IT IS TIME TO SHOW THAT RUSSIA IS *NOT* THE DESCENDANT OF TINY *SLAVIC STATES* IN EASTERN EUROPE, BUT OF THE GOLDEN HORDE, WHICH UNITED EAST AND WEST! *PAN-MONGOLISM*, NOT PAN-SLAVISM, WILL LEAD US, JUST AS LEV NIKOLAEVICH GUMILYOV PROPHESIED IN THE LAST CENTURY...
DO YOU UNDERSTAND WHAT I'M TALKING ABOUT? NO? WHERE'S YOUR *IMAGINATION*, COMRADES?

CHECHNYA. MILITARY
UNIT # 1331582

CLIC!

HEH.
FUCK...

ONE
MORE?

MY
TURN.

THE
VODKA'S
GONE.

СХЕМА ПОСТРОЕНИЯ

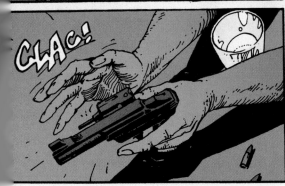

CLAC!

HEY!
FUCKING
WARRIORS!
MORE
VODKA!

9

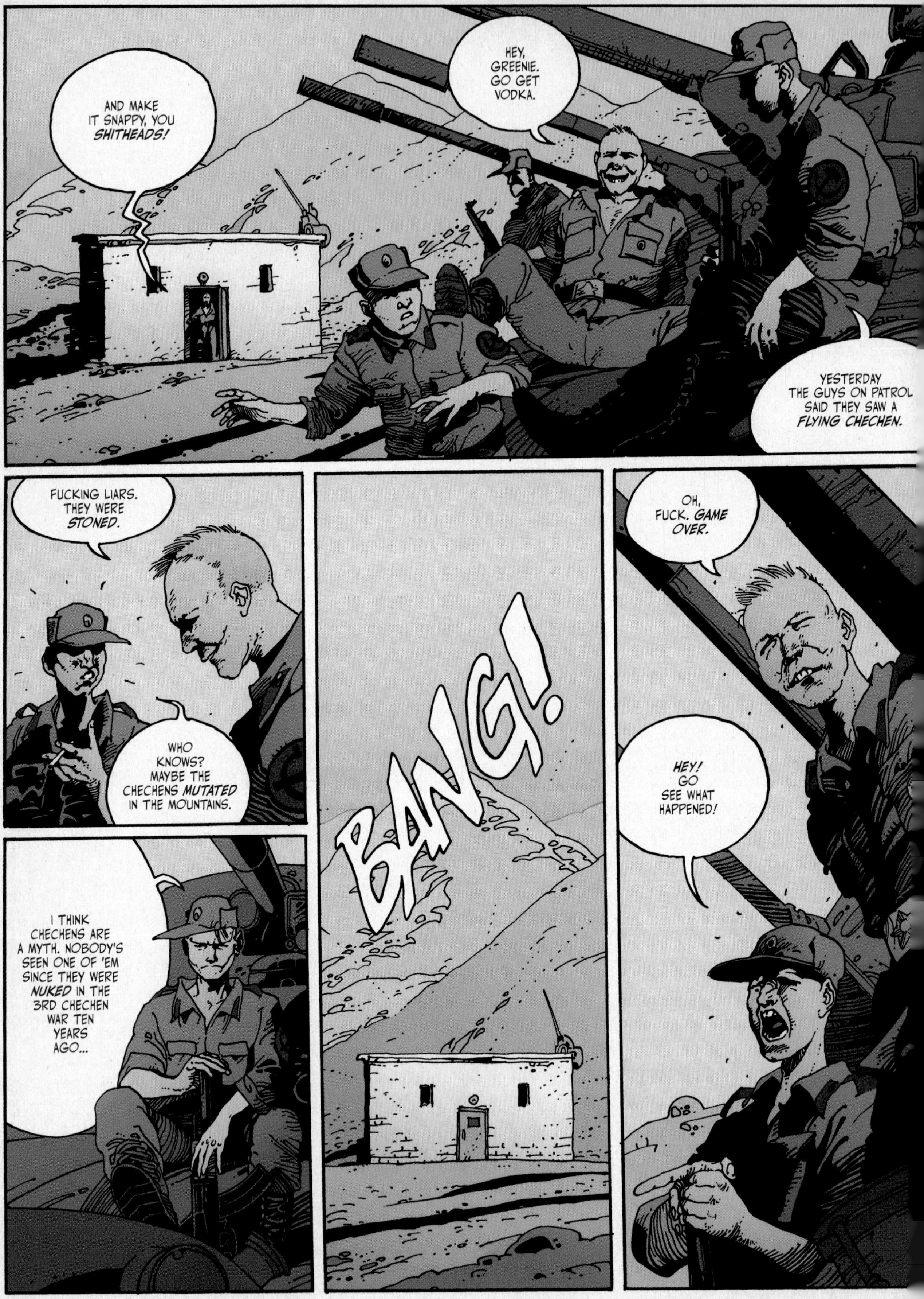
AND MAKE IT SNAPPY, YOU *SHITHEADS!*
HEY, GREENIE. GO GET VODKA.
YESTERDAY THE GUYS ON PATROL SAID THEY SAW A *FLYING CHECHEN.*
FUCKING LIARS. THEY WERE *STONED.*
WHO KNOWS? MAYBE THE CHECHENS *MUTATED* IN THE MOUNTAINS.
I THINK CHECHENS ARE A MYTH. NOBODY'S SEEN ONE OF 'EM SINCE THEY WERE *NUKED* IN THE 3RD CHECHEN WAR TEN YEARS AGO...
BANG!
OH, FUCK. *GAME OVER.*
HEY! GO SEE WHAT HAPPENED!

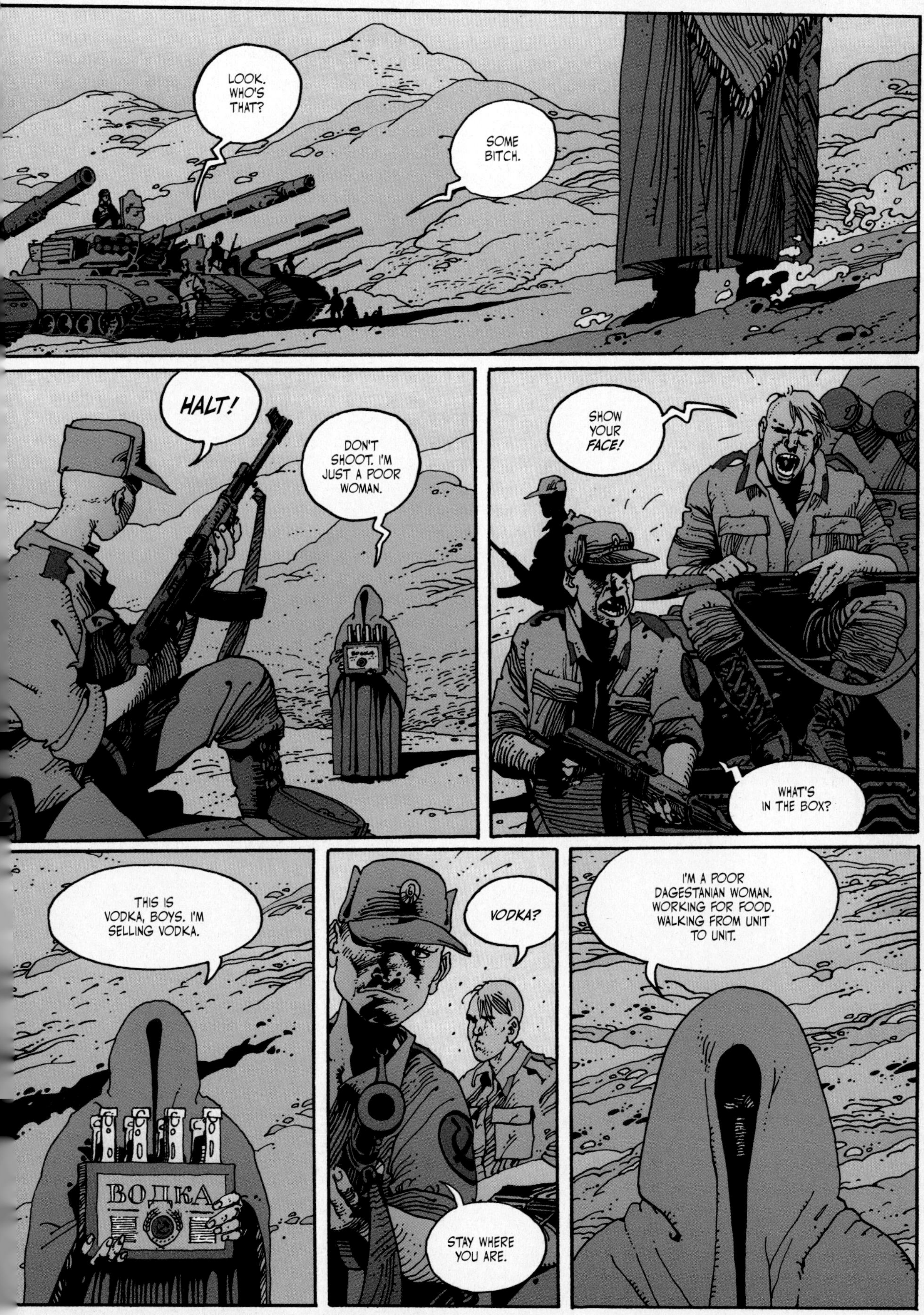

LOOK. WHO'S THAT?
SOME BITCH.
HALT!
DON'T SHOOT. I'M JUST A POOR WOMAN.
SHOW YOUR FACE!
WHAT'S IN THE BOX?
THIS IS VODKA, BOYS. I'M SELLING VODKA.
ВОДКА
VODKA?
STAY WHERE YOU ARE.
I'M A POOR DAGESTANIAN WOMAN. WORKING FOR FOOD. WALKING FROM UNIT TO UNIT.

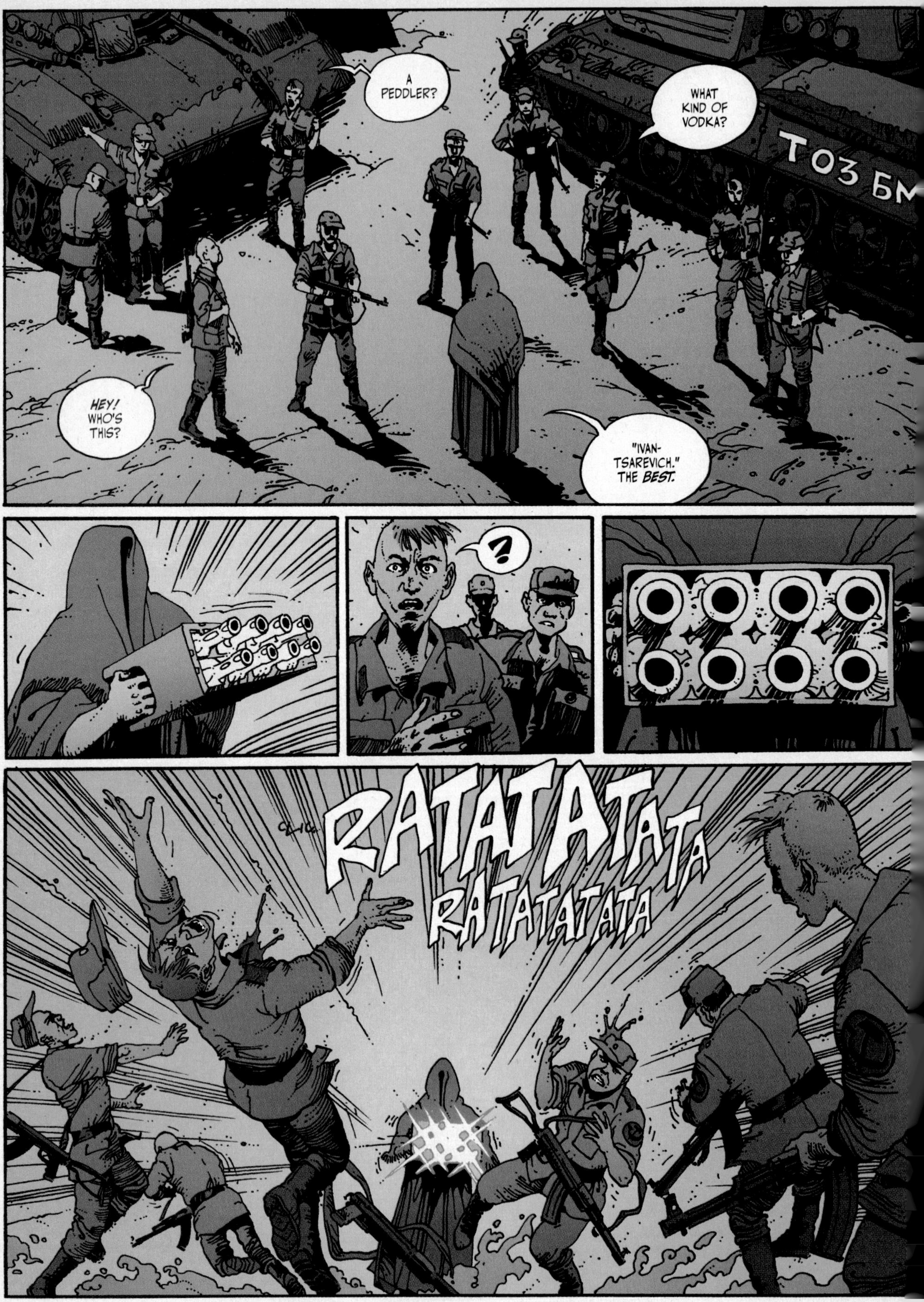
HEY! WHO'S THIS?
A PEDDLER?
WHAT KIND OF VODKA?
"IVAN-TSAREVICH." THE *BEST.*
T 03 БМ
?
CLICK
RATATATATA
RATATATATA

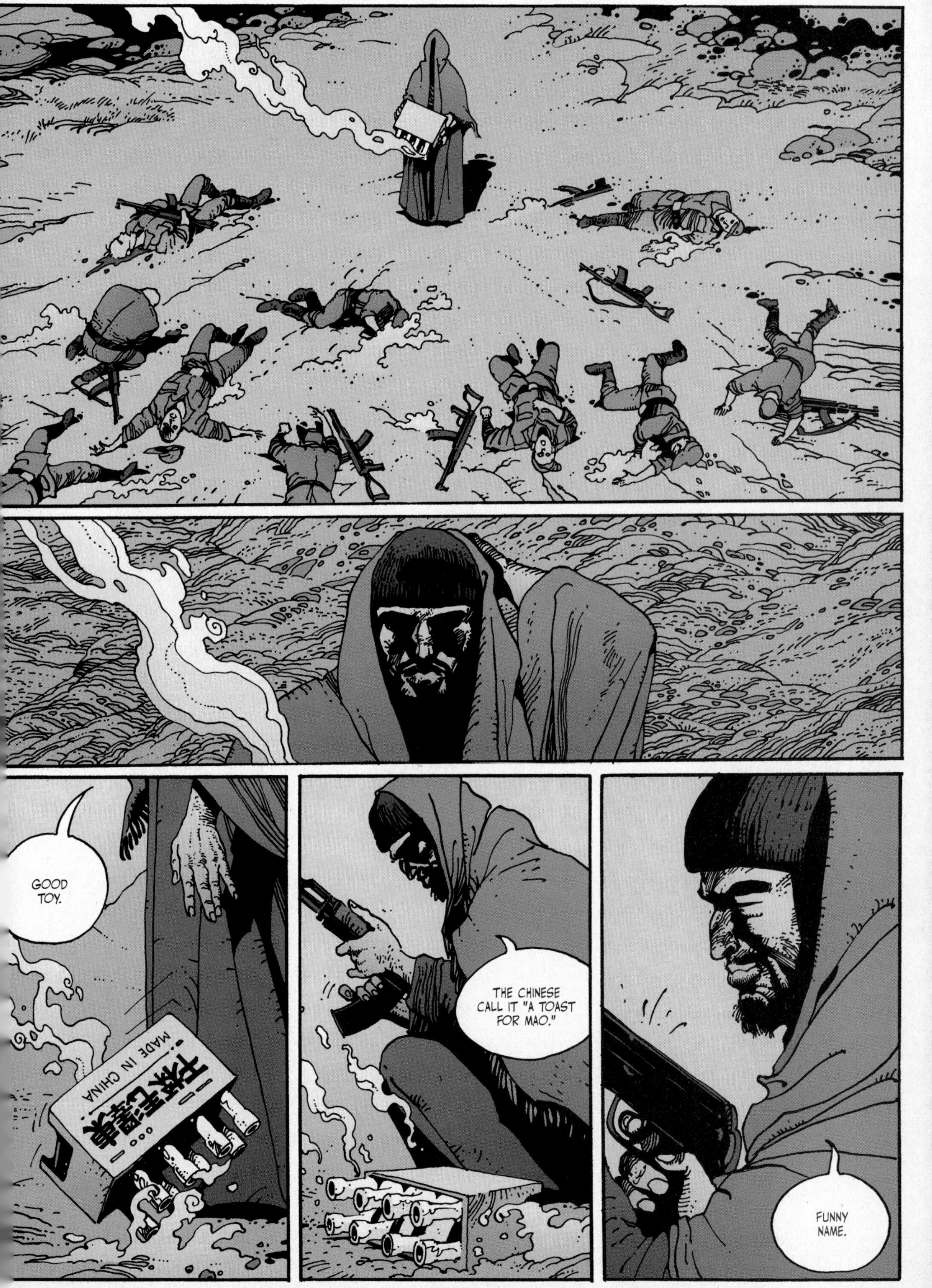
GOOD TOY.
MADE IN CHINA
THE CHINESE CALL IT "A TOAST FOR MAO."
FUNNY NAME.

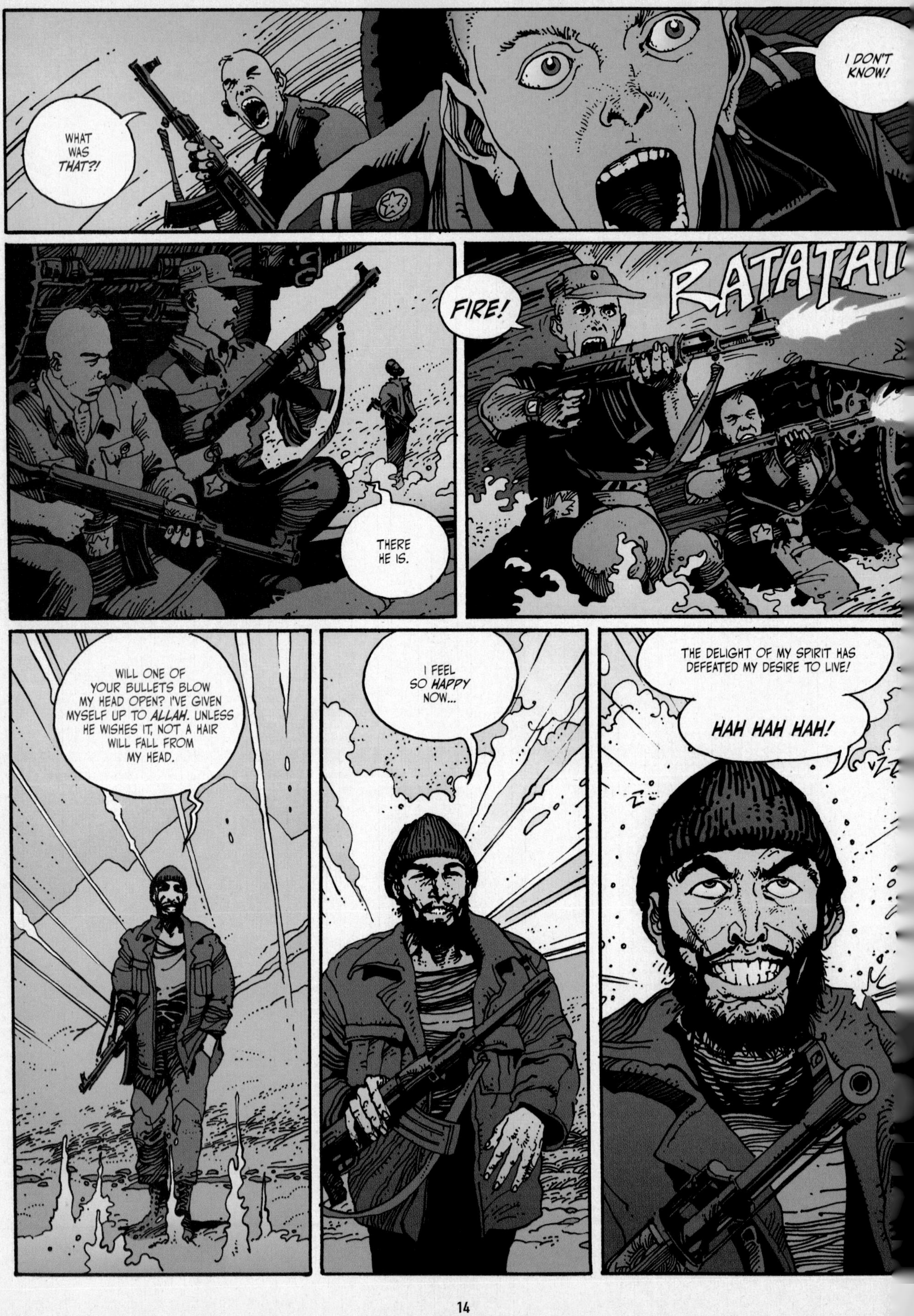
WHAT WAS THAT?!
I DON'T KNOW!
THERE HE IS.
FIRE!
RATATAT
WILL ONE OF YOUR BULLETS BLOW MY HEAD OPEN? I'VE GIVEN MYSELF UP TO ALLAH. UNLESS HE WISHES IT, NOT A HAIR WILL FALL FROM MY HEAD.
I FEEL SO HAPPY NOW...
THE DELIGHT OF MY SPIRIT HAS DEFEATED MY DESIRE TO LIVE!
HAH HAH HAH!

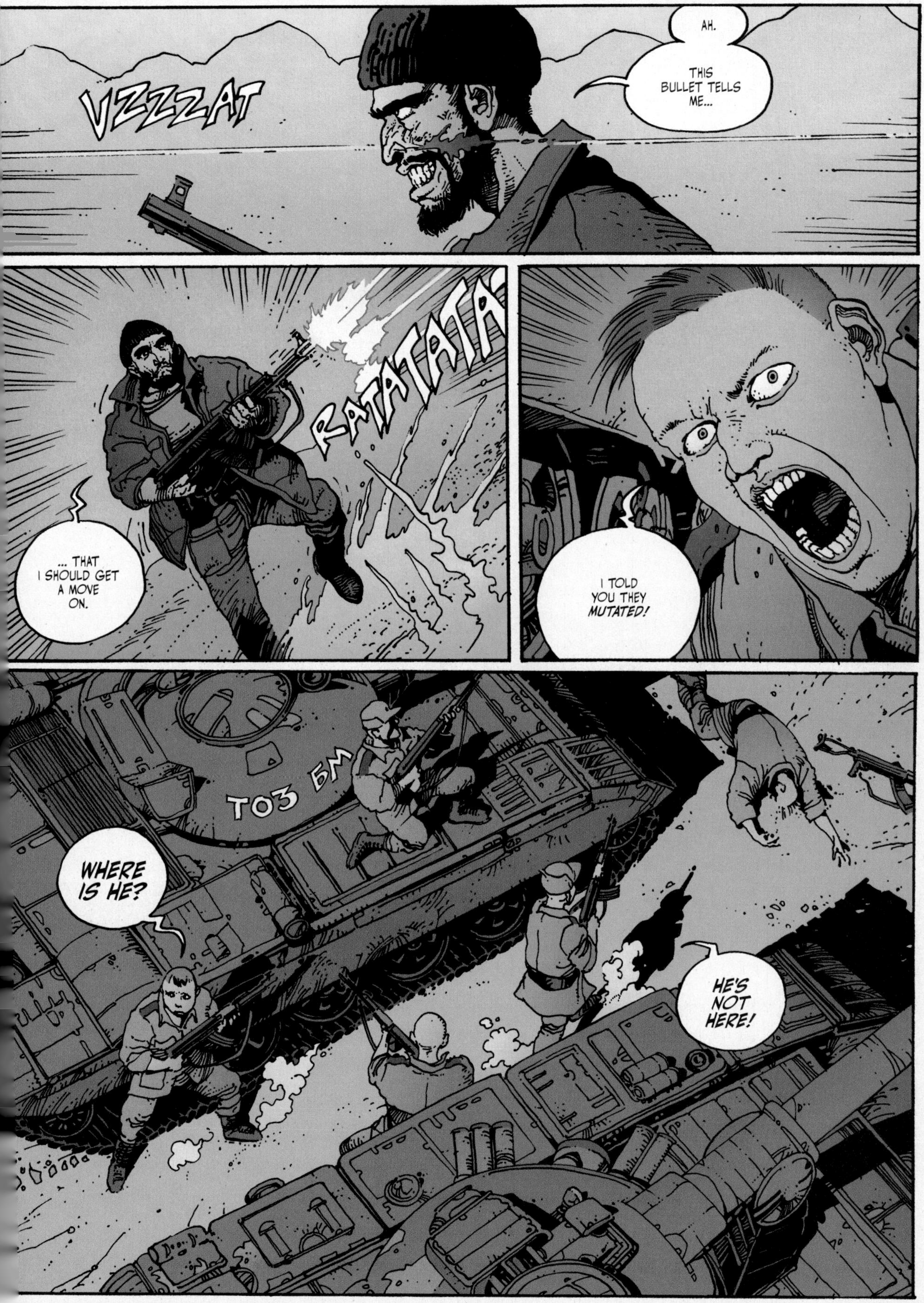
VZZZAT
AH.
THIS BULLET TELLS ME...
RATATATA
... THAT I SHOULD GET A MOVE ON.
I TOLD YOU THEY MUTATED!
TO3 БМ
WHERE IS HE?
HE'S NOT HERE!

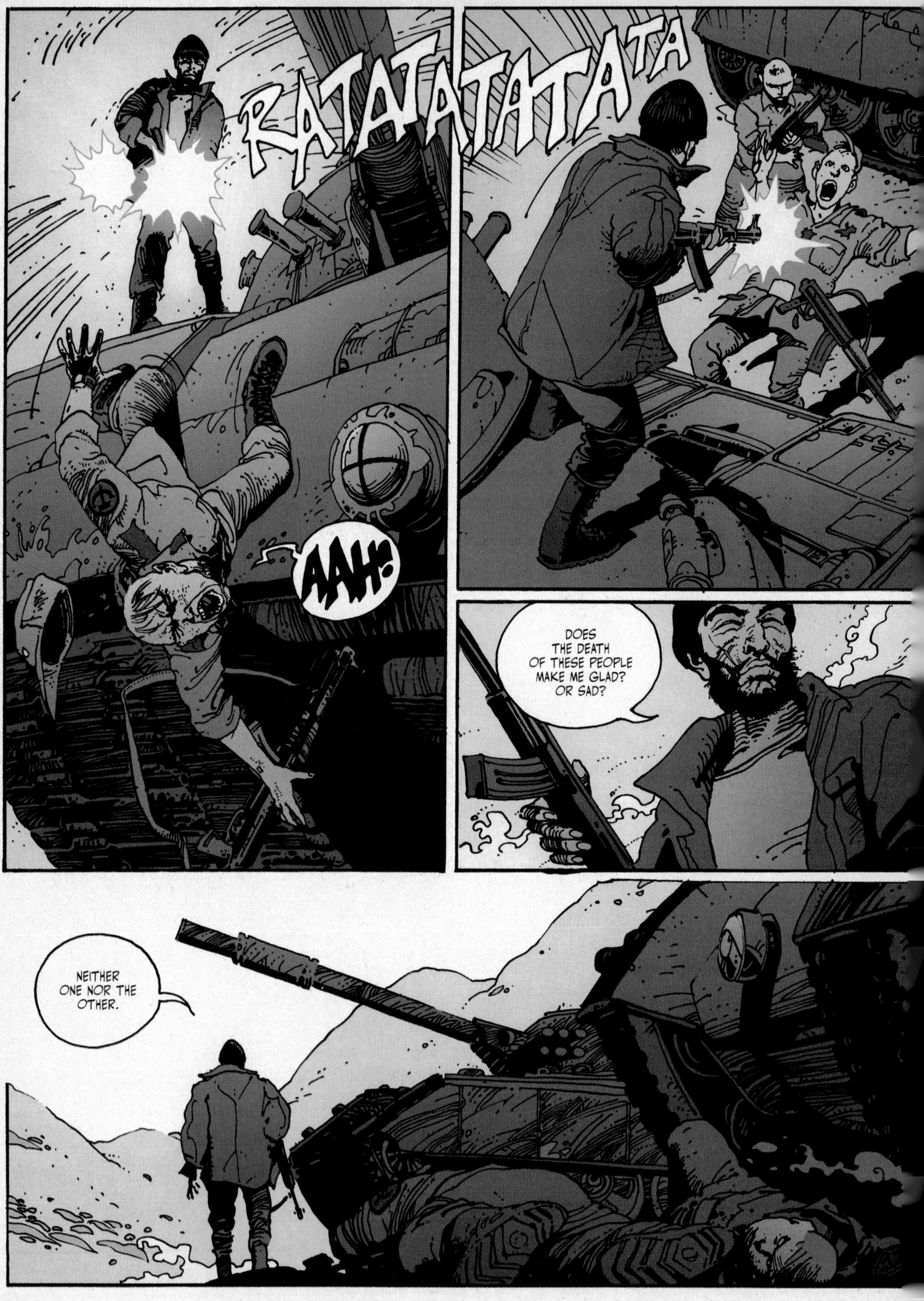
RATATATATATATA
AAH!
DOES THE DEATH OF THESE PEOPLE MAKE ME GLAD? OR SAD?
NEITHER ONE NOR THE OTHER.

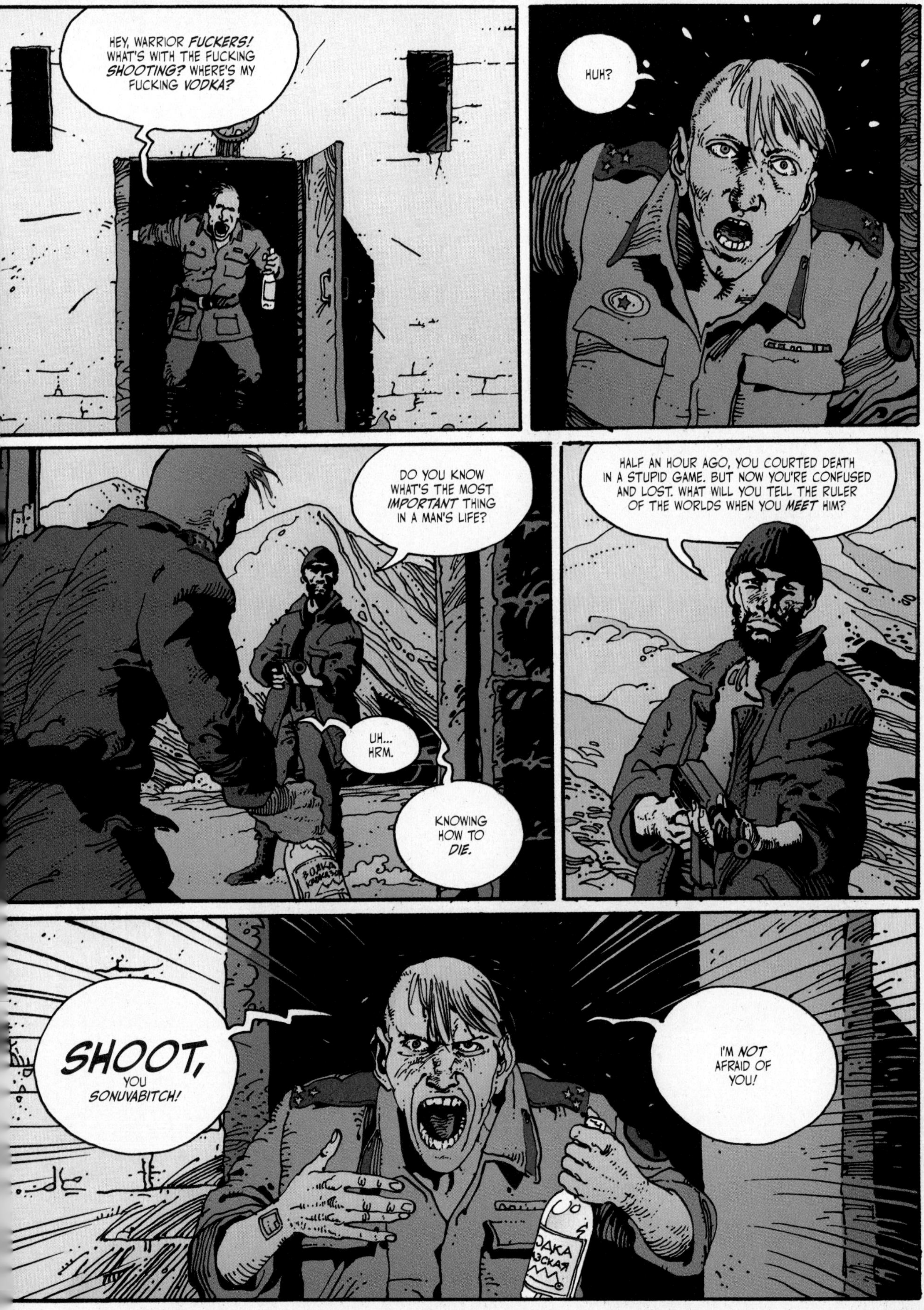
HEY, WARRIOR FUCKERS! WHAT'S WITH THE FUCKING SHOOTING? WHERE'S MY FUCKING VODKA?
HUH?
DO YOU KNOW WHAT'S THE MOST IMPORTANT THING IN A MAN'S LIFE?
UH... HRM.
KNOWING HOW TO DIE.
HALF AN HOUR AGO, YOU COURTED DEATH IN A STUPID GAME. BUT NOW YOU'RE CONFUSED AND LOST. WHAT WILL YOU TELL THE RULER OF THE WORLDS WHEN YOU MEET HIM?
SHOOT, YOU SONUVABITCH!
I'M NOT AFRAID OF YOU!

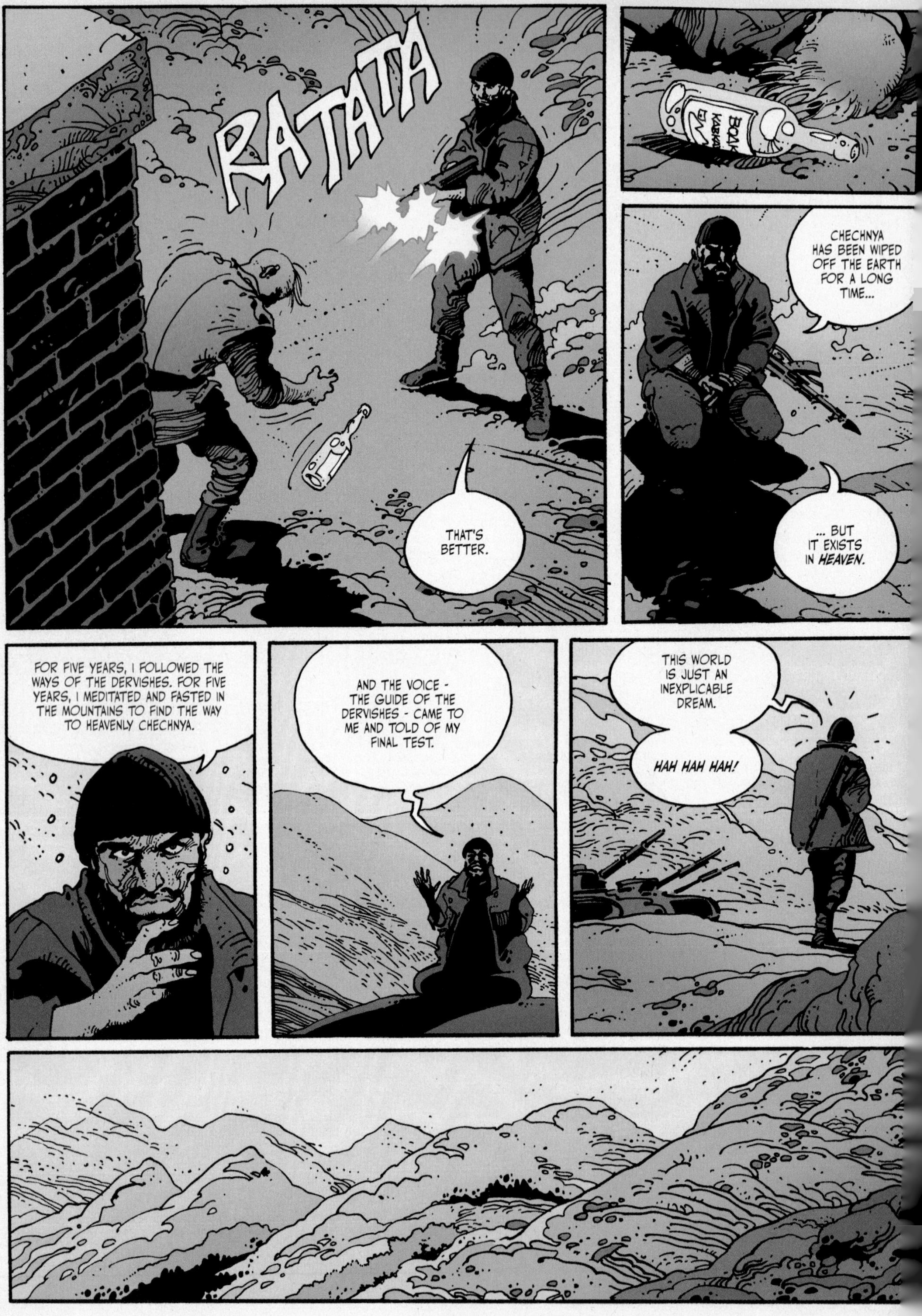
RATATA
THAT'S BETTER.
CHECHNYA HAS BEEN WIPED OFF THE EARTH FOR A LONG TIME...
... BUT IT EXISTS IN *HEAVEN.*
FOR FIVE YEARS, I FOLLOWED THE WAYS OF THE DERVISHES. FOR FIVE YEARS, I MEDITATED AND FASTED IN THE MOUNTAINS TO FIND THE WAY TO HEAVENLY CHECHNYA.
AND THE VOICE - THE GUIDE OF THE DERVISHES - CAME TO ME AND TOLD OF MY FINAL TEST.
THIS WORLD IS JUST AN INEXPLICABLE DREAM.
HAH HAH HAH!

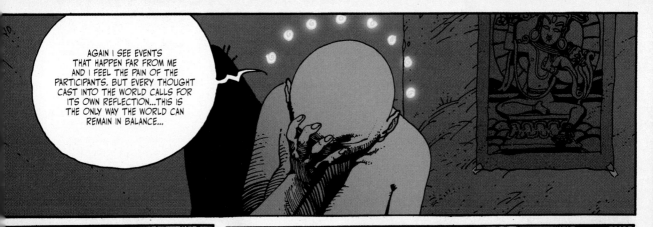

AGAIN I SEE EVENTS THAT HAPPEN FAR FROM ME AND I FEEL THE PAIN OF THE PARTICIPANTS. BUT EVERY THOUGHT CAST INTO THE WORLD CALLS FOR ITS OWN REFLECTION...THIS IS THE ONLY WAY THE WORLD CAN REMAIN IN BALANCE...

HE IS *SHIVA* THE DESTROYER... AND HIS PRESENCE MAKES ME COLD.

AND WHEN THE ONE WHO HAS POWER - MOVED BY GREED - ATTEMPTS TO LIVE ETERNALLY...

... AT THAT MOMENT, ANOTHER ONE - DETACHED AND FRIGHTENING - COMES INTO THE WORLD SEEKING DEATH.

BUT WHO MOVES THE PLAYERS? WHY DO THEY COME TO ME? WHO AM I IN THIS STORY?

MY QUEST IS TO UNDERSTAND.

OM MANI PADME HUM....

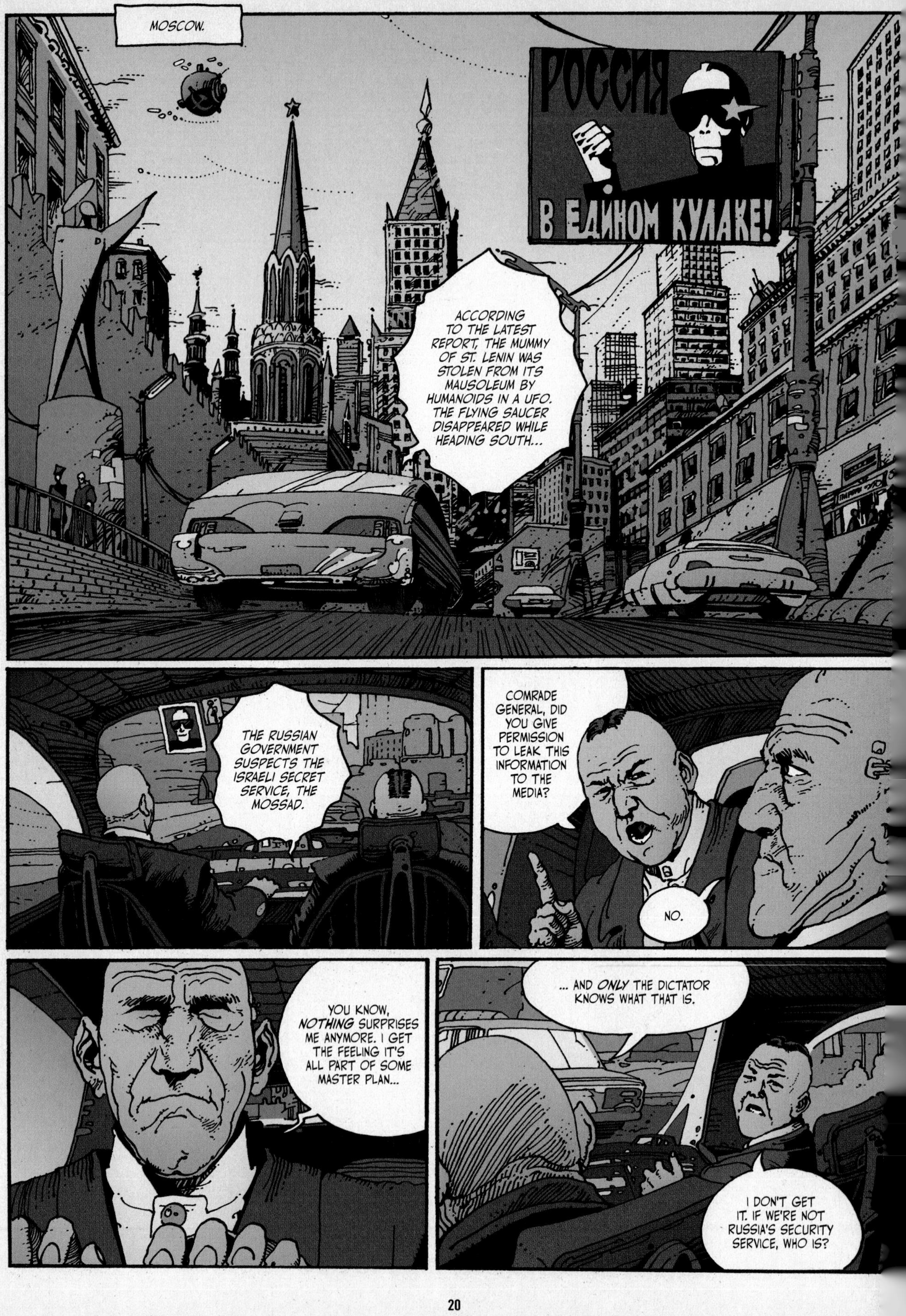
MOSCOW.
РОССИЯ
В ЕДИНОМ КУЛАКЕ!
ACCORDING TO THE LATEST REPORT, THE MUMMY OF ST. LENIN WAS STOLEN FROM ITS MAUSOLEUM BY HUMANOIDS IN A UFO. THE FLYING SAUCER DISAPPEARED WHILE HEADING SOUTH...
THE RUSSIAN GOVERNMENT SUSPECTS THE ISRAELI SECRET SERVICE, THE MOSSAD.
COMRADE GENERAL, DID YOU GIVE PERMISSION TO LEAK THIS INFORMATION TO THE MEDIA?
NO.
YOU KNOW, NOTHING SURPRISES ME ANYMORE. I GET THE FEELING IT'S ALL PART OF SOME MASTER PLAN...
... AND ONLY THE DICTATOR KNOWS WHAT THAT IS.
I DON'T GET IT. IF WE'RE NOT RUSSIA'S SECURITY SERVICE, WHO IS?

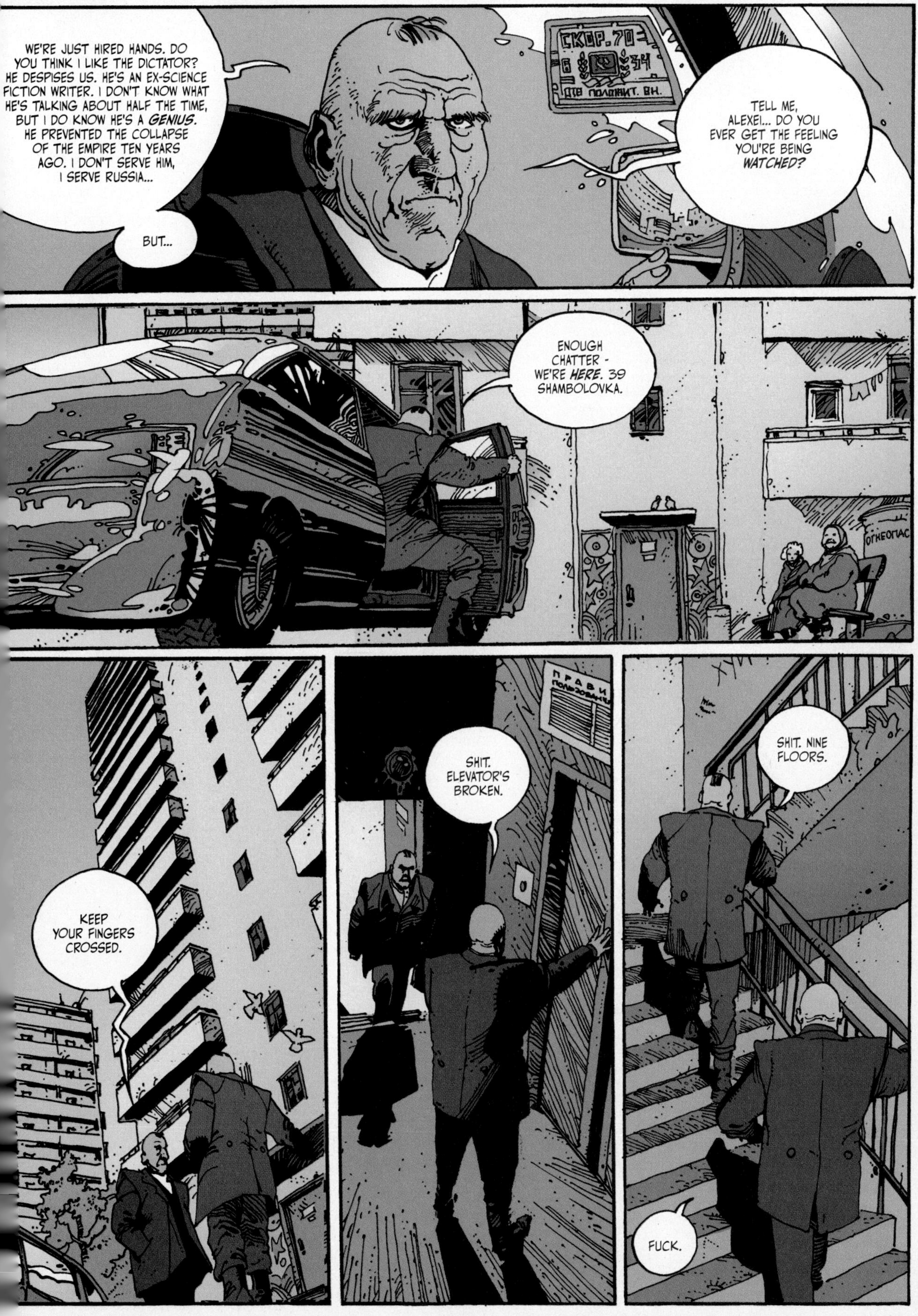
WE'RE JUST HIRED HANDS. DO YOU THINK I LIKE THE DICTATOR? HE DESPISES US. HE'S AN EX-SCIENCE FICTION WRITER. I DON'T KNOW WHAT HE'S TALKING ABOUT HALF THE TIME, BUT I DO KNOW HE'S A GENIUS. HE PREVENTED THE COLLAPSE OF THE EMPIRE TEN YEARS AGO. I DON'T SERVE HIM, I SERVE RUSSIA...
BUT...
TELL ME, ALEXEI... DO YOU EVER GET THE FEELING YOU'RE BEING WATCHED?
ENOUGH CHATTER - WE'RE HERE. 39 SHAMBOLOVKA.
ОГНЕОПАС
KEEP YOUR FINGERS CROSSED.
SHIT. ELEVATOR'S BROKEN.
SHIT. NINE FLOORS.
FUCK.

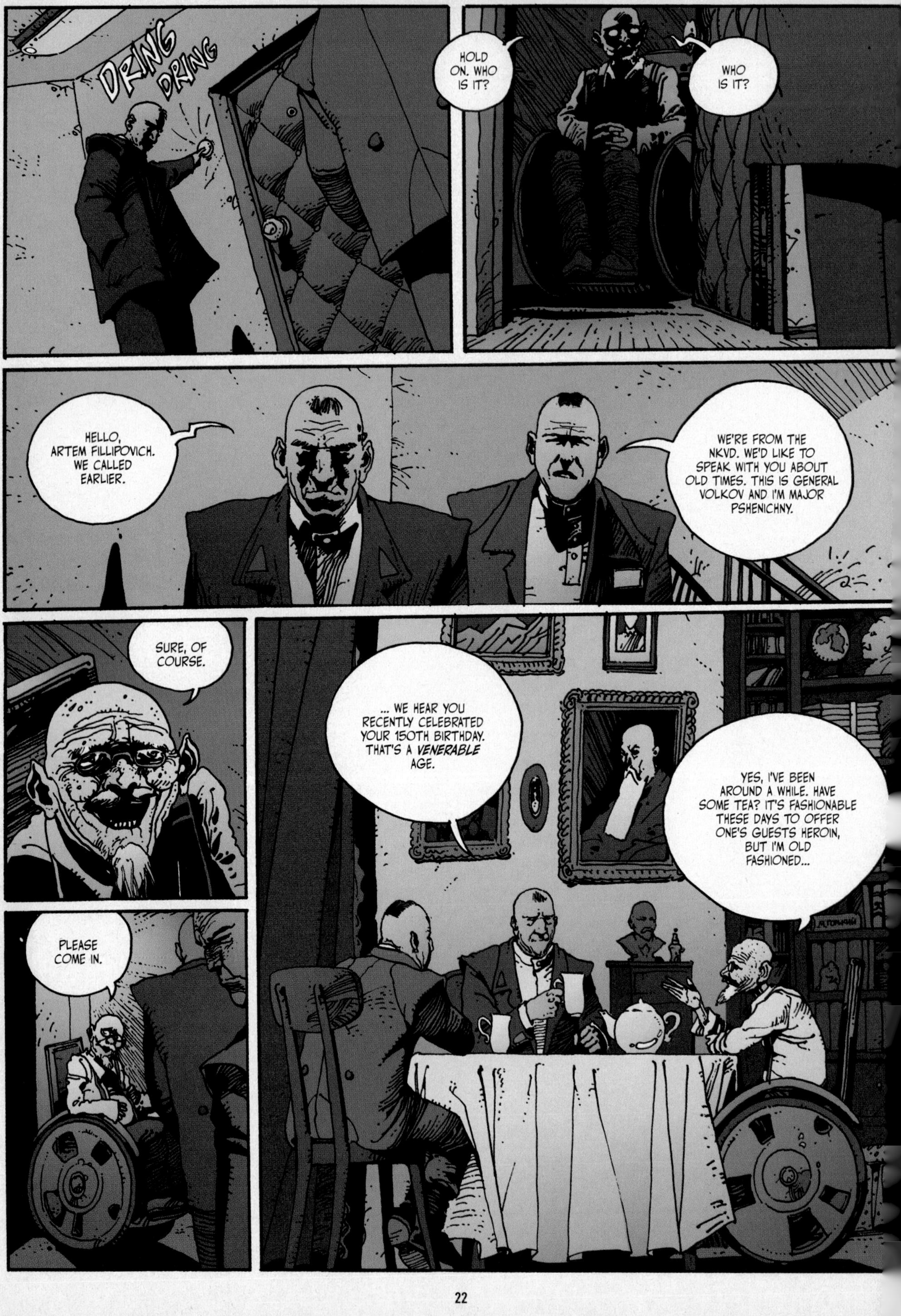
DRING DRING
HOLD ON. WHO IS IT?
WHO IS IT?
HELLO, ARTEM FILLIPOVICH. WE CALLED EARLIER.
WE'RE FROM THE NKVD. WE'D LIKE TO SPEAK WITH YOU ABOUT OLD TIMES. THIS IS GENERAL VOLKOV AND I'M MAJOR PSHENICHNY.
SURE, OF COURSE.
PLEASE COME IN.
... WE HEAR YOU RECENTLY CELEBRATED YOUR 150TH BIRTHDAY. THAT'S A *VENERABLE* AGE.
YES, I'VE BEEN AROUND A WHILE. HAVE SOME TEA? IT'S FASHIONABLE THESE DAYS TO OFFER ONE'S GUESTS HEROIN, BUT I'M OLD FASHIONED...

AND THIS IS MY GRANDSON, VLADLEN. LIKE A TRUE PATRIOT, HE FOUGHT IN THE 2ND TATAR WAR TO KEEP RUSSIA WHOLE.

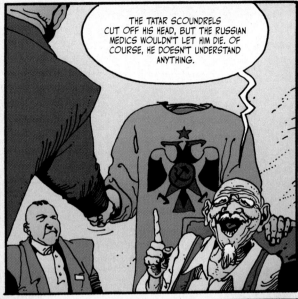

THE TATAR SCOUNDRELS CUT OFF HIS HEAD, BUT THE RUSSIAN MEDICS WOULDN'T LET HIM DIE. OF COURSE, HE DOESN'T UNDERSTAND ANYTHING.

GO OUT FOR A BIT, VLADIK.

I'M SO PROUD OF HIM, SO HAPPY FOR HIM. HE LITERALLY GAVE UP HIS HEAD FOR OUR EMPIRE.

ARTEM FILLIPOVICH, WE CAME HERE FOR INFORMATION VITAL TO RUSSIA. YOUR WORK WITH ROERICH IN THE 1920'S...

WILL YOU SPEAK WITH US ABOUT IT?

OH YEAH, SURE... ROUGH, TROUBLING YEARS... YOUTH, REVOLUTION...

"YOUTHS LED US/ON AN ARMED MARCH,/YOUTH FLUNG US/ONTO THE KRONSTADT ICE/THE BATTLE HORSES CARRIED US/ON THE WIDE SQUARE THEY KILLED US.../BUT IN THE FEVERISH BLOOD WE ROSE/AND OUR BLINDED EYES..."

YES, YES - WE REMEMBER BAGRITSKY'S VERSES. BUT WHAT ABOUT ROERICH?

NIKOLAI KONSTANTINOVICH ROERICH... I REMEMBER THE PASSIONS OF THOSE YEARS - SPIRITUALISM, THE OCCULT... WE WERE DIVIDED INTO MYSTICS AND ATHEISTS...

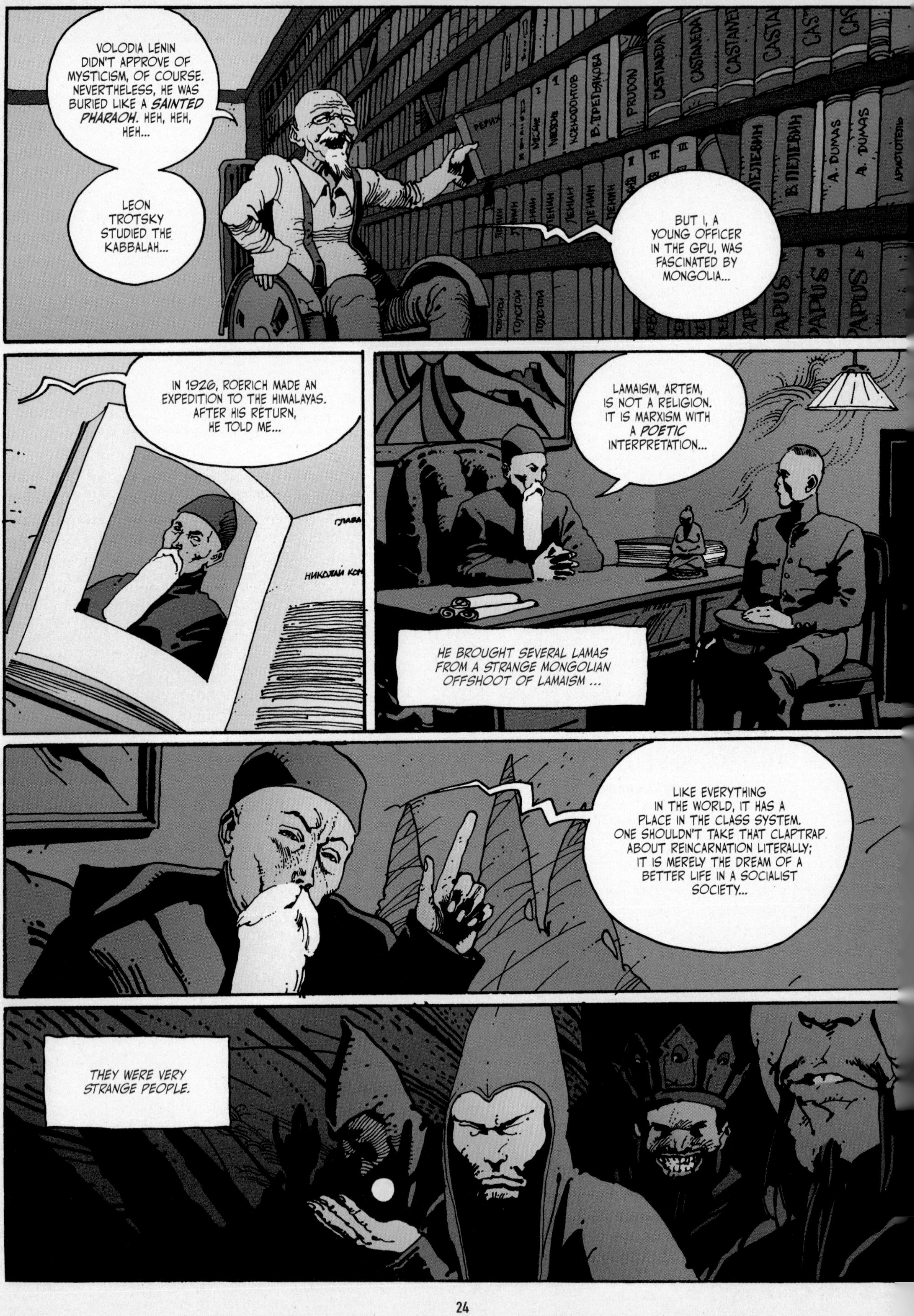
VOLODIA LENIN DIDN'T APPROVE OF MYSTICISM, OF COURSE. NEVERTHELESS, HE WAS BURIED LIKE A SAINTED PHARAOH. HEH, HEH, HEH...
LEON TROTSKY STUDIED THE KABBALAH...
BUT I, A YOUNG OFFICER IN THE GPU, WAS FASCINATED BY MONGOLIA...
IN 1926, ROERICH MADE AN EXPEDITION TO THE HIMALAYAS. AFTER HIS RETURN, HE TOLD ME...
LAMAISM, ARTEM, IS NOT A RELIGION. IT IS MARXISM WITH A POETIC INTERPRETATION...
HE BROUGHT SEVERAL LAMAS FROM A STRANGE MONGOLIAN OFFSHOOT OF LAMAISM ...
LIKE EVERYTHING IN THE WORLD, IT HAS A PLACE IN THE CLASS SYSTEM. ONE SHOULDN'T TAKE THAT CLAPTRAP ABOUT REINCARNATION LITERALLY; IT IS MERELY THE DREAM OF A BETTER LIFE IN A SOCIALIST SOCIETY...
THEY WERE VERY STRANGE PEOPLE.

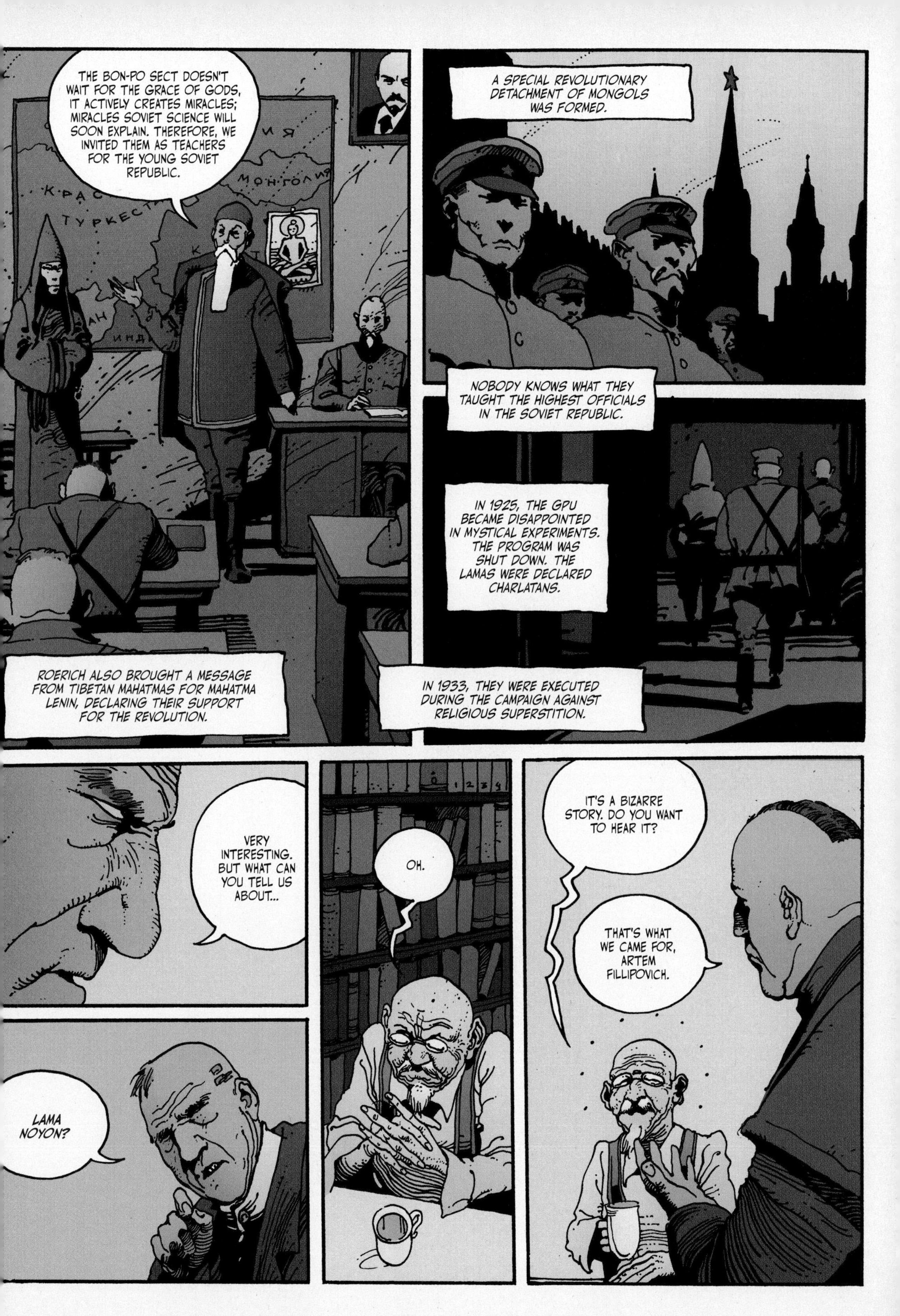

THE BON-PO SECT DOESN'T WAIT FOR THE GRACE OF GODS, IT ACTIVELY CREATES MIRACLES; MIRACLES SOVIET SCIENCE WILL SOON EXPLAIN. THEREFORE, WE INVITED THEM AS TEACHERS FOR THE YOUNG SOVIET REPUBLIC.
МОНГОЛИЯ
ROERICH ALSO BROUGHT A MESSAGE FROM TIBETAN MAHATMAS FOR MAHATMA LENIN, DECLARING THEIR SUPPORT FOR THE REVOLUTION.
A SPECIAL REVOLUTIONARY DETACHMENT OF MONGOLS WAS FORMED.
NOBODY KNOWS WHAT THEY TAUGHT THE HIGHEST OFFICIALS IN THE SOVIET REPUBLIC.
IN 1925, THE GPU BECAME DISAPPOINTED IN MYSTICAL EXPERIMENTS. THE PROGRAM WAS SHUT DOWN. THE LAMAS WERE DECLARED CHARLATANS.
IN 1933, THEY WERE EXECUTED DURING THE CAMPAIGN AGAINST RELIGIOUS SUPERSTITION.
VERY INTERESTING. BUT WHAT CAN YOU TELL US ABOUT...
LAMA NOYON?
OH.
IT'S A BIZARRE STORY. DO YOU WANT TO HEAR IT?
THAT'S WHAT WE CAME FOR, ARTEM FILLIPOVICH.

HE WAS A YOUNG MONGOL LAMA. VERY AMBITIOUS. HE HELD THE RANK OF COMMISSAR. SAID HE KNEW THE SECRET OF IMMORTALITY...

AND MOST IMPORTANTLY, HE CLAIMED TO BE THE REINCARNATION OF *GENGHIS KHAN*.

HERE HE IS.

FOR MONGOLS, GENGHIS KHAN IS NOT JUST A FRIGHTENING HISTORICAL FIGURE. FOR THEM, HE IS SOMEWHERE BETWEEN DRACULA AND JESUS CHRIST.

NOYON WAS ACCUSED OF ATTEMPTING TO ASSASSINATE STALIN, OF TROTSKYISM, AND OF LEFTIST OPPORTUNISM.

HE MADE HIS MISTAKE WHEN HE ADVISED STALIN TO EAT THE MUMMY OF LENIN TO GAIN THE GREAT MAN'S WISDOM.

ACTUALLY, THAT'S AN OLD TRADITION OF THE BON-PO.

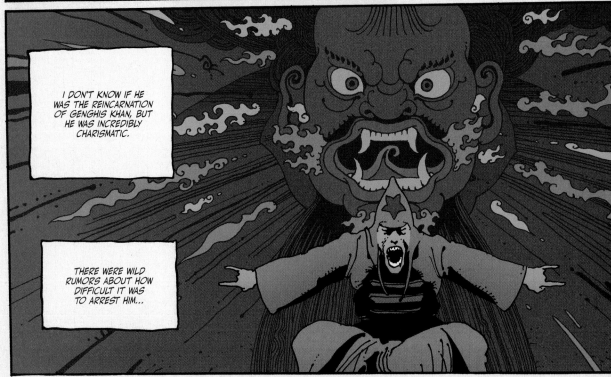

I DON'T KNOW IF HE WAS THE REINCARNATION OF GENGHIS KHAN, BUT HE WAS INCREDIBLY CHARISMATIC.

THERE WERE WILD RUMORS ABOUT HOW DIFFICULT IT WAS TO ARREST HIM...

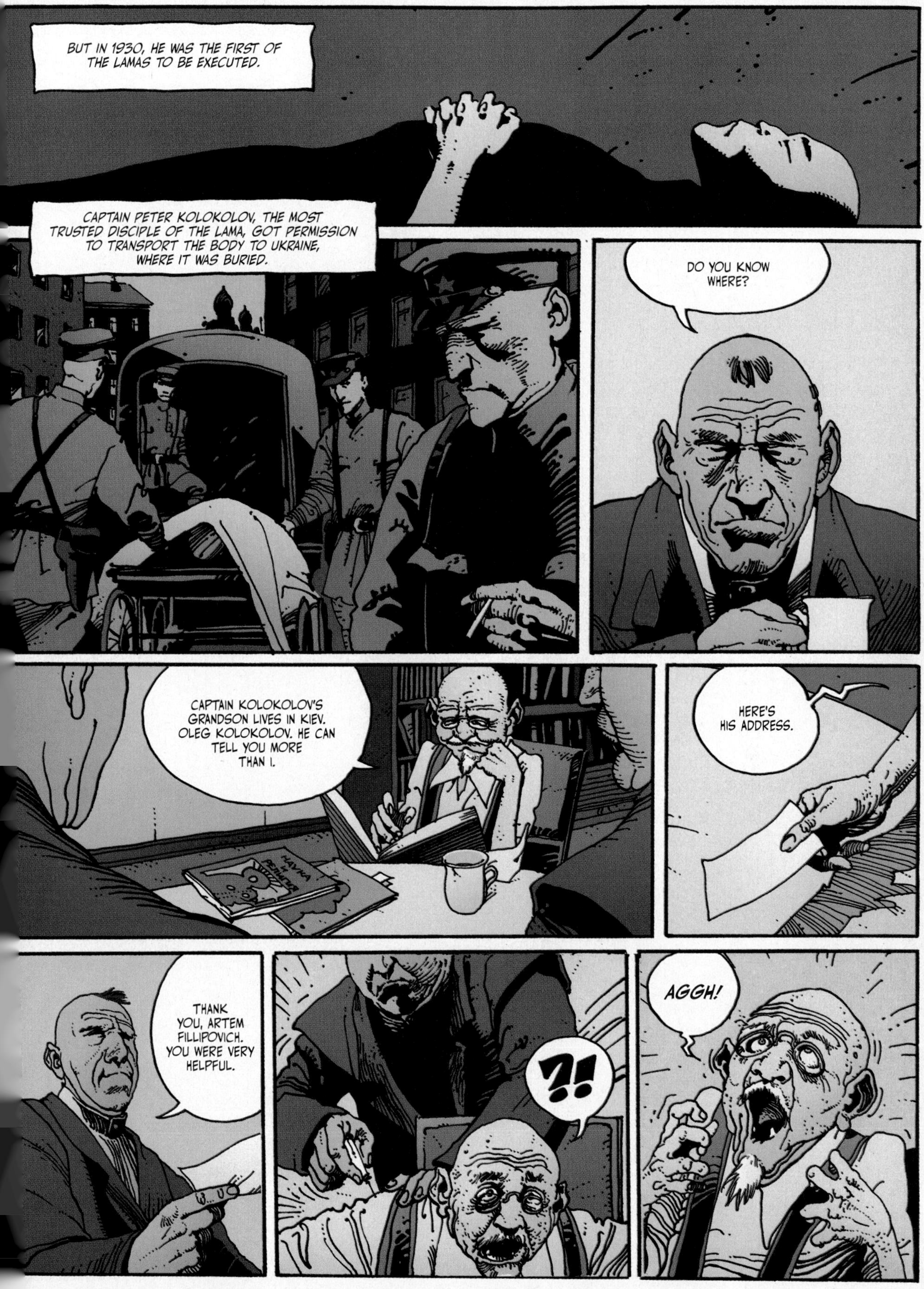
BUT IN 1930, HE WAS THE FIRST OF THE LAMAS TO BE EXECUTED.
CAPTAIN PETER KOLOKOLOV, THE MOST TRUSTED DISCIPLE OF THE LAMA, GOT PERMISSION TO TRANSPORT THE BODY TO UKRAINE, WHERE IT WAS BURIED.
DO YOU KNOW WHERE?
CAPTAIN KOLOKOLOV'S GRANDSON LIVES IN KIEV. OLEG KOLOKOLOV. HE CAN TELL YOU MORE THAN I.
HERE'S HIS ADDRESS.
THANK YOU, ARTEM FILLIPOVICH. YOU WERE VERY HELPFUL.
?!
AGGH!

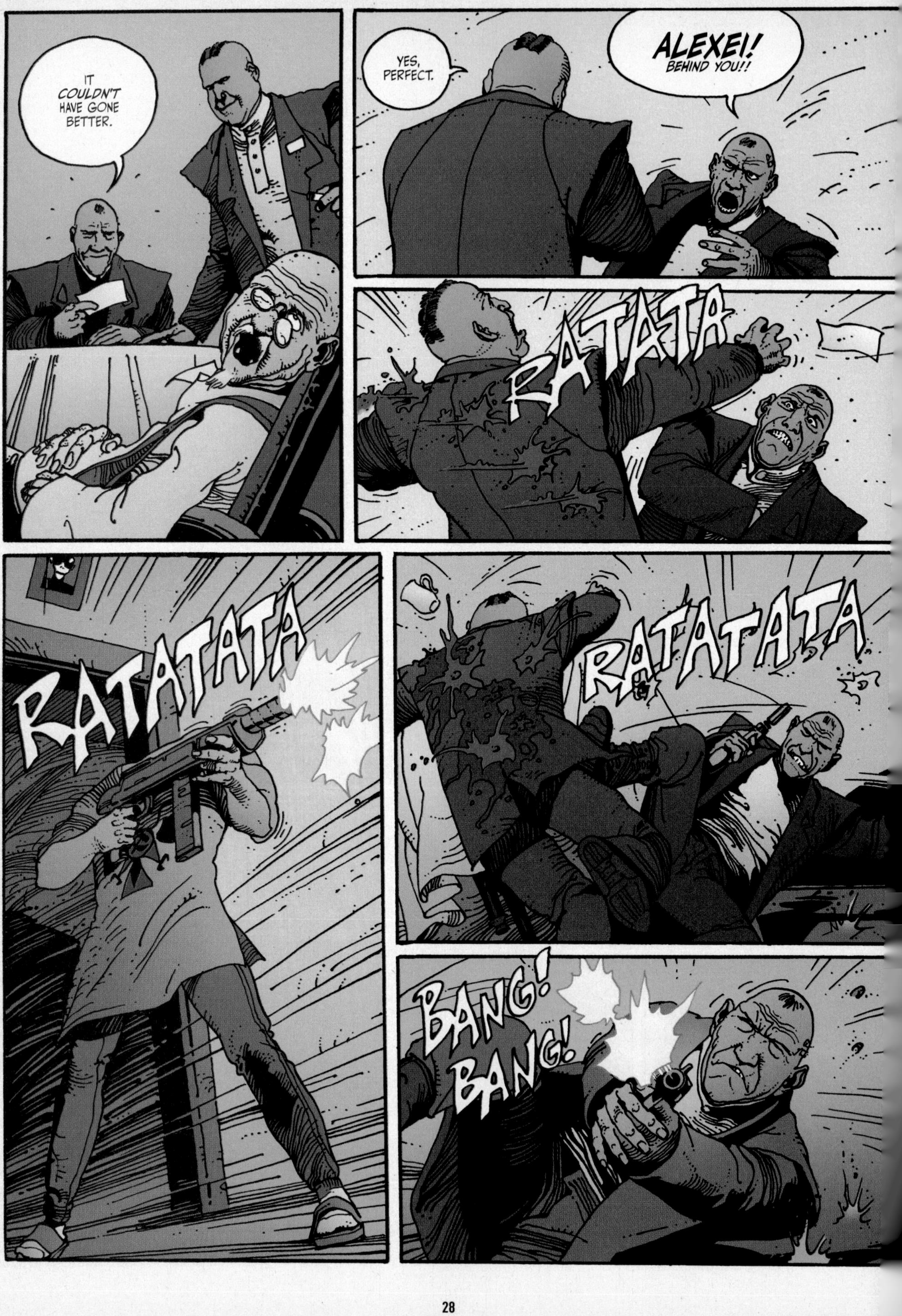
IT COULDN'T HAVE GONE BETTER.
YES, PERFECT.
ALEXEI! BEHIND YOU!!
RATATATA
RATATATA
RATATATA
BANG! BANG!

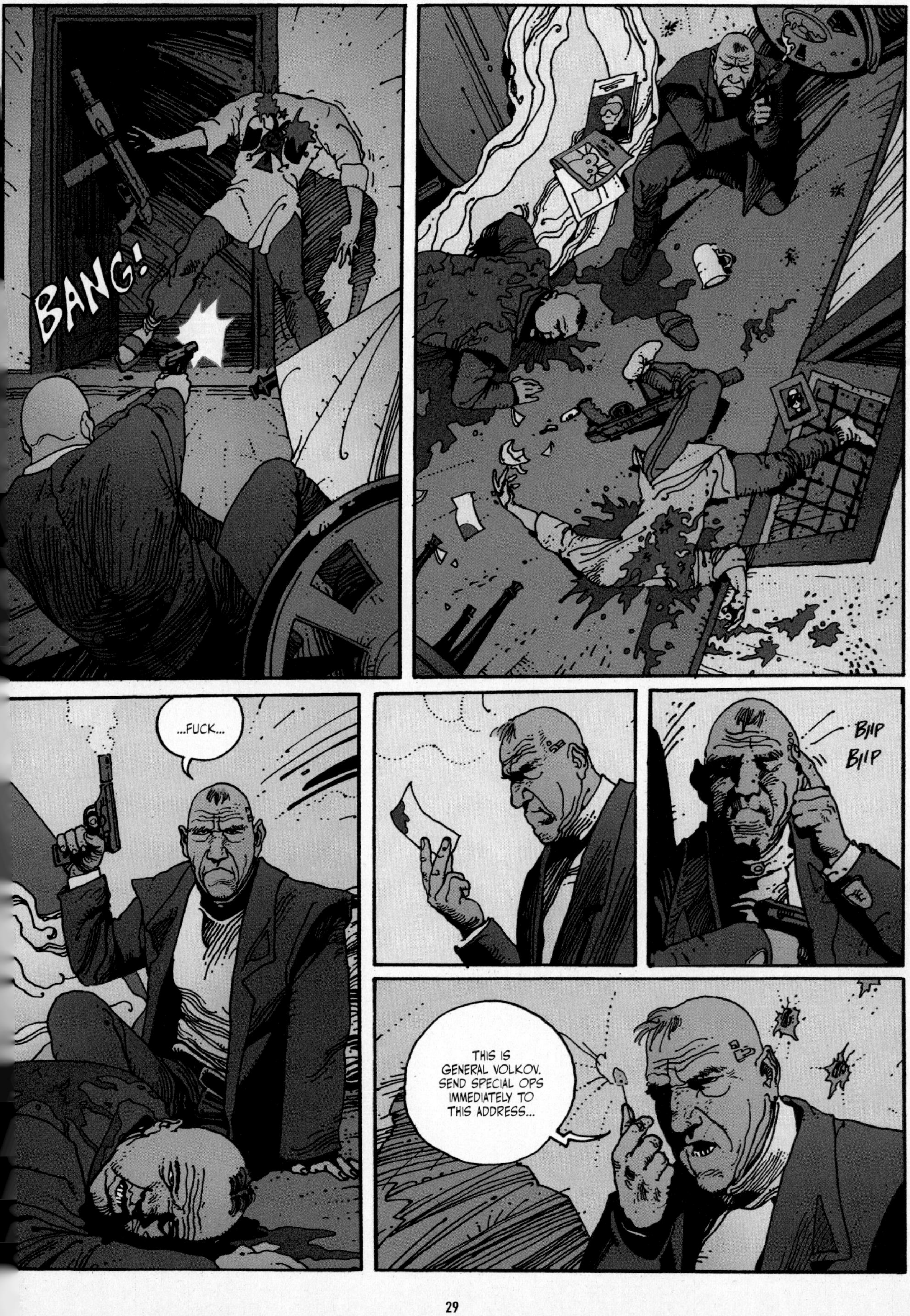
BANG!
...FUCK...
BIIP
BIIP
THIS IS GENERAL VOLKOV. SEND SPECIAL OPS IMMEDIATELY TO THIS ADDRESS...

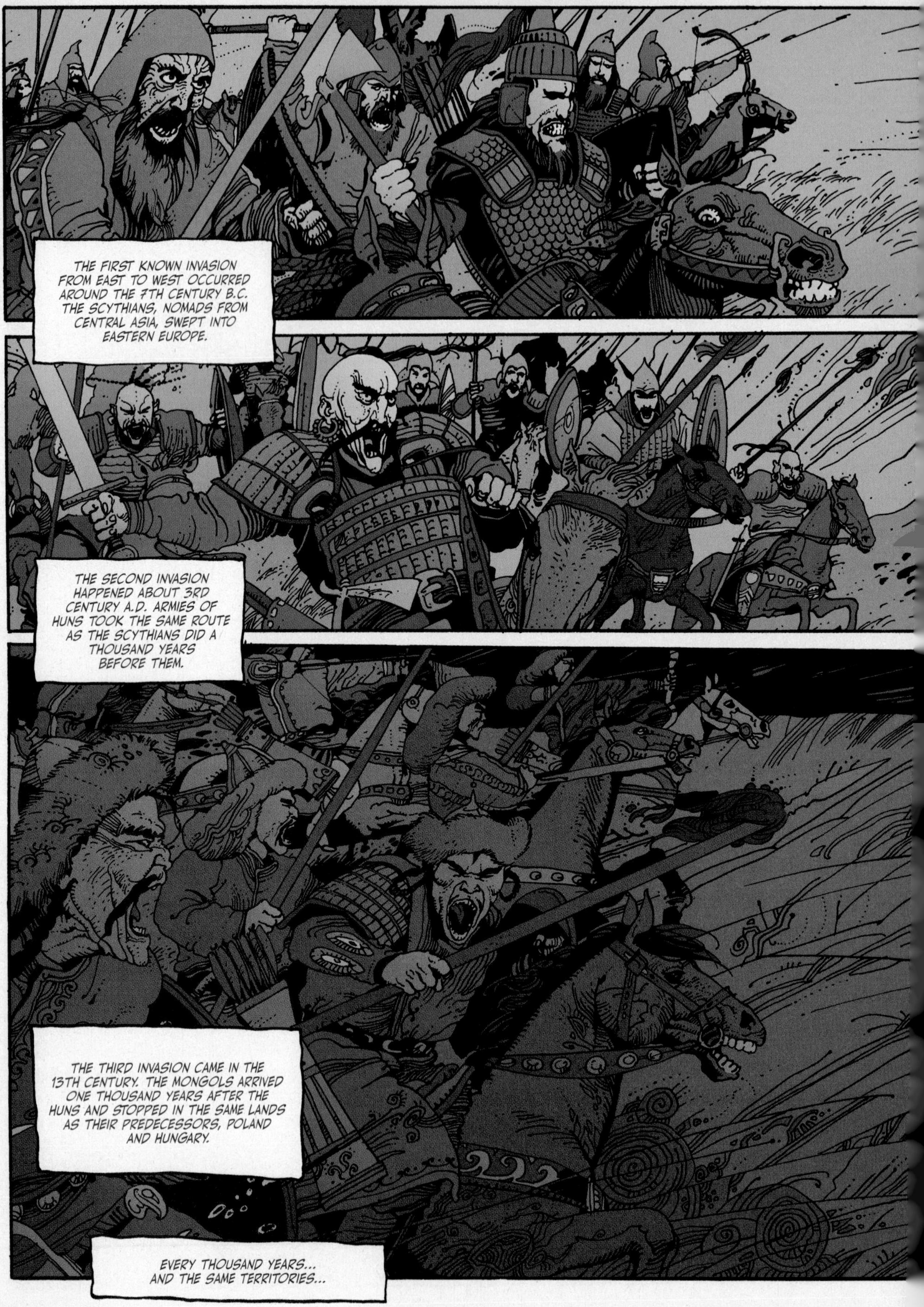
THE FIRST KNOWN INVASION FROM EAST TO WEST OCCURRED AROUND THE 7TH CENTURY B.C. THE SCYTHIANS, NOMADS FROM CENTRAL ASIA, SWEPT INTO EASTERN EUROPE.
THE SECOND INVASION HAPPENED ABOUT 3RD CENTURY A.D. ARMIES OF HUNS TOOK THE SAME ROUTE AS THE SCYTHIANS DID A THOUSAND YEARS BEFORE THEM.
THE THIRD INVASION CAME IN THE 13TH CENTURY. THE MONGOLS ARRIVED ONE THOUSAND YEARS AFTER THE HUNS AND STOPPED IN THE SAME LANDS AS THEIR PREDECESSORS, POLAND AND HUNGARY.
EVERY THOUSAND YEARS... AND THE SAME TERRITORIES...

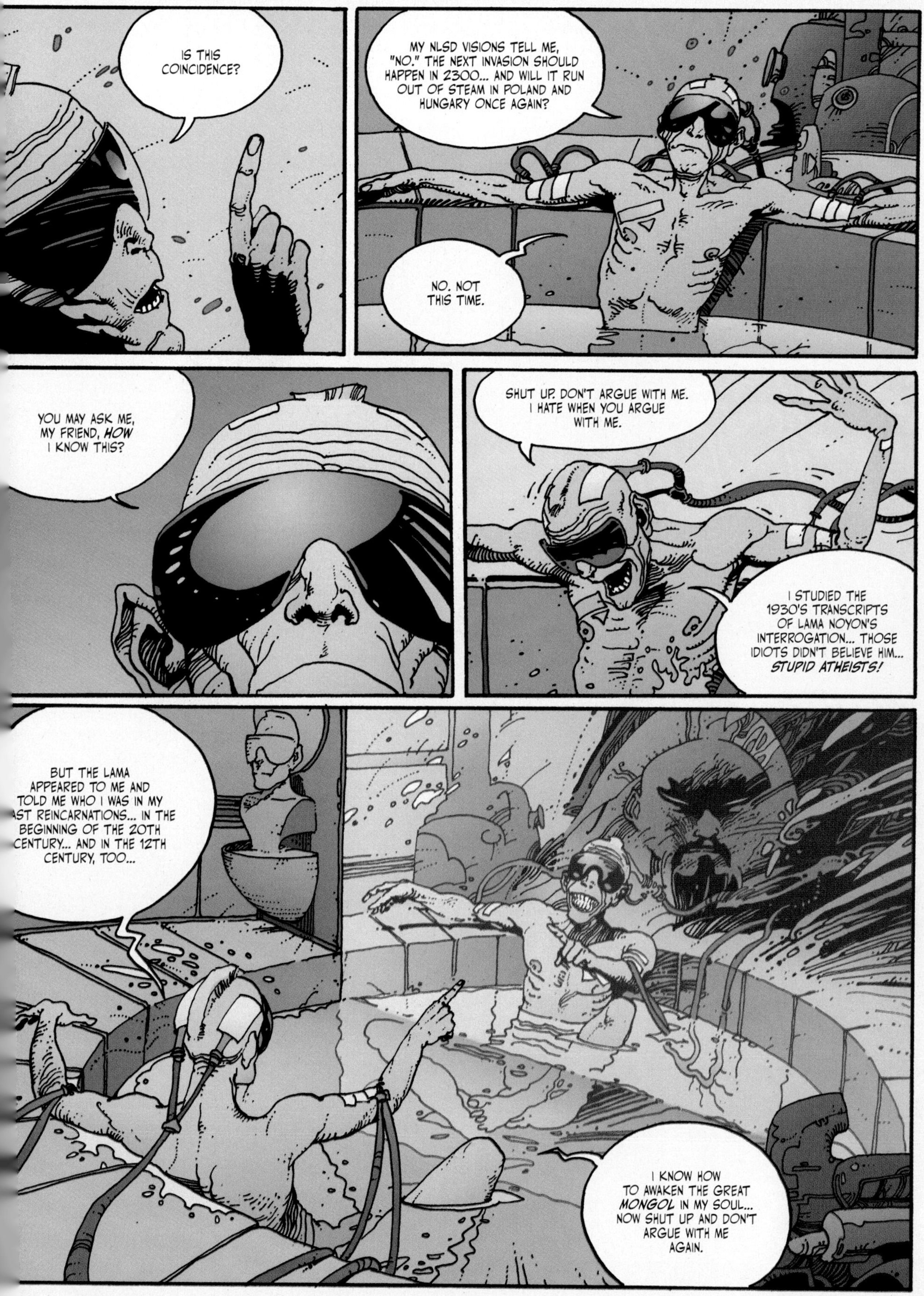
IS THIS COINCIDENCE?
MY NLSD VISIONS TELL ME, "NO." THE NEXT INVASION SHOULD HAPPEN IN 2300... AND WILL IT RUN OUT OF STEAM IN POLAND AND HUNGARY ONCE AGAIN?
NO. NOT THIS TIME.
YOU MAY ASK ME, MY FRIEND, *HOW* I KNOW THIS?
SHUT UP. DON'T ARGUE WITH ME. I HATE WHEN YOU ARGUE WITH ME.
I STUDIED THE 1930'S TRANSCRIPTS OF LAMA NOYON'S INTERROGATION... THOSE IDIOTS DIDN'T BELIEVE HIM... *STUPID ATHEISTS!*
BUT THE LAMA APPEARED TO ME AND TOLD ME WHO I WAS IN MY AST REINCARNATIONS... IN THE BEGINNING OF THE 20TH CENTURY... AND IN THE 12TH CENTURY, TOO...
I KNOW HOW TO AWAKEN THE GREAT *MONGOL* IN MY SOUL... NOW SHUT UP AND DON'T ARGUE WITH ME AGAIN.

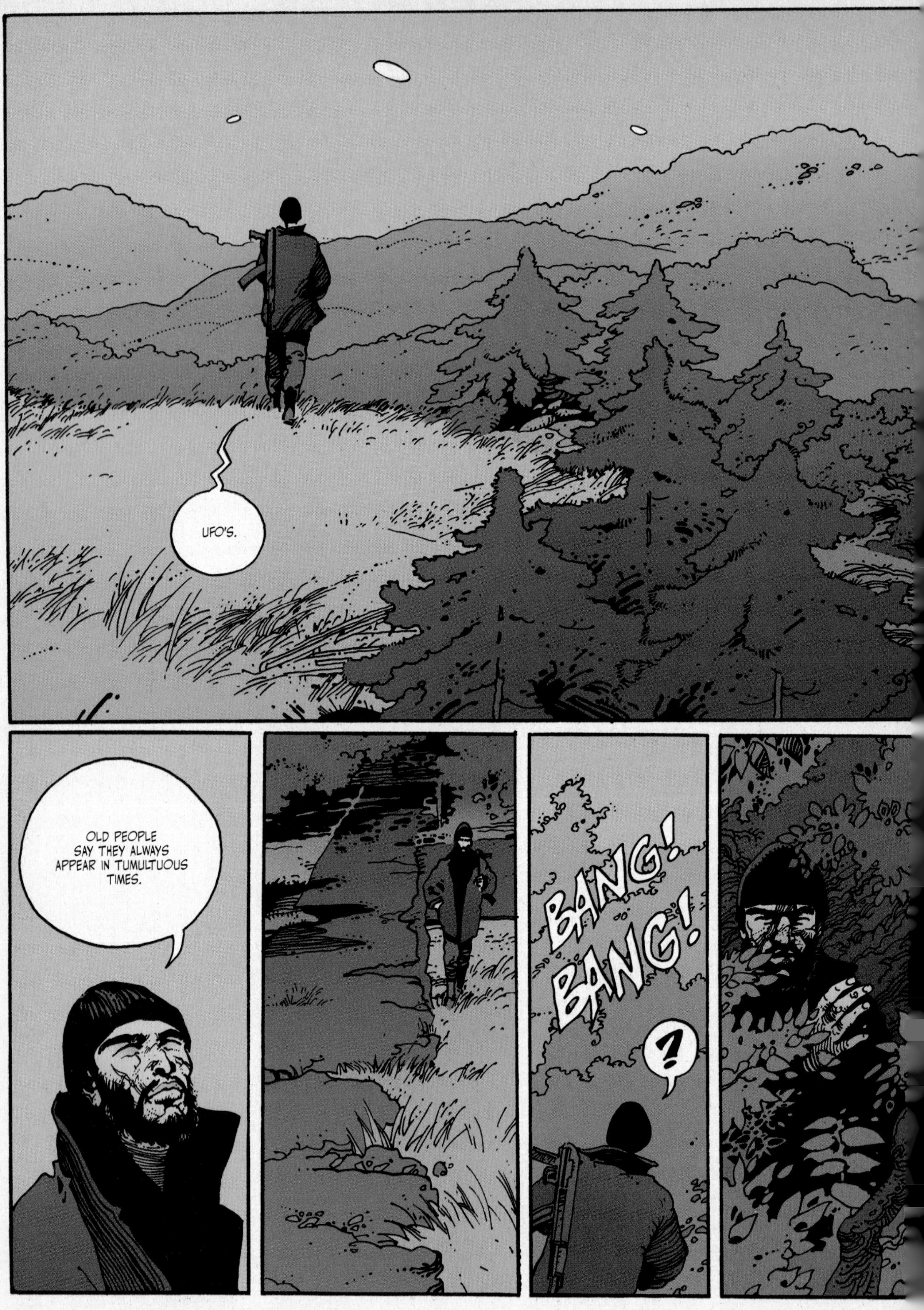
UFO'S.
OLD PEOPLE SAY THEY ALWAYS APPEAR IN TUMULTUOUS TIMES.
BANG!
BANG!
?

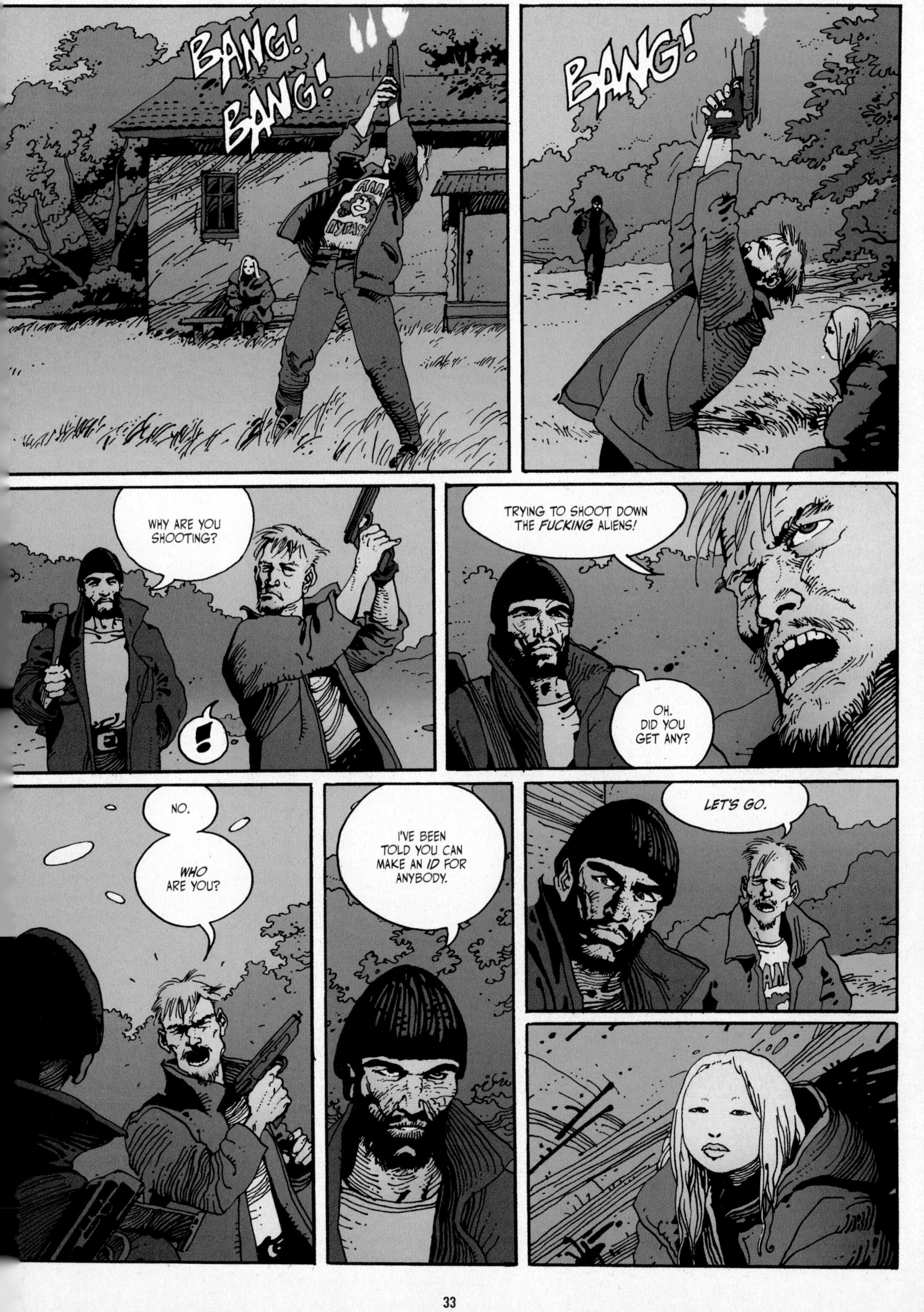
BANG! BANG!
BANG!
WHY ARE YOU SHOOTING?
!
TRYING TO SHOOT DOWN THE *FUCKING* ALIENS!
OH. DID YOU GET ANY?
NO.
WHO ARE YOU?
I'VE BEEN TOLD YOU CAN MAKE AN *ID* FOR ANYBODY.
LET'S GO.

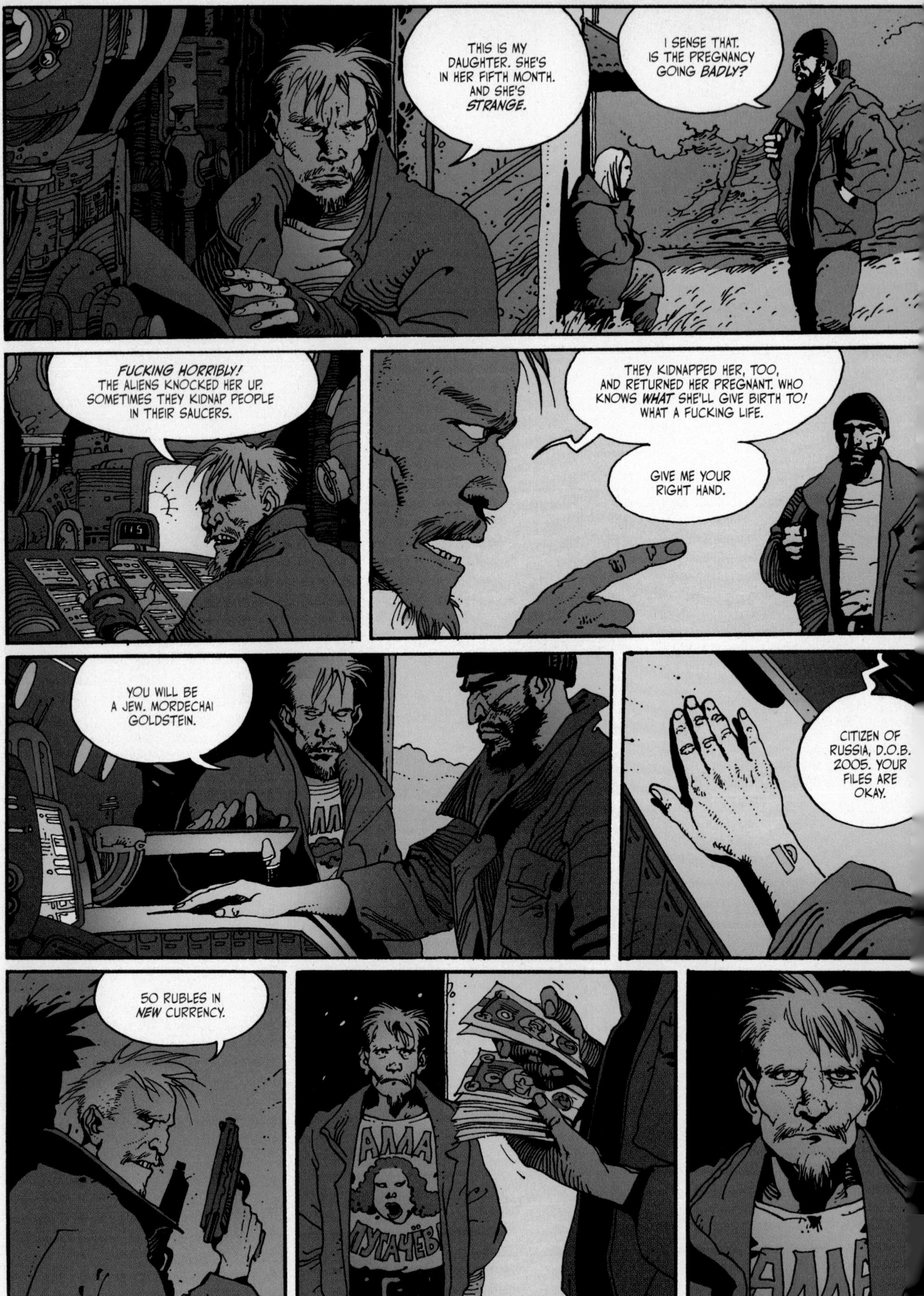
THIS IS MY DAUGHTER. SHE'S IN HER FIFTH MONTH. AND SHE'S *STRANGE.*
I SENSE THAT. IS THE PREGNANCY GOING *BADLY?*
FUCKING HORRIBLY! THE ALIENS KNOCKED HER UP. SOMETIMES THEY KIDNAP PEOPLE IN THEIR SAUCERS.
THEY KIDNAPPED HER, TOO, AND RETURNED HER PREGNANT. WHO KNOWS *WHAT* SHE'LL GIVE BIRTH TO! WHAT A FUCKING LIFE.
GIVE ME YOUR RIGHT HAND.
YOU WILL BE A JEW. MORDECHAI GOLDSTEIN.
CITIZEN OF RUSSIA, D.O.B. 2005. YOUR FILES ARE OKAY.
50 RUBLES IN *NEW* CURRENCY.
АЛЛА
ПУГАЧЁВА

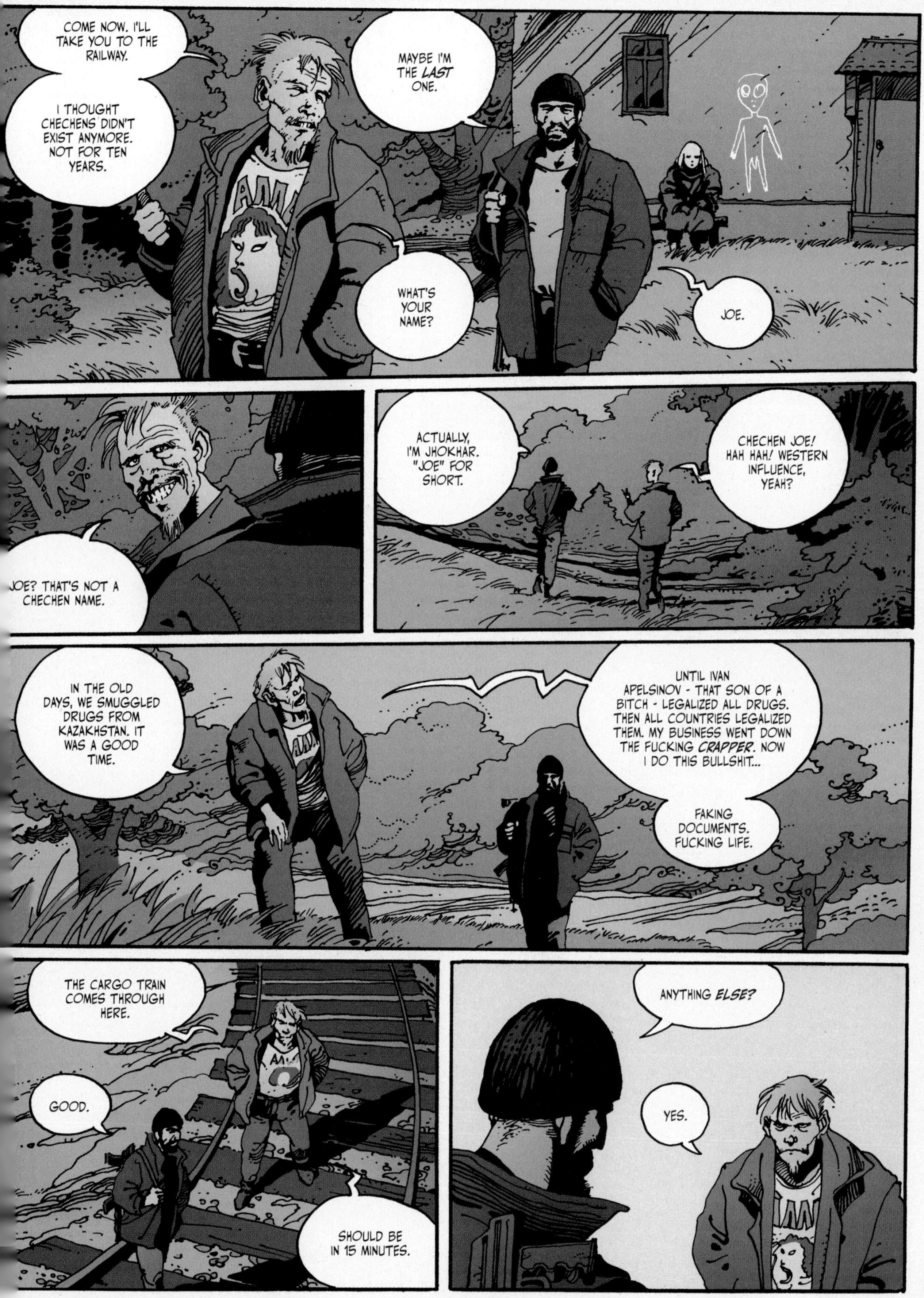

COME NOW. I'LL TAKE YOU TO THE RAILWAY.
I THOUGHT CHECHENS DIDN'T EXIST ANYMORE. NOT FOR TEN YEARS.
MAYBE I'M THE *LAST* ONE.
WHAT'S YOUR NAME?
JOE.
JOE? THAT'S NOT A CHECHEN NAME.
ACTUALLY, I'M JHOKHAR. "JOE" FOR SHORT.
CHECHEN JOE! HAH HAH! WESTERN INFLUENCE, YEAH?
IN THE OLD DAYS, WE SMUGGLED DRUGS FROM KAZAKHSTAN. IT WAS A GOOD TIME.
UNTIL IVAN APELSINOV - THAT SON OF A BITCH - LEGALIZED ALL DRUGS. THEN ALL COUNTRIES LEGALIZED THEM. MY BUSINESS WENT DOWN THE FUCKING *CRAPPER*. NOW I DO THIS BULLSHIT...
FAKING DOCUMENTS. FUCKING LIFE.
THE CARGO TRAIN COMES THROUGH HERE.
GOOD.
SHOULD BE IN 15 MINUTES.
ANYTHING *ELSE?*
YES.

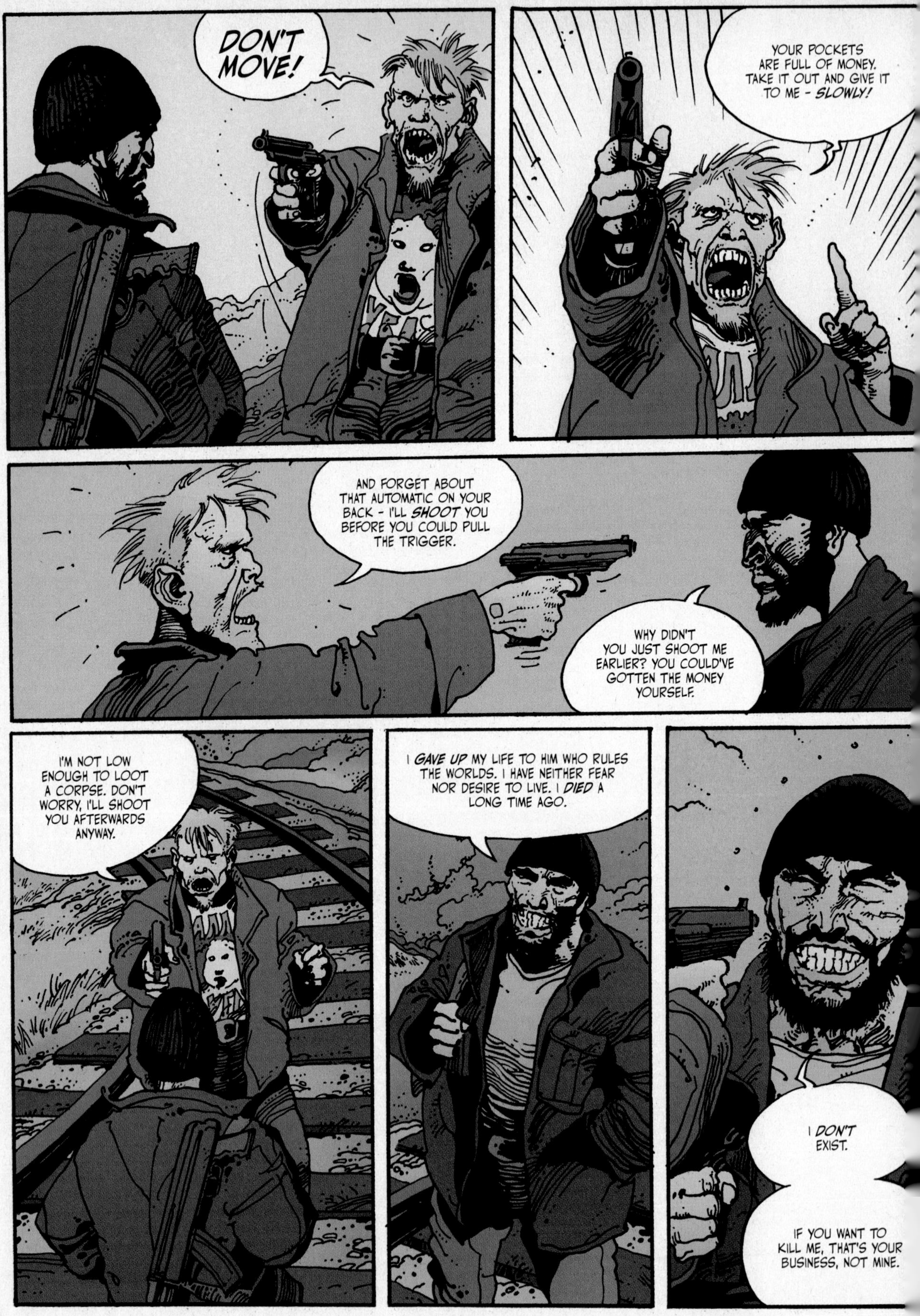
DON'T MOVE!
YOUR POCKETS ARE FULL OF MONEY. TAKE IT OUT AND GIVE IT TO ME - SLOWLY!
AND FORGET ABOUT THAT AUTOMATIC ON YOUR BACK - I'LL SHOOT YOU BEFORE YOU COULD PULL THE TRIGGER.
WHY DIDN'T YOU JUST SHOOT ME EARLIER? YOU COULD'VE GOTTEN THE MONEY YOURSELF.
I'M NOT LOW ENOUGH TO LOOT A CORPSE. DON'T WORRY, I'LL SHOOT YOU AFTERWARDS ANYWAY.
I GAVE UP MY LIFE TO HIM WHO RULES THE WORLDS. I HAVE NEITHER FEAR NOR DESIRE TO LIVE. I DIED A LONG TIME AGO.
I DON'T EXIST.
IF YOU WANT TO KILL ME, THAT'S YOUR BUSINESS, NOT MINE.

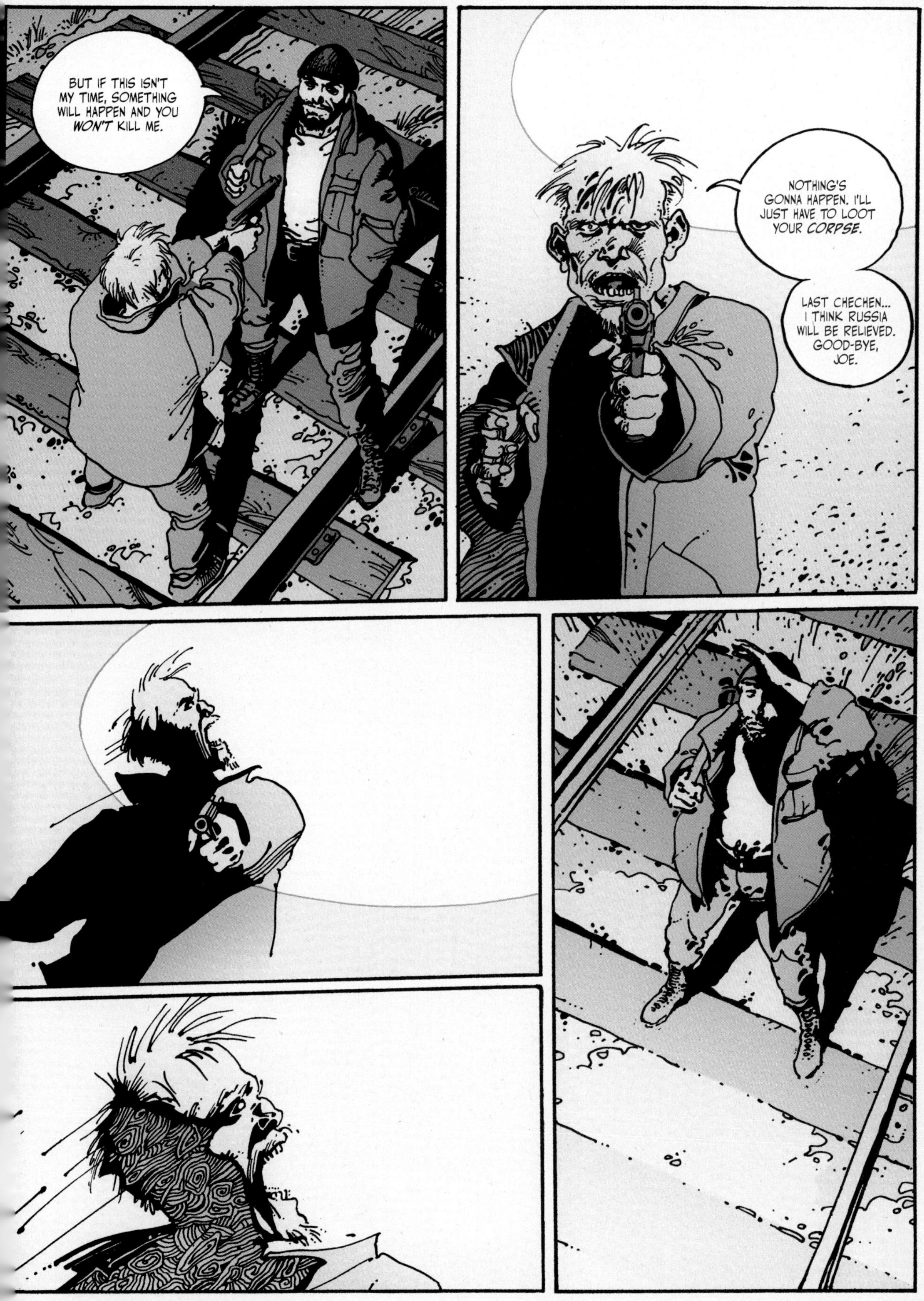
BUT IF THIS ISN'T MY TIME, SOMETHING WILL HAPPEN AND YOU WON'T KILL ME.
NOTHING'S GONNA HAPPEN. I'LL JUST HAVE TO LOOT YOUR CORPSE.
LAST CHECHEN... I THINK RUSSIA WILL BE RELIEVED. GOOD-BYE, JOE.

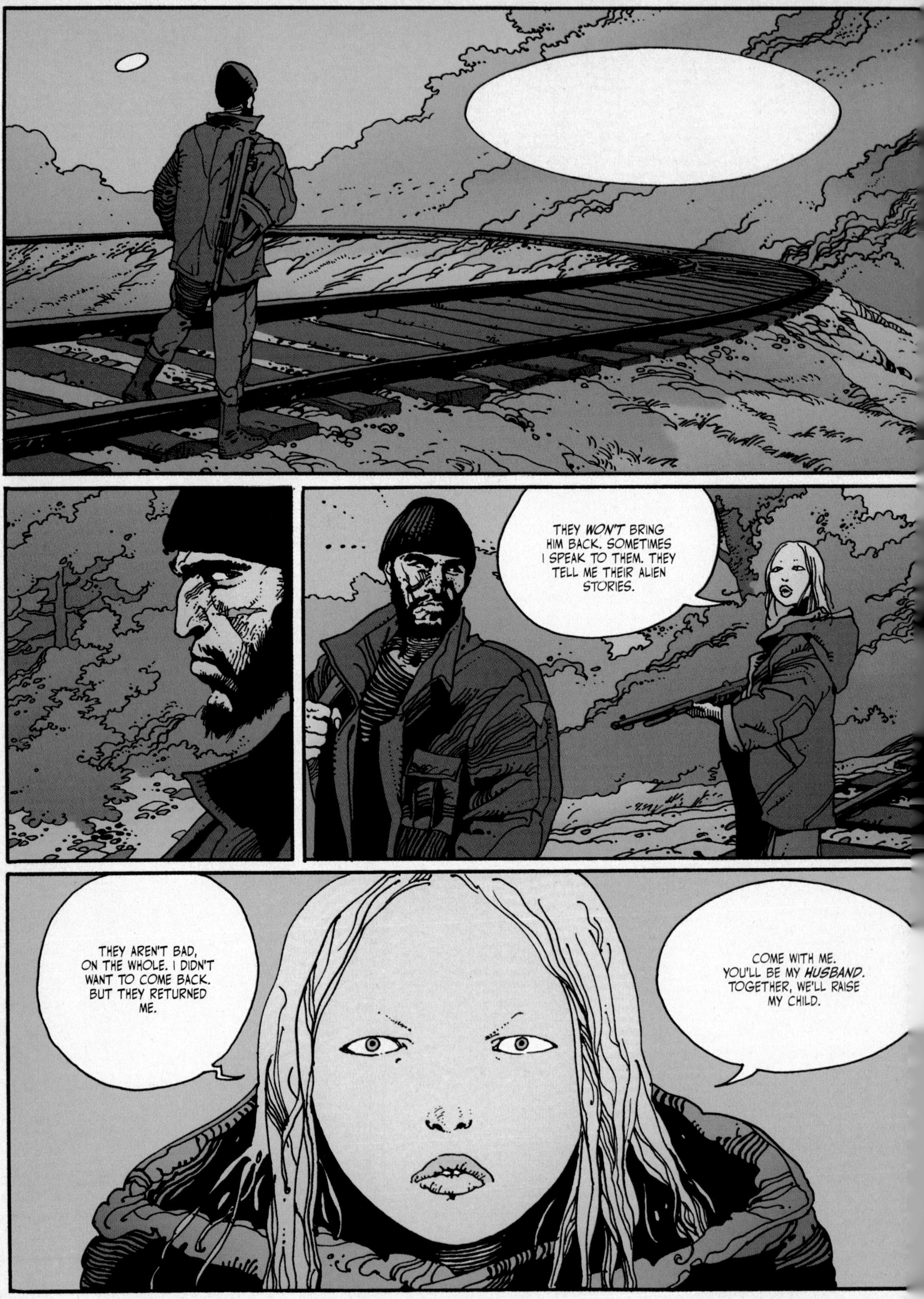
THEY WON'T BRING HIM BACK. SOMETIMES I SPEAK TO THEM. THEY TELL ME THEIR ALIEN STORIES.
THEY AREN'T BAD, ON THE WHOLE. I DIDN'T WANT TO COME BACK. BUT THEY RETURNED ME.
COME WITH ME. YOU'LL BE MY HUSBAND. TOGETHER, WE'LL RAISE MY CHILD.

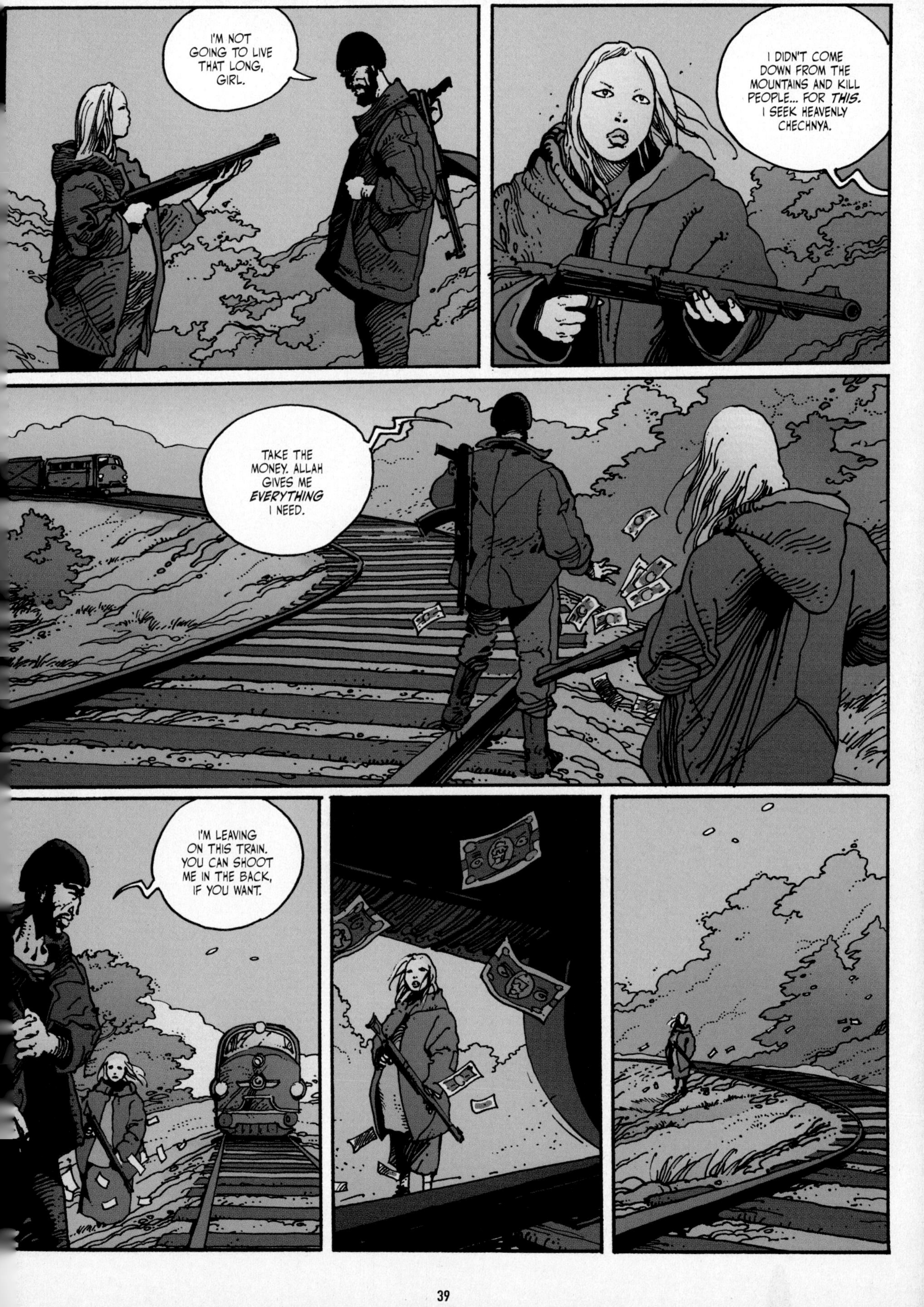
I'M NOT GOING TO LIVE THAT LONG, GIRL.
I DIDN'T COME DOWN FROM THE MOUNTAINS AND KILL PEOPLE... FOR *THIS.* I SEEK HEAVENLY CHECHNYA.
TAKE THE MONEY. ALLAH GIVES ME *EVERYTHING* I NEED.
I'M LEAVING ON THIS TRAIN. YOU CAN SHOOT ME IN THE BACK, IF YOU WANT.

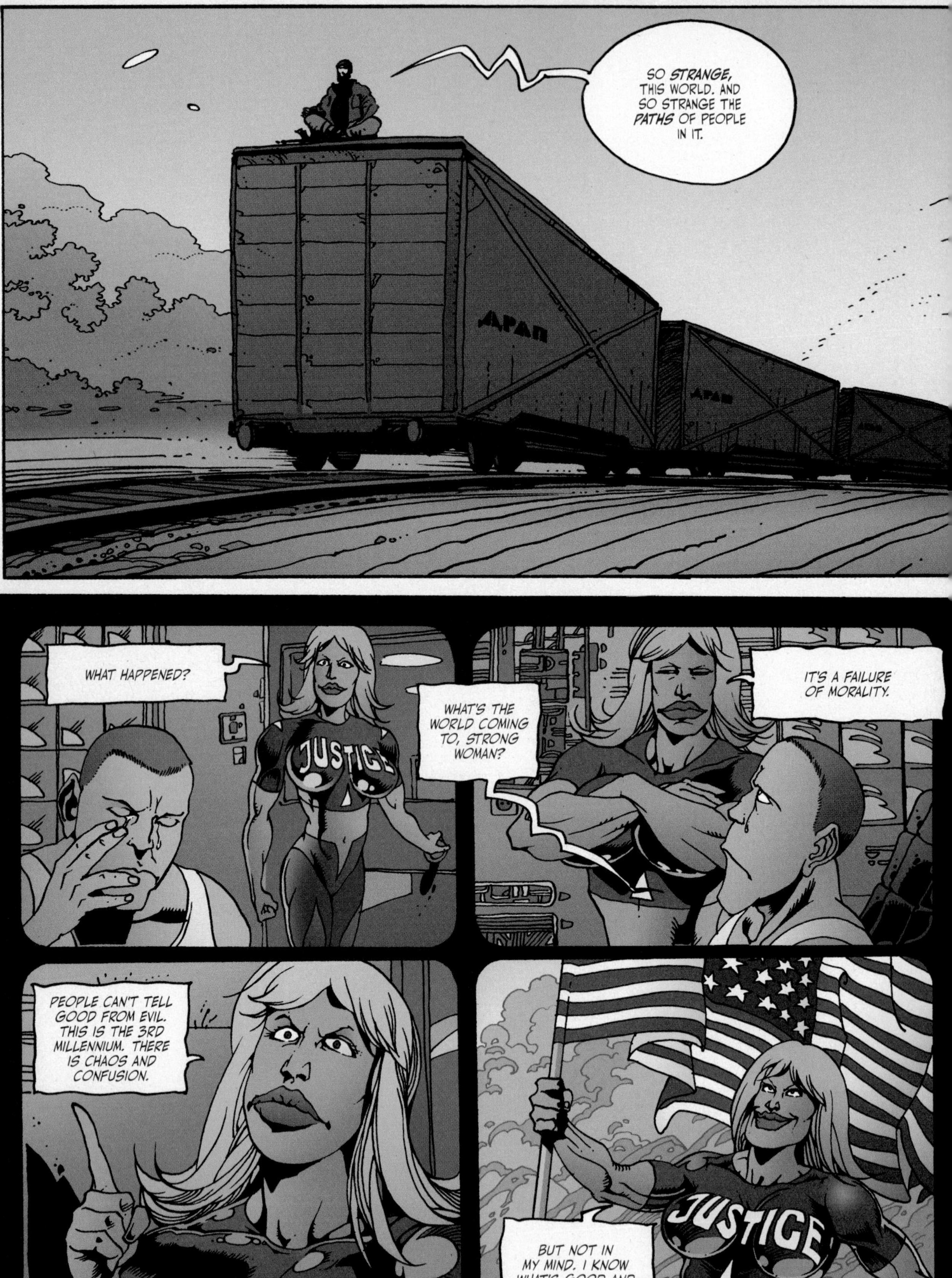
SO STRANGE, THIS WORLD. AND SO STRANGE THE PATHS OF PEOPLE IN IT.
WHAT HAPPENED?
WHAT'S THE WORLD COMING TO, STRONG WOMAN?
IT'S A FAILURE OF MORALITY.
PEOPLE CAN'T TELL GOOD FROM EVIL. THIS IS THE 3RD MILLENNIUM. THERE IS CHAOS AND CONFUSION.
BUT NOT IN MY MIND. I KNOW WHAT'S GOOD AND WHAT'S BAD!

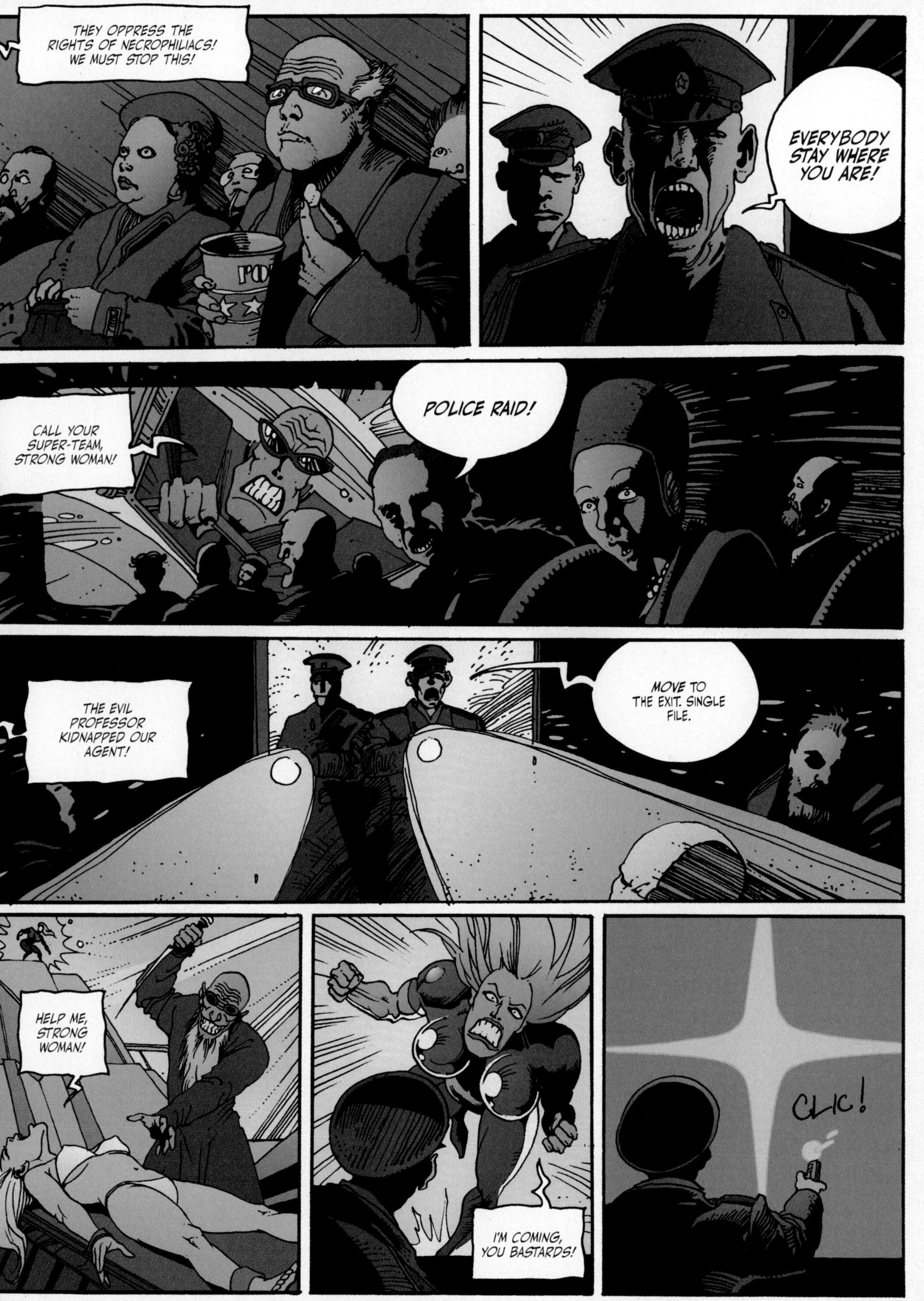
THEY OPPRESS THE RIGHTS OF NECROPHILIACS! WE MUST STOP THIS!
EVERYBODY STAY WHERE YOU ARE!
CALL YOUR SUPER-TEAM, STRONG WOMAN!
POLICE RAID!
THE EVIL PROFESSOR KIDNAPPED OUR AGENT!
MOVE TO THE EXIT. SINGLE FILE.
HELP ME, STRONG WOMAN!
I'M COMING, YOU BASTARDS!
CLIC!

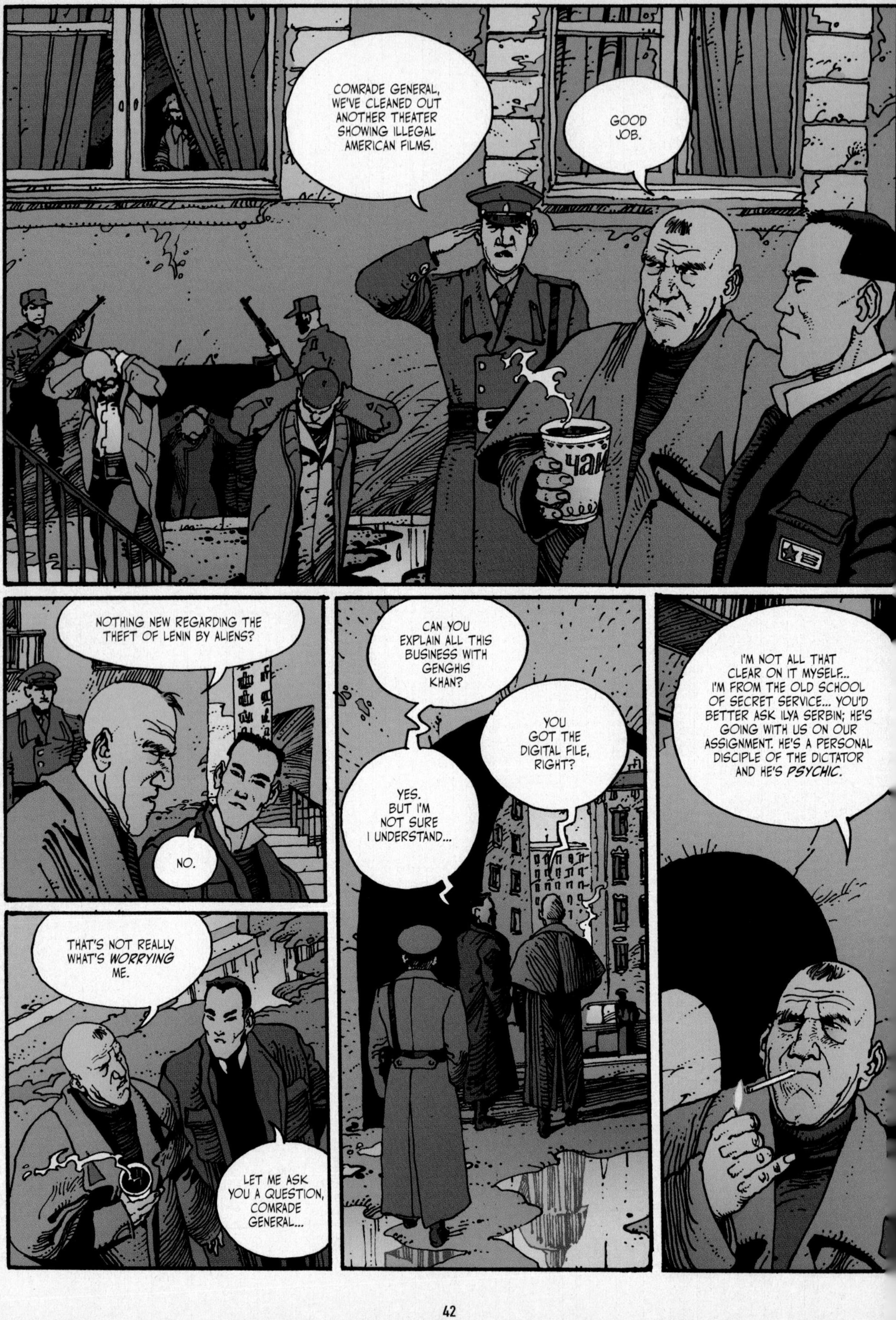
COMRADE GENERAL, WE'VE CLEANED OUT ANOTHER THEATER SHOWING ILLEGAL AMERICAN FILMS.
GOOD JOB.
NOTHING NEW REGARDING THE THEFT OF LENIN BY ALIENS?
NO.
THAT'S NOT REALLY WHAT'S *WORRYING* ME.
LET ME ASK YOU A QUESTION, COMRADE GENERAL...
CAN YOU EXPLAIN ALL THIS BUSINESS WITH GENGHIS KHAN?
YOU GOT THE DIGITAL FILE, RIGHT?
YES. BUT I'M NOT SURE I UNDERSTAND...
I'M NOT ALL THAT CLEAR ON IT MYSELF... I'M FROM THE OLD SCHOOL OF SECRET SERVICE... YOU'D BETTER ASK ILYA SERBIN; HE'S GOING WITH US ON OUR ASSIGNMENT. HE'S A PERSONAL DISCIPLE OF THE DICTATOR AND HE'S *PSYCHIC*.

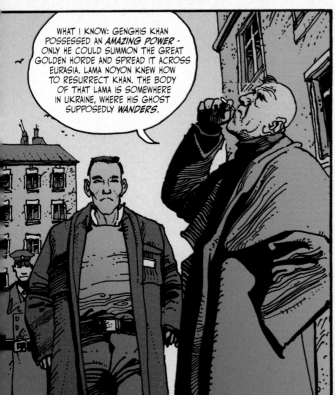

WHAT I KNOW: GENGHIS KHAN POSSESSED AN *AMAZING POWER* - ONLY HE COULD SUMMON THE GREAT GOLDEN HORDE AND SPREAD IT ACROSS EURASIA. LAMA NOYON KNEW HOW TO RESURRECT KHAN. THE BODY OF THAT LAMA IS SOMEWHERE IN UKRAINE, WHERE HIS GHOST SUPPOSEDLY *WANDERS*.

OUR TASK IS TO FIND THE BODY OF THE LAMA AND BRING IT BACK TO MOSCOW.

ALL THIS IN THE INTEREST OF THE EMPIRE.

YOUR MISSION IS TO POSE AS THE DESCENDANT OF LAMA NOYON. YOU'LL GO TO UKRAINE TO EXHUME THE BODY OF YOUR GREAT-GREAT-GRANDFATHER, TO RE-BURY IT IN THE FAMILY CRYPT. EVERYTHING SHOULD GO SMOOTHLY.

ONE MORE QUESTION, COMRADE GENERAL - WHY NOT FLY TO KIEV?

BECAUSE TRAINS ATTRACT LESS ATTENTION.

LIKE THE DICTATOR SAYS, "DON'T RUSH ME, I'VE GOT *ALL* THE TIME IN THE WORLD."

BY THE WAY, DOES ANYBODY KNOW WHAT THE HELL'S GOING ON RIGHT NOW IN UKRAINE?

Я ПОМНЮ

O BAC!

VRUMMMM

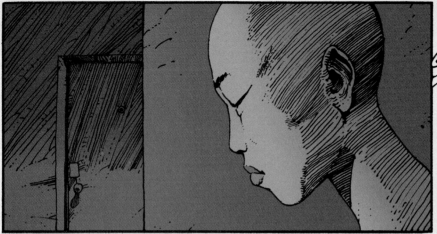

SLAM!

LET'S CHECK OUT THIS ONE.

SLAM!

HUH. NOTHING AGAIN.

THEY SOLD EVERYTHING WHEN THEY ESCAPED THE FLOOD.

HEY. LOOK!

I'D HEARD THOSE CRAZY BUDDHIST MONKS TURNED THESE VACATED APARTMENTS INTO MEDITATION CELLS.

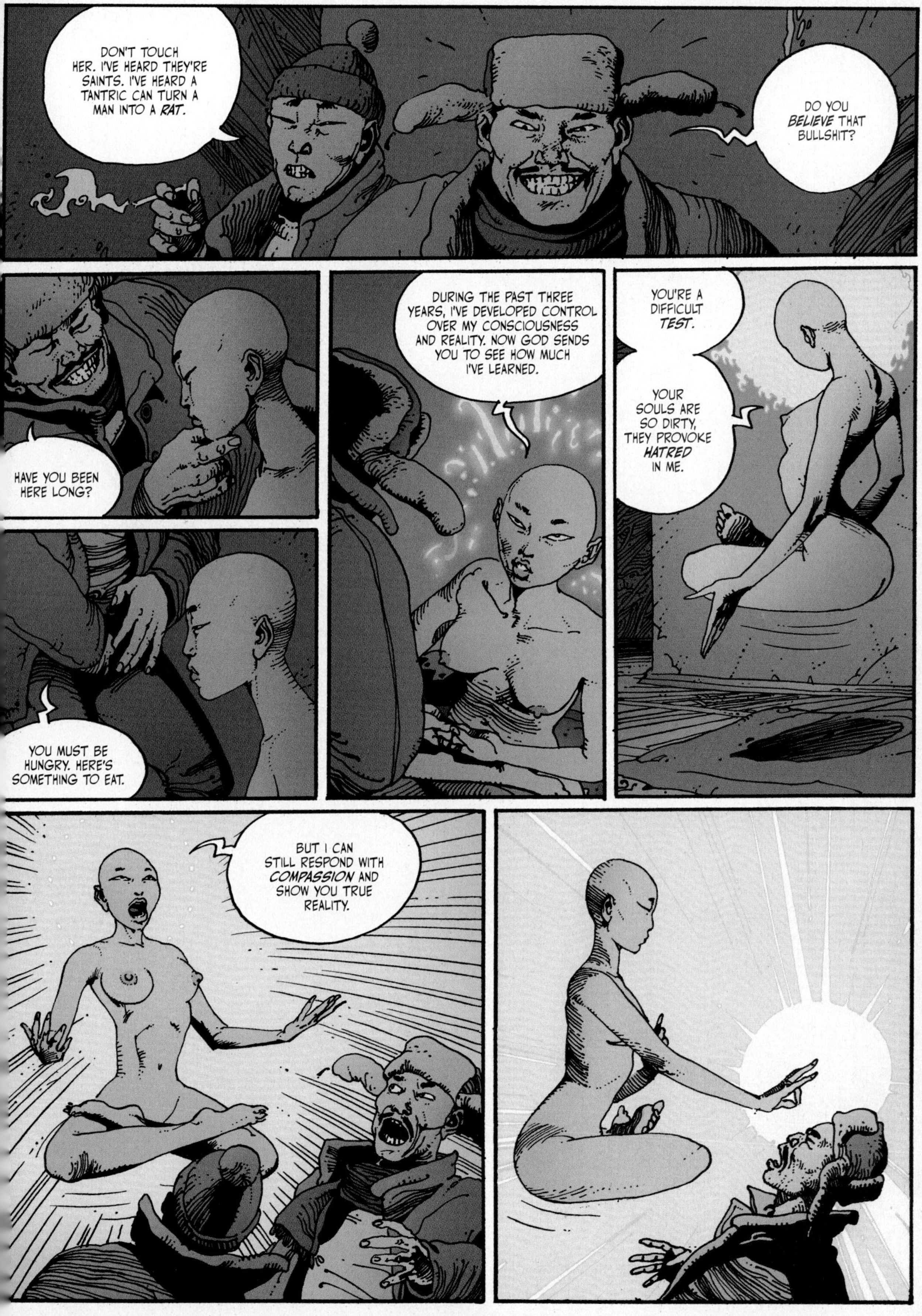

DON'T TOUCH HER. I'VE HEARD THEY'RE SAINTS. I'VE HEARD A TANTRIC CAN TURN A MAN INTO A *RAT*.
DO YOU *BELIEVE* THAT BULLSHIT?
HAVE YOU BEEN HERE LONG?
YOU MUST BE HUNGRY. HERE'S SOMETHING TO EAT.
DURING THE PAST THREE YEARS, I'VE DEVELOPED CONTROL OVER MY CONSCIOUSNESS AND REALITY. NOW GOD SENDS YOU TO SEE HOW MUCH I'VE LEARNED.
YOU'RE A DIFFICULT *TEST*.
YOUR SOULS ARE SO DIRTY, THEY PROVOKE *HATRED* IN ME.
BUT I CAN STILL RESPOND WITH *COMPASSION* AND SHOW YOU TRUE REALITY.

AAAAH!
IT'S HORRIBLE!

WHAT'S WITH YOU?

I'M A MONSTER! BLACK WORMS... INSIDE OF ME! EACH OF THEM IS ME!

?

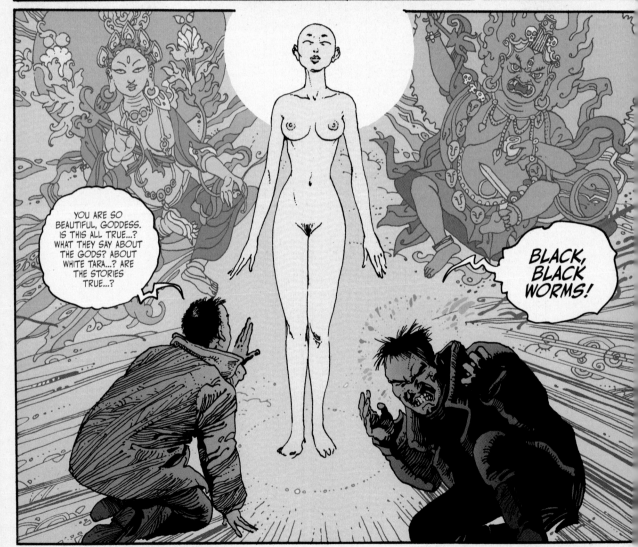

YOU ARE SO BEAUTIFUL, GODDESS. IS THIS ALL TRUE...? WHAT THEY SAY ABOUT THE GODS? ABOUT WHITE TARA...? ARE THE STORIES TRUE...?

BLACK, BLACK WORMS!

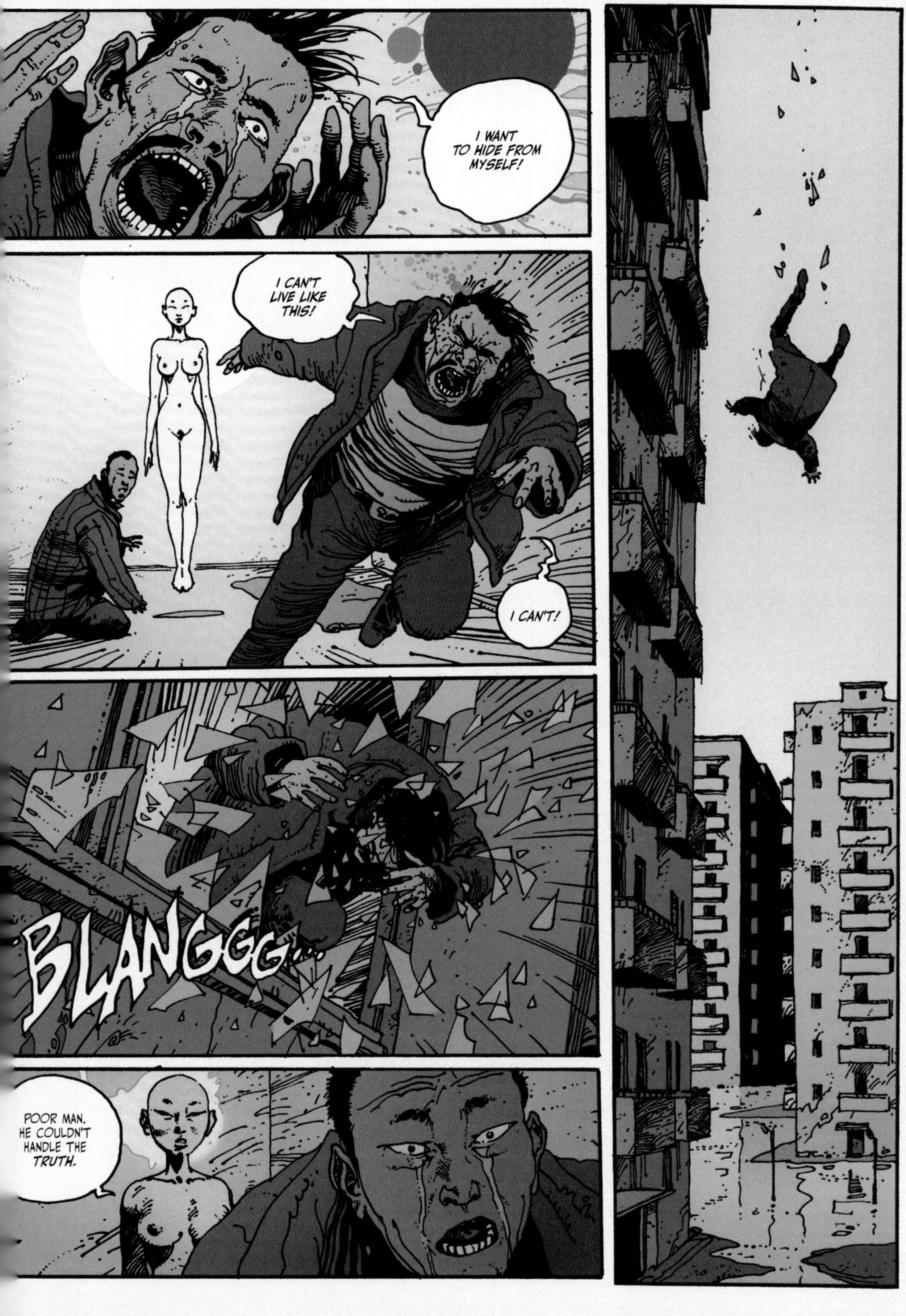
I WANT TO HIDE FROM MYSELF!
I CAN'T LIVE LIKE THIS!
I CAN'T!
BLANGGG...
POOR MAN. HE COULDN'T HANDLE THE TRUTH.

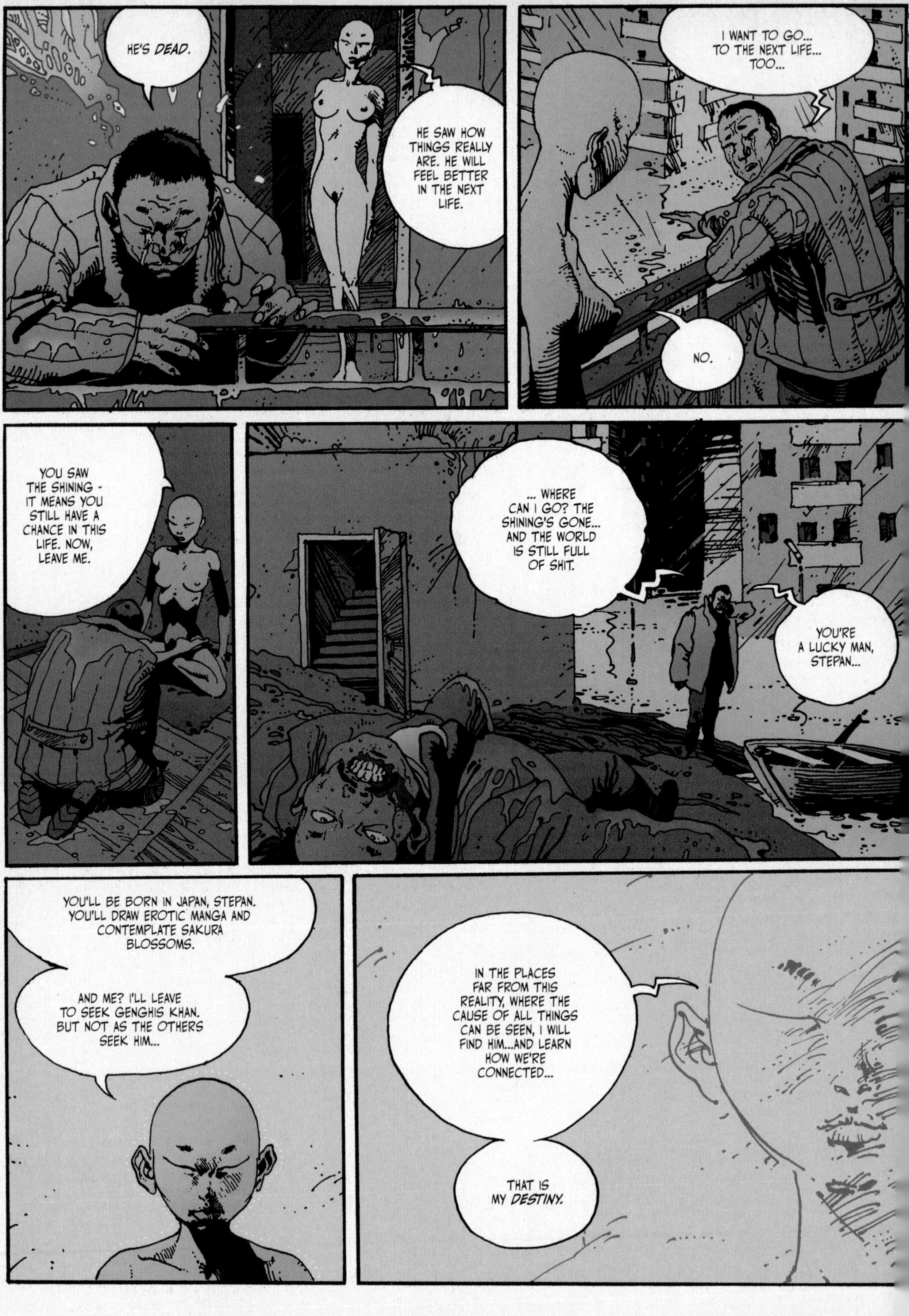
HE'S *DEAD*.
HE SAW HOW THINGS REALLY ARE. HE WILL FEEL BETTER IN THE NEXT LIFE.
I WANT TO GO... TO THE NEXT LIFE... TOO...
NO.
YOU SAW THE SHINING - IT MEANS YOU STILL HAVE A CHANCE IN THIS LIFE. NOW, LEAVE ME.
... WHERE CAN I GO? THE SHINING'S GONE... AND THE WORLD IS STILL FULL OF SHIT.
YOU'RE A LUCKY MAN, STEPAN...
YOU'LL BE BORN IN JAPAN, STEPAN. YOU'LL DRAW EROTIC MANGA AND CONTEMPLATE SAKURA BLOSSOMS.
AND ME? I'LL LEAVE TO SEEK GENGHIS KHAN. BUT NOT AS THE OTHERS SEEK HIM...
IN THE PLACES FAR FROM THIS REALITY, WHERE THE CAUSE OF ALL THINGS CAN BE SEEN, I WILL FIND HIM...AND LEARN HOW WE'RE CONNECTED...
THAT IS MY *DESTINY*.

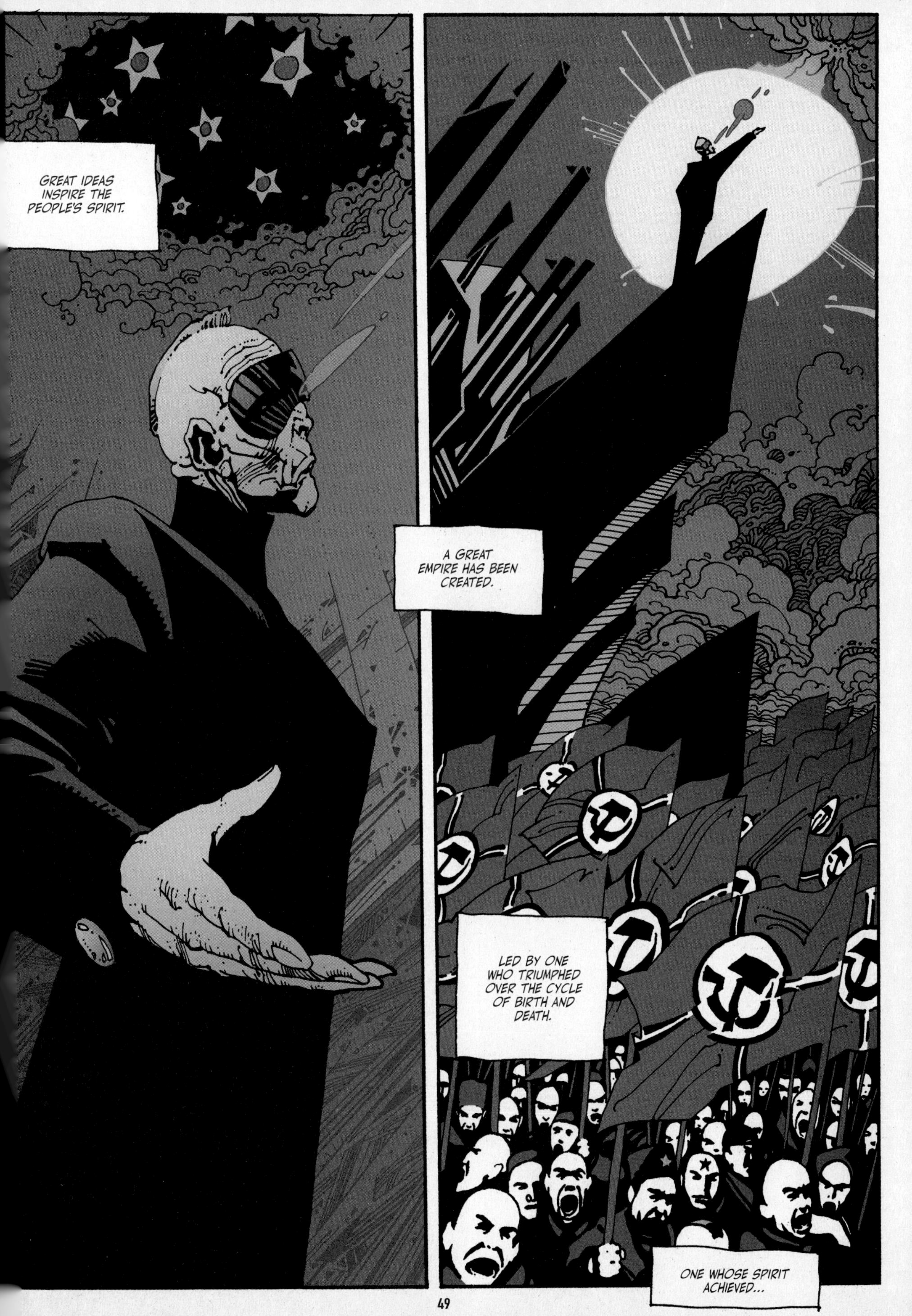
GREAT IDEAS INSPIRE THE PEOPLE'S SPIRIT.
A GREAT EMPIRE HAS BEEN CREATED.
LED BY ONE WHO TRIUMPHED OVER THE CYCLE OF BIRTH AND DEATH.
ONE WHOSE SPIRIT ACHIEVED...

... WHOSE SPIRIT ACHIEVED...

IS THAT ME THERE? TRYING TO FLY?

THAT'S YOU.

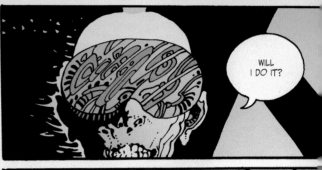

WILL I DO IT?

MAYBE YOU WILL... OR MAYBE YOU'LL DIE.

IT'S HARD TO SAY.

TELL ME... AND ONLY ME...

WHAT COULD POSSIBLY KILL ME?

IT'S UP TO YOU. MAYBE PEN AND INK.

CHEERS.

WHAT PEN?

WHERE ARE YOU?

COMMISSAR NOYON?!

HE'S DEAD!

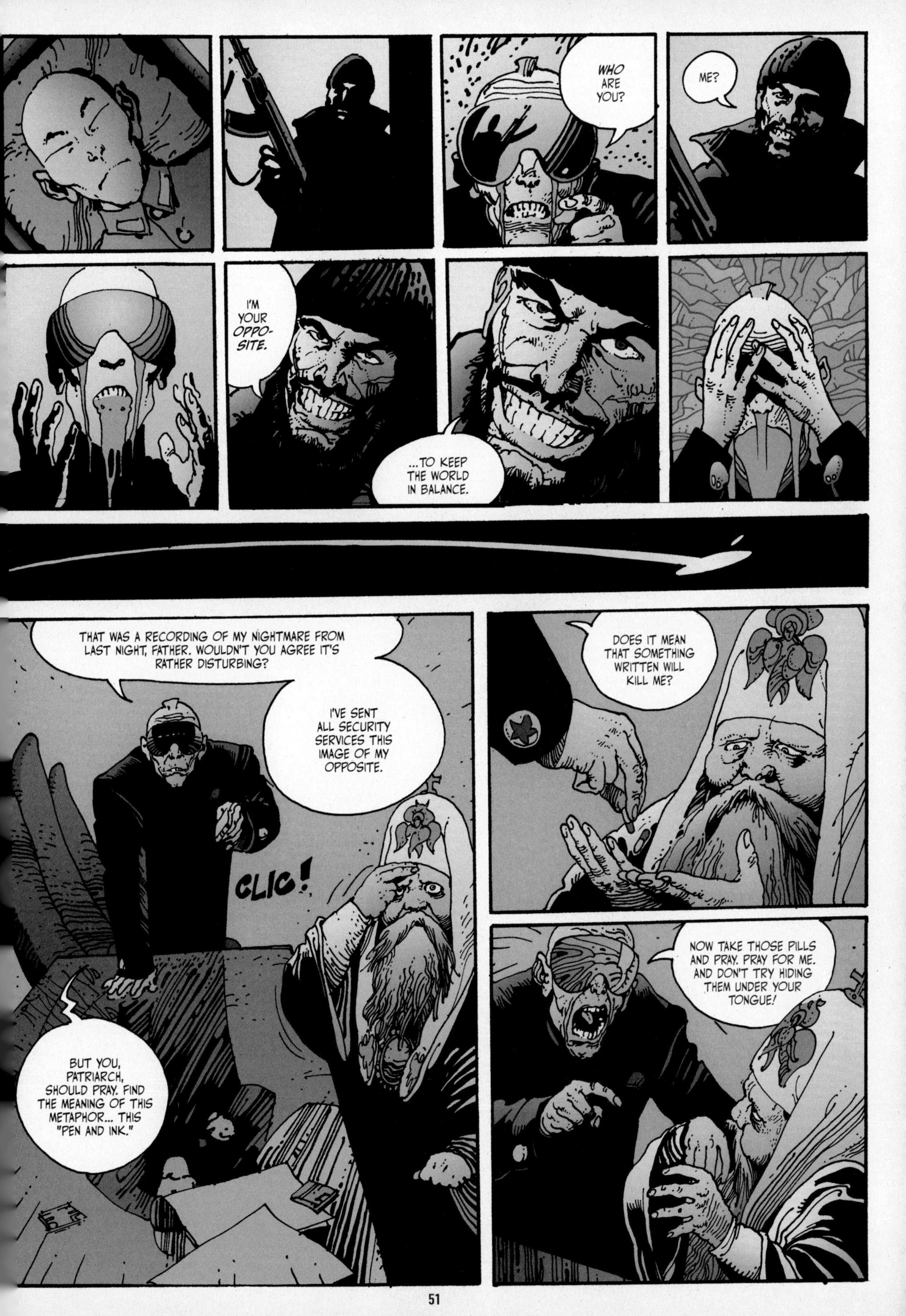
WHO ARE YOU?
ME?
I'M YOUR OPPO-SITE.
...TO KEEP THE WORLD IN BALANCE.
THAT WAS A RECORDING OF MY NIGHTMARE FROM LAST NIGHT, FATHER. WOULDN'T YOU AGREE IT'S RATHER DISTURBING?
I'VE SENT ALL SECURITY SERVICES THIS IMAGE OF MY OPPOSITE.
CLIC!
BUT YOU, PATRIARCH, SHOULD PRAY. FIND THE MEANING OF THIS METAPHOR... THIS "PEN AND INK."
DOES IT MEAN THAT SOMETHING WRITTEN WILL KILL ME?
NOW TAKE THOSE PILLS AND PRAY. PRAY FOR ME. AND DON'T TRY HIDING THEM UNDER YOUR TONGUE!

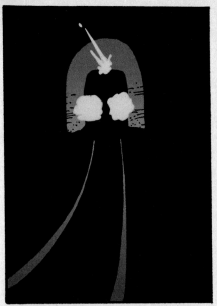

YOU ARE LISTENING TO UKRAINIAN RADIO...

...BECAUSE OF ITS GEOGRAPHICAL AND POLITICAL SITUATION, UKRAINE IS THE ONLY NEUTRAL STATE LEFT IN EUROPE AFTER THE FAILURE OF GLOBALIZATION IN THE YEAR 2024. IT IS THE LAST BASTION OF PEACE AND PROGRESS...

LADIES AND GENTLEMEN, WE ARE NOW APPROACHING THE UKRAINIAN FRONTIER.

I HATE UKRAINIAN.

IT SOUNDS LIKE A PARODY OF RUSSIAN. WHY DO WE STILL PUT UP WITH THEIR INDEPENDENCE?

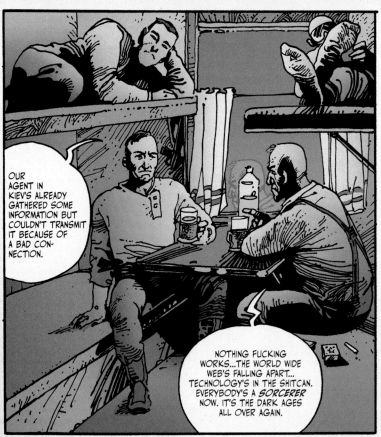

OUR AGENT IN KIEV'S ALREADY GATHERED SOME INFORMATION BUT COULDN'T TRANSMIT IT BECAUSE OF A BAD CONNECTION.

NOTHING FUCKING WORKS...THE WORLD WIDE WEB'S FALLING APART... TECHNOLOGY'S IN THE SHITCAN. EVERYBODY'S A *SORCERER* NOW. IT'S THE DARK AGES ALL OVER AGAIN.

WE EVEN HAVE AN OCCULT AGENT AMONG US.

HEAR THAT, ILYA? I'M TALKING ABOUT YOU.

YOU'RE JUST OLD FASHIONED, VLADIMIR VLADIMIROVICH... YOUR METHODS ARE *OBSOLETE.* WE'RE FINALLY GETTING BACK TO REAL RUSSIAN SPIRITUALITY. THE DICTATOR UNDERSTANDS HOW THINGS ARE.

IS THAT WHY YOU RAIDED HIS CLOSET FOR A PAIR OF GLASSES?

LEAVE ME ALONE, COMRADE GENERAL.

VZAT

HELLO, YOU HANDSOME HUNKS. WANT ME TO TELL YOUR FORTUNE? YOUR FUTURE LOVE LIFE? CROSS MY PALM WITH A LITTLE GOLD.

I WON'T BE TOO GREEDY AND I'LL TELL YOU EVERYTHING.

DAMN! WHO LET HER IN THIS CAR?

CHRIST, BUDULAY! WHAT AM I SUPPOSED TO DO?! IN ONE COMPARTMENT THERE'S A JEW WHO'S NOT A JEW AT ALL...

... AND IN ANOTHER COMPARTMENT, A PACK OF UNDER-COVER AGENTS...

OOPS! EXCUSE ME, SIR!

SLAM!

VZZAT

56Б

GYPSIES. I HATE GYPSIES.

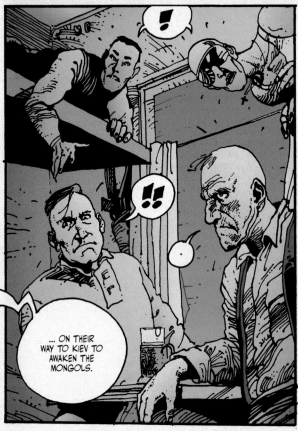

!

!!

... ON THEIR WAY TO KIEV TO AWAKEN THE MONGOLS.

YOU! DON'T MOVE!

HOW COULD SHE KNOW?!

HAVEN'T YOU HEARD? A GYPSY KNOWS EVERYTHING.

ТУАЛЕТ

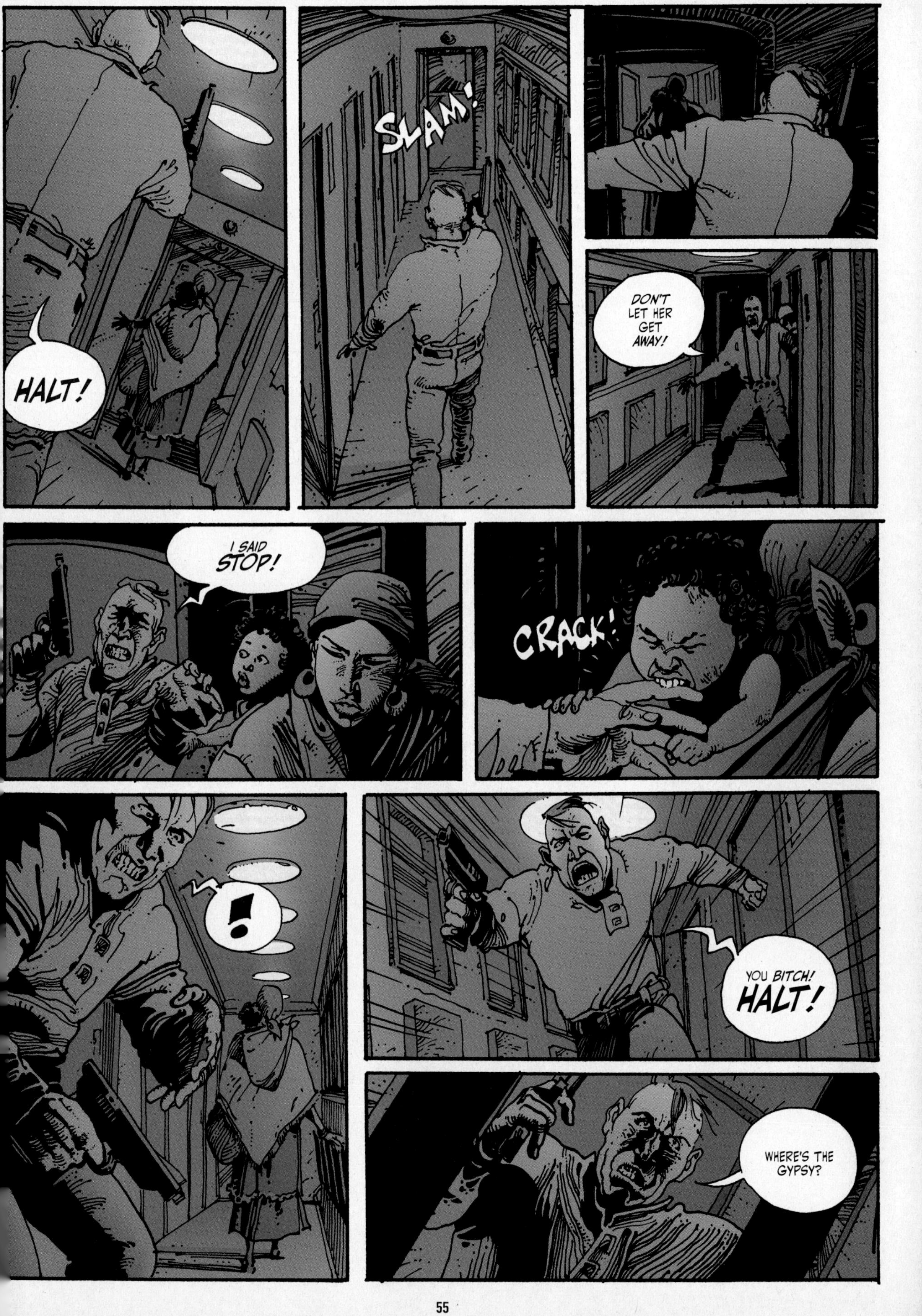
HALT!
SLAM!
DON'T LET HER GET AWAY!
I SAID STOP!
CRACK!
!
YOU BITCH! HALT!
WHERE'S THE GYPSY?

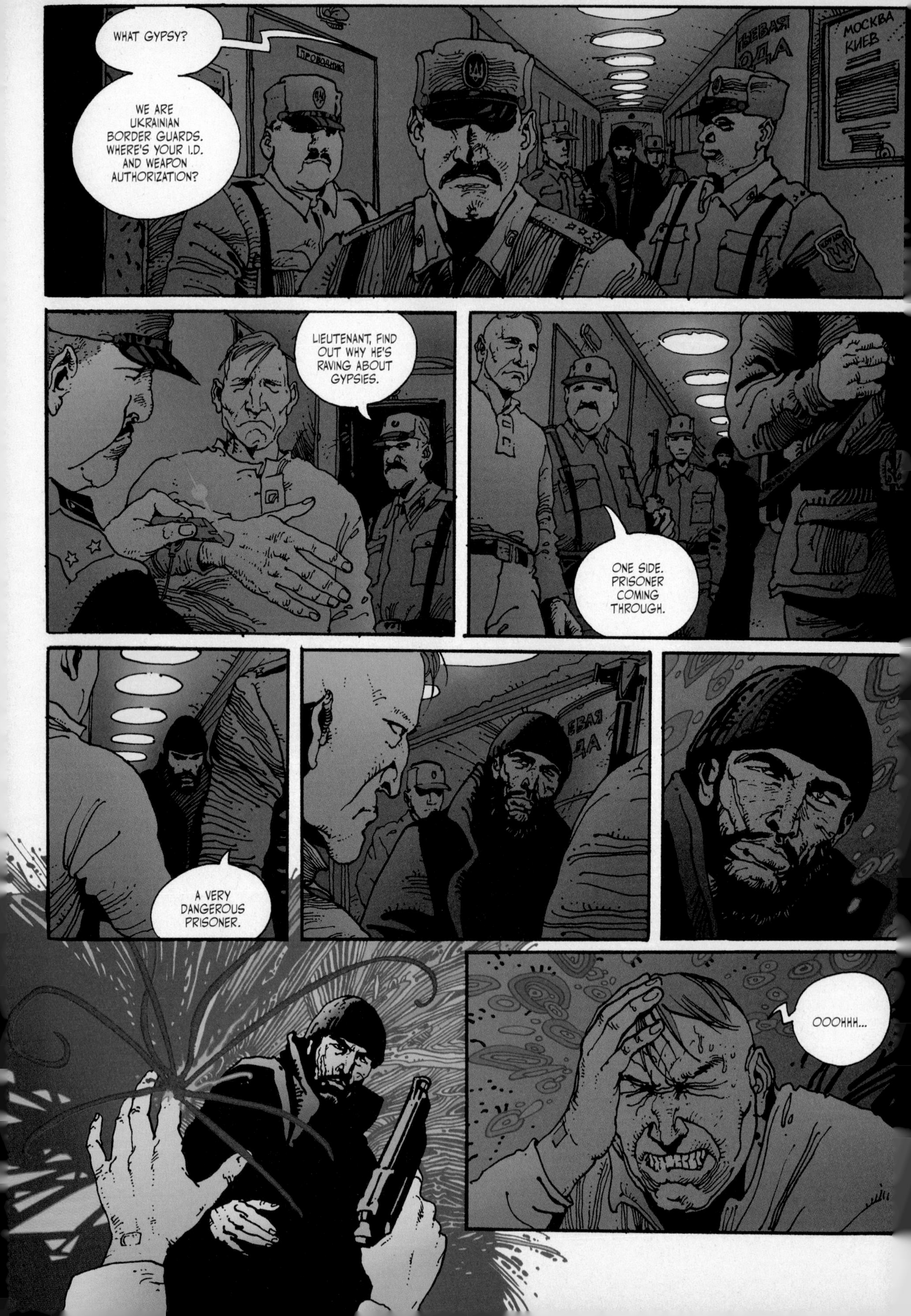

WHAT GYPSY?
WE ARE UKRAINIAN BORDER GUARDS. WHERE'S YOUR I.D. AND WEAPON AUTHORIZATION?
МОСКВА
КИЕВ
LIEUTENANT, FIND OUT WHY HE'S RAVING ABOUT GYPSIES.
ONE SIDE. PRISONER COMING THROUGH.
A VERY DANGEROUS PRISONER.
OOOHHH...

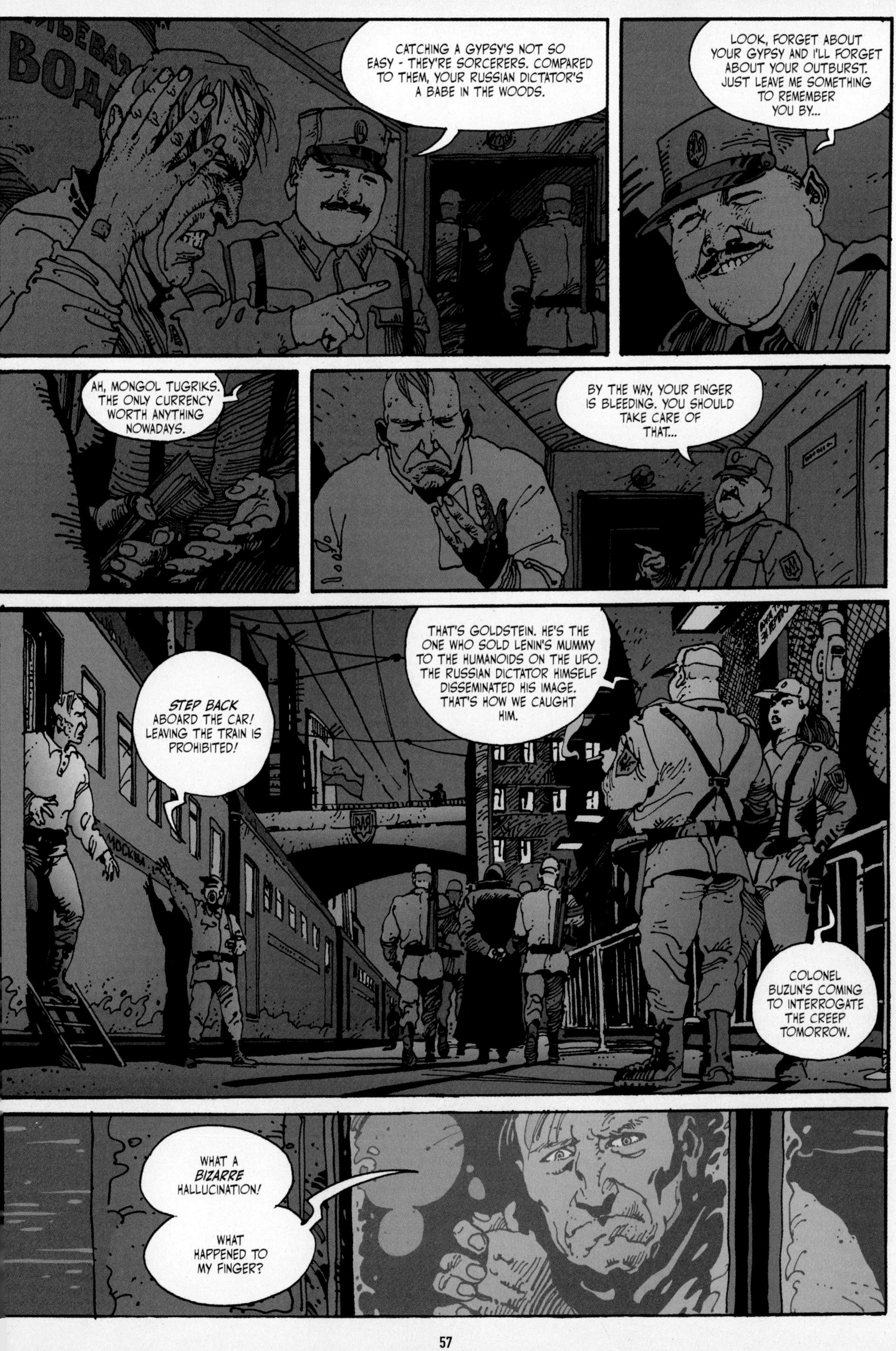
CATCHING A GYPSY'S NOT SO EASY - THEY'RE SORCERERS. COMPARED TO THEM, YOUR RUSSIAN DICTATOR'S A BABE IN THE WOODS.
LOOK, FORGET ABOUT YOUR GYPSY AND I'LL FORGET ABOUT YOUR OUTBURST. JUST LEAVE ME SOMETHING TO REMEMBER YOU BY...
AH, MONGOL TUGRIKS. THE ONLY CURRENCY WORTH ANYTHING NOWADAYS.
BY THE WAY, YOUR FINGER IS BLEEDING. YOU SHOULD TAKE CARE OF THAT...
STEP BACK ABOARD THE CAR! LEAVING THE TRAIN IS PROHIBITED!
THAT'S GOLDSTEIN. HE'S THE ONE WHO SOLD LENIN'S MUMMY TO THE HUMANOIDS ON THE UFO. THE RUSSIAN DICTATOR HIMSELF DISSEMINATED HIS IMAGE. THAT'S HOW WE CAUGHT HIM.
МОСКВА
COLONEL BUZUN'S COMING TO INTERROGATE THE CREEP TOMORROW.
WHAT A BIZARRE HALLUCINATION!
WHAT HAPPENED TO MY FINGER?

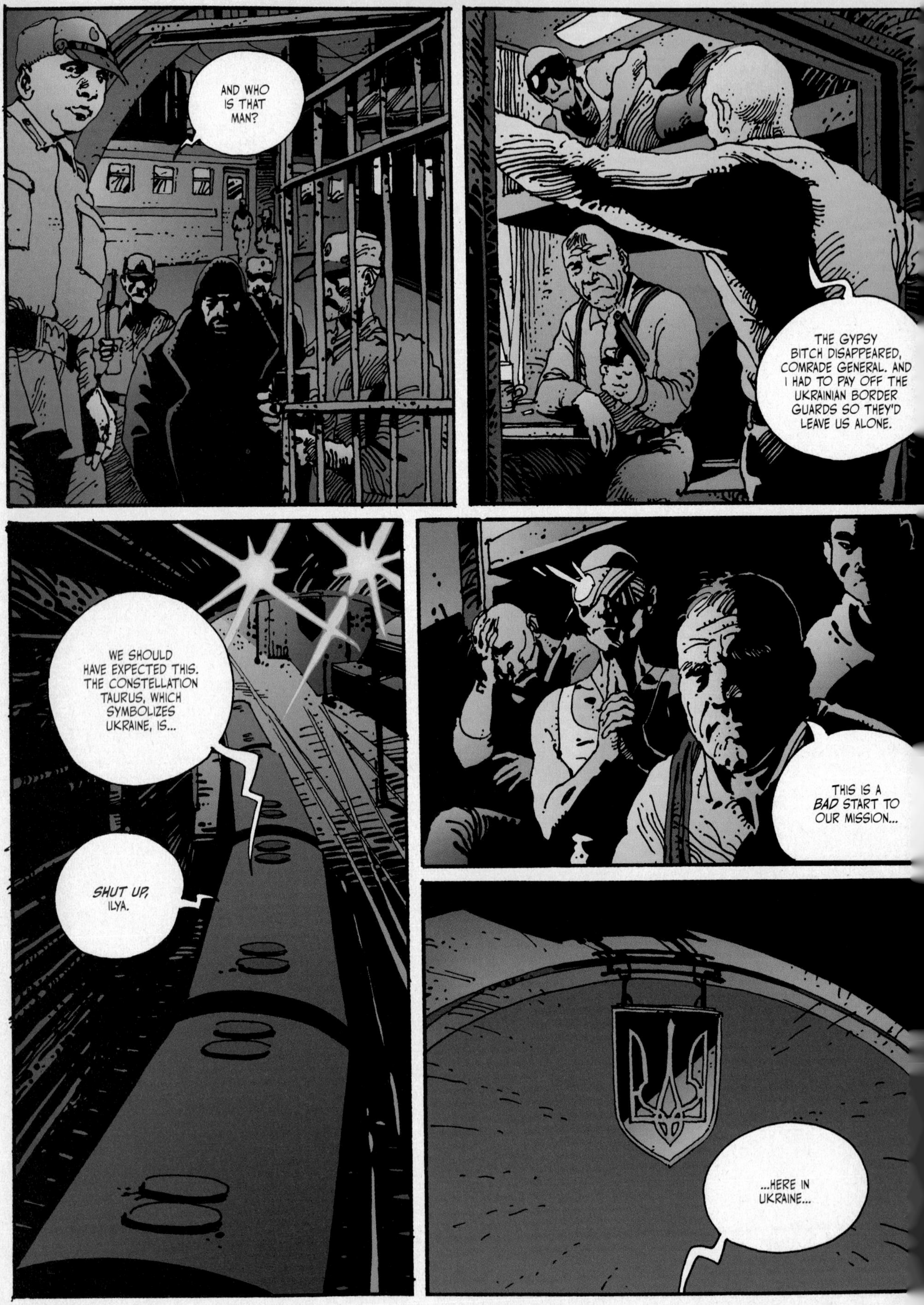
AND WHO IS THAT MAN?
THE GYPSY BITCH DISAPPEARED, COMRADE GENERAL. AND I HAD TO PAY OFF THE UKRAINIAN BORDER GUARDS SO THEY'D LEAVE US ALONE.
WE SHOULD HAVE EXPECTED THIS. THE CONSTELLATION TAURUS, WHICH SYMBOLIZES UKRAINE, IS...
SHUT UP, ILYA.
THIS IS A BAD START TO OUR MISSION...
...HERE IN UKRAINE...

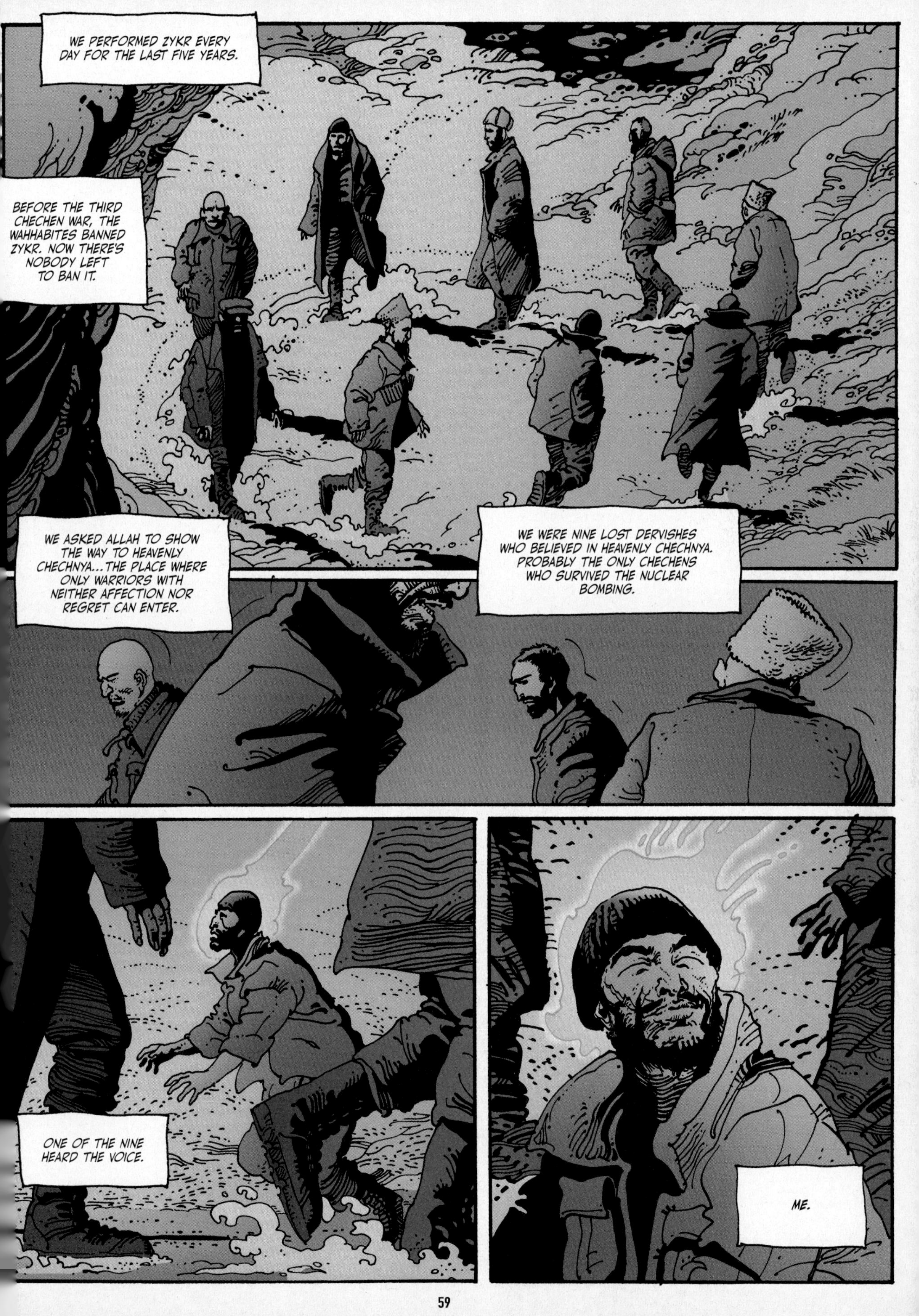
WE PERFORMED ZYKR EVERY DAY FOR THE LAST FIVE YEARS.
BEFORE THE THIRD CHECHEN WAR, THE WAHHABITES BANNED ZYKR. NOW THERE'S NOBODY LEFT TO BAN IT.
WE ASKED ALLAH TO SHOW THE WAY TO HEAVENLY CHECHNYA...THE PLACE WHERE ONLY WARRIORS WITH NEITHER AFFECTION NOR REGRET CAN ENTER.
WE WERE NINE LOST DERVISHES WHO BELIEVED IN HEAVENLY CHECHNYA. PROBABLY THE ONLY CHECHENS WHO SURVIVED THE NUCLEAR BOMBING.
ONE OF THE NINE HEARD THE VOICE.
ME.

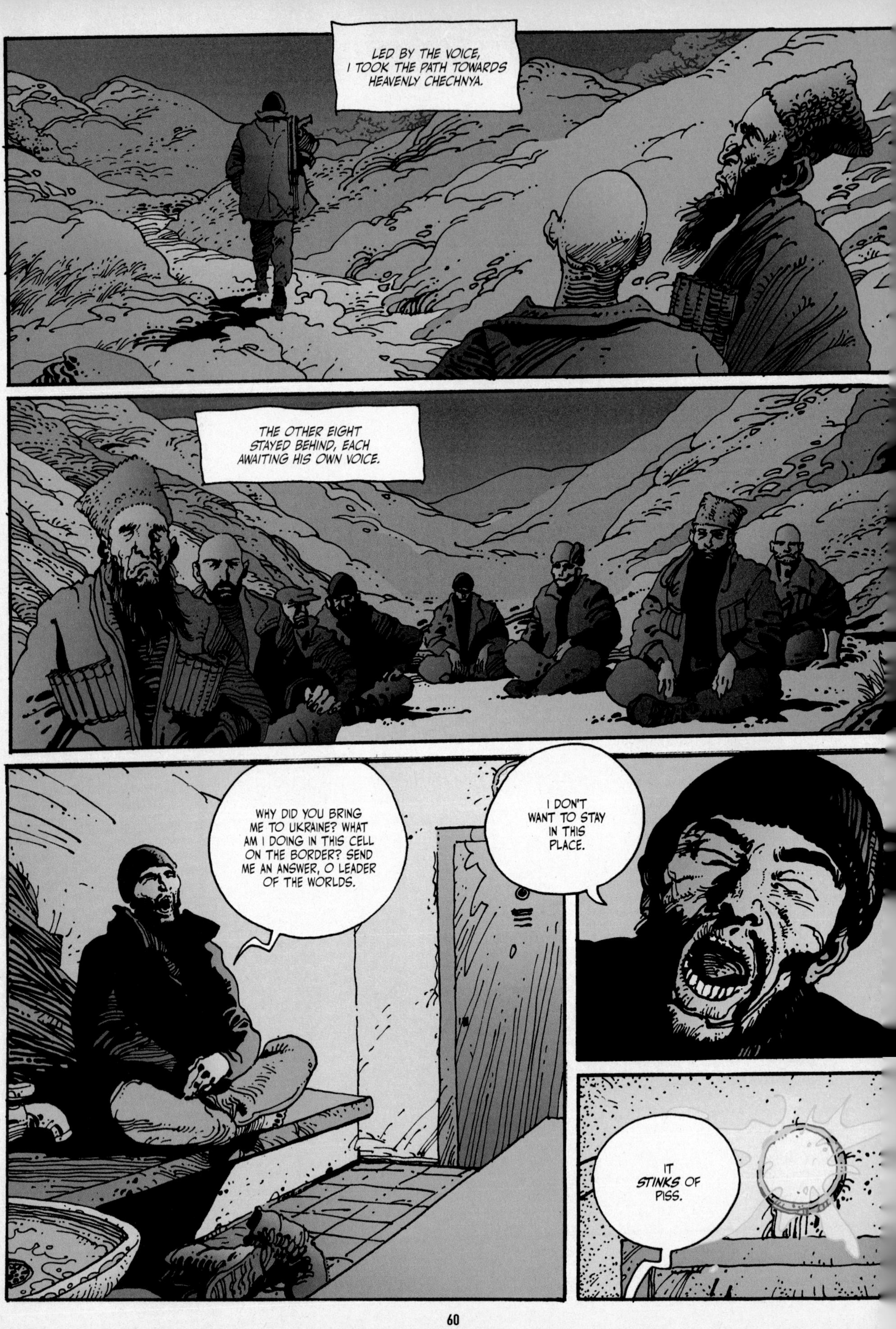
LED BY THE VOICE, I TOOK THE PATH TOWARDS HEAVENLY CHECHNYA.
THE OTHER EIGHT STAYED BEHIND, EACH AWAITING HIS OWN VOICE.
WHY DID YOU BRING ME TO UKRAINE? WHAT AM I DOING IN THIS CELL ON THE BORDER? SEND ME AN ANSWER, O LEADER OF THE WORLDS.
I DON'T WANT TO STAY IN THIS PLACE.
IT STINKS OF PISS.

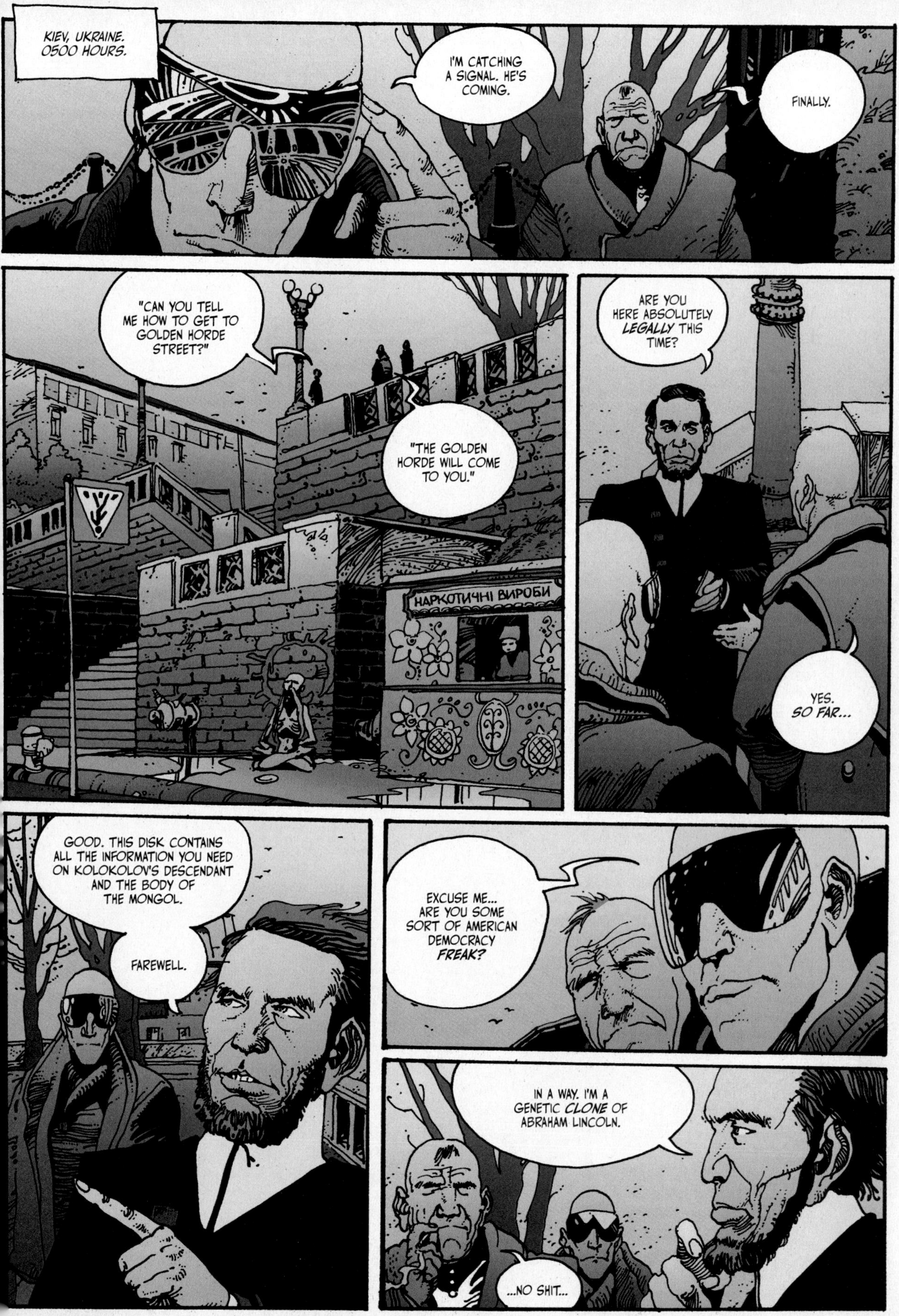
KIEV, UKRAINE.
0500 HOURS.
I'M CATCHING A SIGNAL. HE'S COMING.
FINALLY.
"CAN YOU TELL ME HOW TO GET TO GOLDEN HORDE STREET?"
"THE GOLDEN HORDE WILL COME TO YOU."
НАРКОТИЧНІ ВИРОБИ
ARE YOU HERE ABSOLUTELY *LEGALLY* THIS TIME?
YES. *SO FAR...*
GOOD. THIS DISK CONTAINS ALL THE INFORMATION YOU NEED ON KOLOKOLOV'S DESCENDANT AND THE BODY OF THE MONGOL.
FAREWELL.
EXCUSE ME... ARE YOU SOME SORT OF AMERICAN DEMOCRACY *FREAK?*
IN A WAY. I'M A GENETIC *CLONE* OF ABRAHAM LINCOLN.
...NO SHIT...

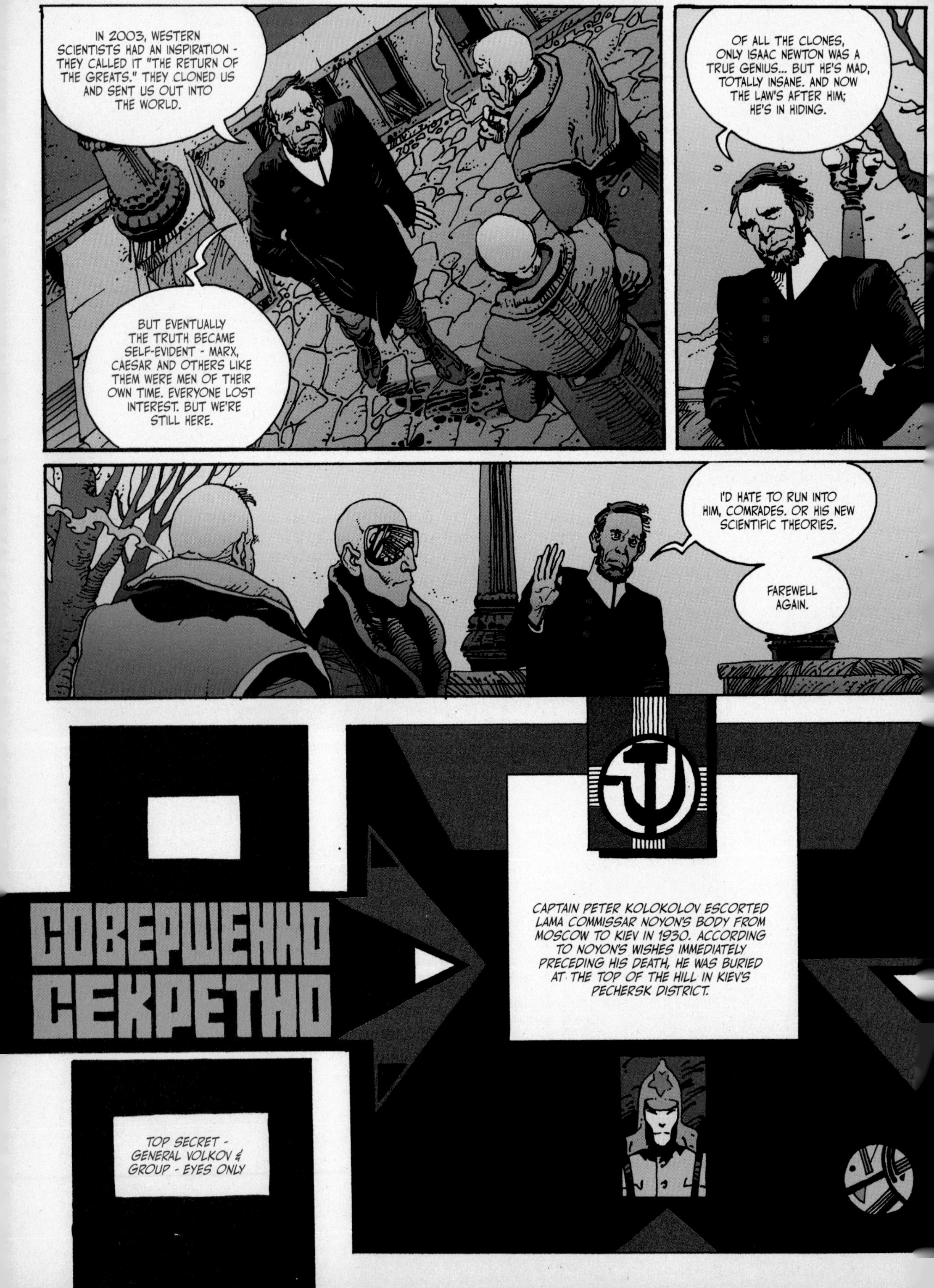
IN 2003, WESTERN SCIENTISTS HAD AN INSPIRATION - THEY CALLED IT "THE RETURN OF THE GREATS." THEY CLONED US AND SENT US OUT INTO THE WORLD.
BUT EVENTUALLY THE TRUTH BECAME SELF-EVIDENT - MARX, CAESAR AND OTHERS LIKE THEM WERE MEN OF THEIR OWN TIME. EVERYONE LOST INTEREST. BUT WE'RE STILL HERE.
OF ALL THE CLONES, ONLY ISAAC NEWTON WAS A TRUE GENIUS... BUT HE'S MAD, TOTALLY INSANE. AND NOW THE LAW'S AFTER HIM; HE'S IN HIDING.
I'D HATE TO RUN INTO HIM, COMRADES. OR HIS NEW SCIENTIFIC THEORIES.
FAREWELL AGAIN.
СОВЕРШЕННО СЕКРЕТНО
CAPTAIN PETER KOLOKOLOV ESCORTED LAMA COMMISSAR NOYON'S BODY FROM MOSCOW TO KIEV IN 1930. ACCORDING TO NOYON'S WISHES IMMEDIATELY PRECEDING HIS DEATH, HE WAS BURIED AT THE TOP OF THE HILL IN KIEV'S PECHERSK DISTRICT.
TOP SECRET - GENERAL VOLKOV & GROUP - EYES ONLY

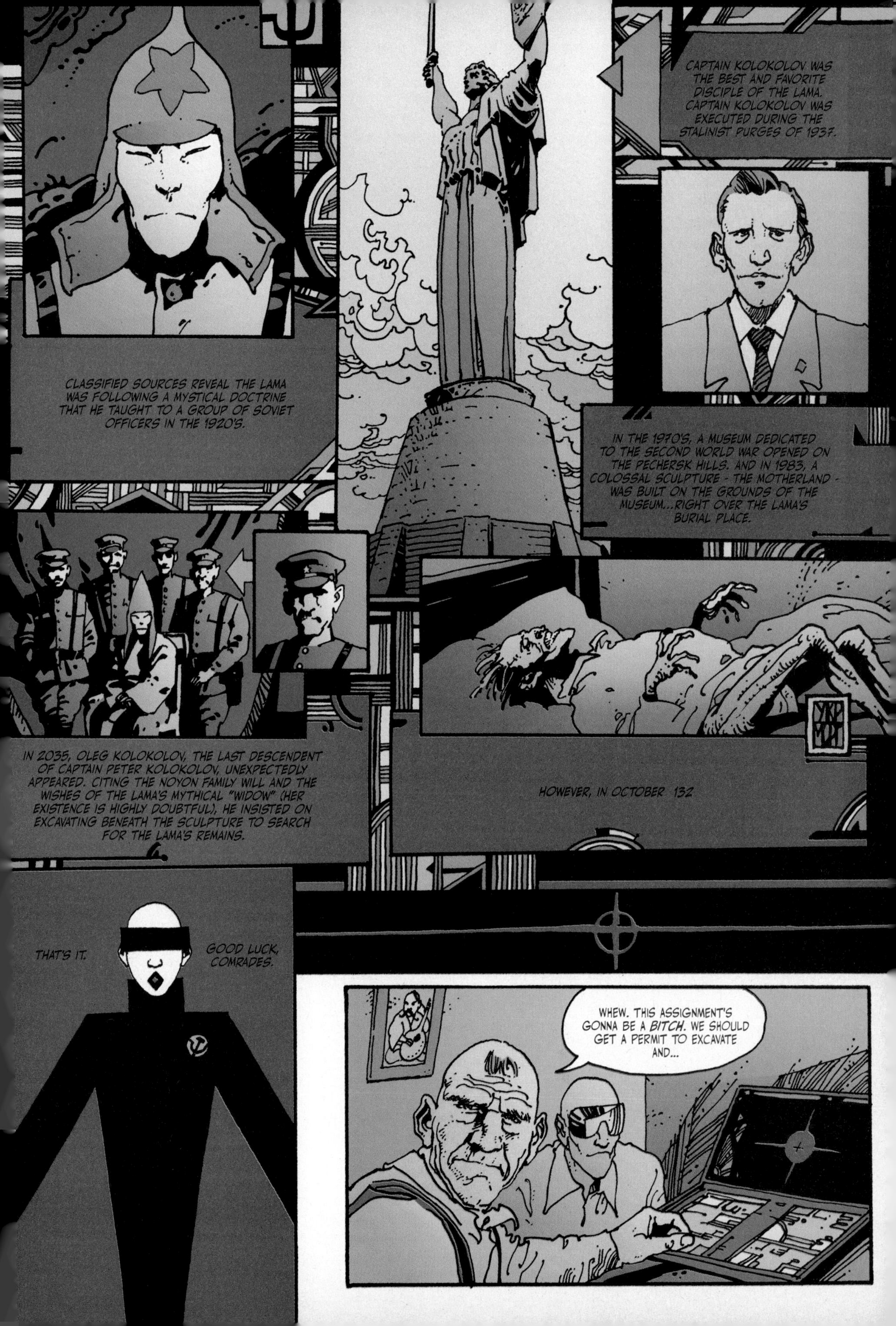
CAPTAIN KOLOKOLOV WAS THE BEST AND FAVORITE DISCIPLE OF THE LAMA. CAPTAIN KOLOKOLOV WAS EXECUTED DURING THE STALINIST PURGES OF 1937.
CLASSIFIED SOURCES REVEAL THE LAMA WAS FOLLOWING A MYSTICAL DOCTRINE THAT HE TAUGHT TO A GROUP OF SOVIET OFFICERS IN THE 1920'S.
IN THE 1970'S, A MUSEUM DEDICATED TO THE SECOND WORLD WAR OPENED ON THE PECHERSK HILLS. AND IN 1983, A COLOSSAL SCULPTURE - THE MOTHERLAND - WAS BUILT ON THE GROUNDS OF THE MUSEUM...RIGHT OVER THE LAMA'S BURIAL PLACE.
IN 2035, OLEG KOLOKOLOV, THE LAST DESCENDENT OF CAPTAIN PETER KOLOKOLOV, UNEXPECTEDLY APPEARED. CITING THE NOYON FAMILY WILL AND THE WISHES OF THE LAMA'S MYTHICAL "WIDOW" (HER EXISTENCE IS HIGHLY DOUBTFUL), HE INSISTED ON EXCAVATING BENEATH THE SCULPTURE TO SEARCH FOR THE LAMA'S REMAINS.
HOWEVER, IN OCTOBER 132
THAT'S IT.
GOOD LUCK, COMRADES.
WHEW. THIS ASSIGNMENT'S GONNA BE A BITCH. WE SHOULD GET A PERMIT TO EXCAVATE AND...

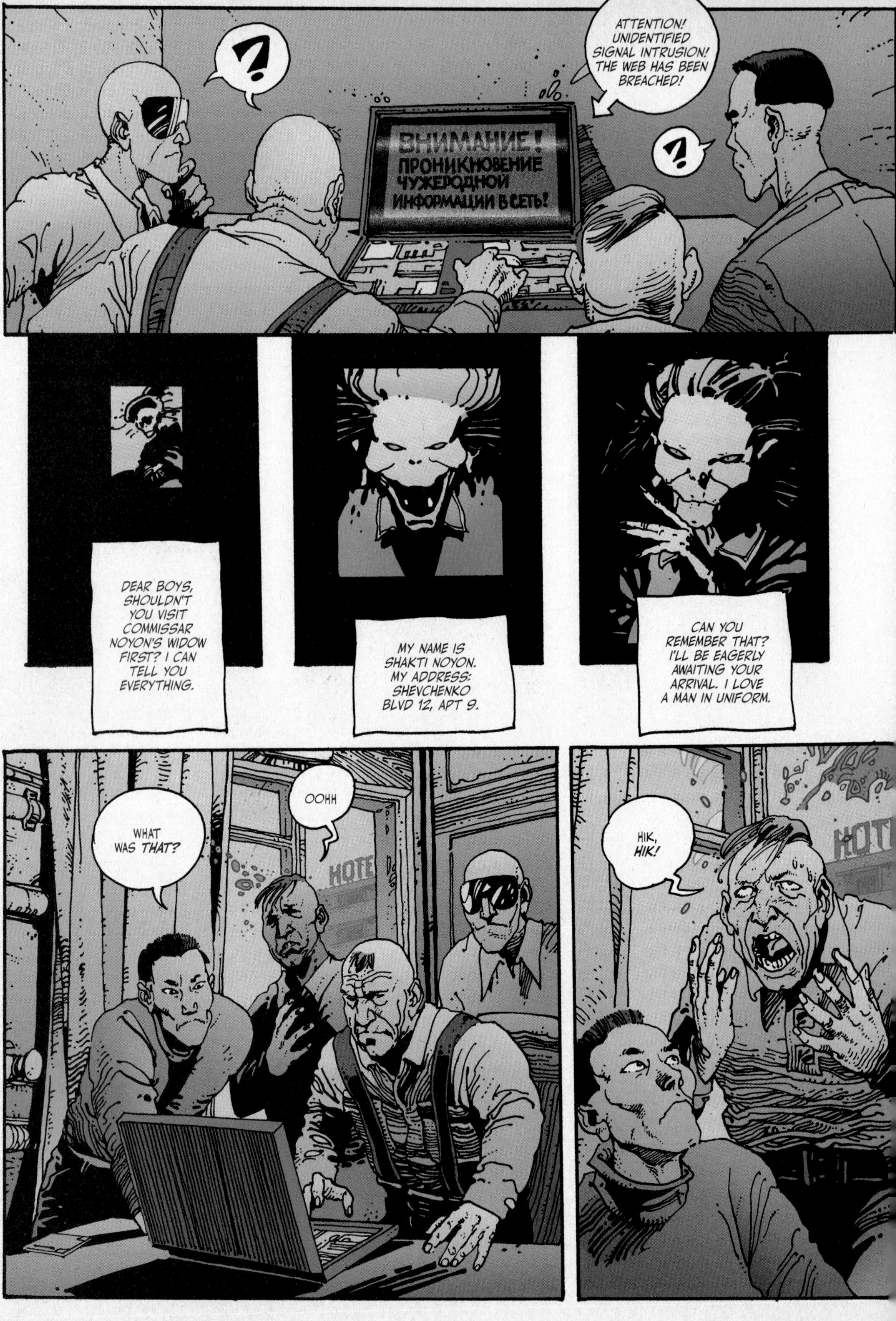
?
ATTENTION! UNIDENTIFIED SIGNAL INTRUSION! THE WEB HAS BEEN BREACHED!
ВНИМАНИЕ! ПРОНИКНОВЕНИЕ ЧУЖЕРОДНОЙ ИНФОРМАЦИИ В СЕТЬ!
?
DEAR BOYS, SHOULDN'T YOU VISIT COMMISSAR NOYON'S WIDOW FIRST? I CAN TELL YOU EVERYTHING.
MY NAME IS SHAKTI NOYON. MY ADDRESS: SHEVCHENKO BLVD 12, APT 9.
CAN YOU REMEMBER THAT? I'LL BE EAGERLY AWAITING YOUR ARRIVAL. I LOVE A MAN IN UNIFORM.
WHAT WAS THAT?
OOHH
HIK, HIK!

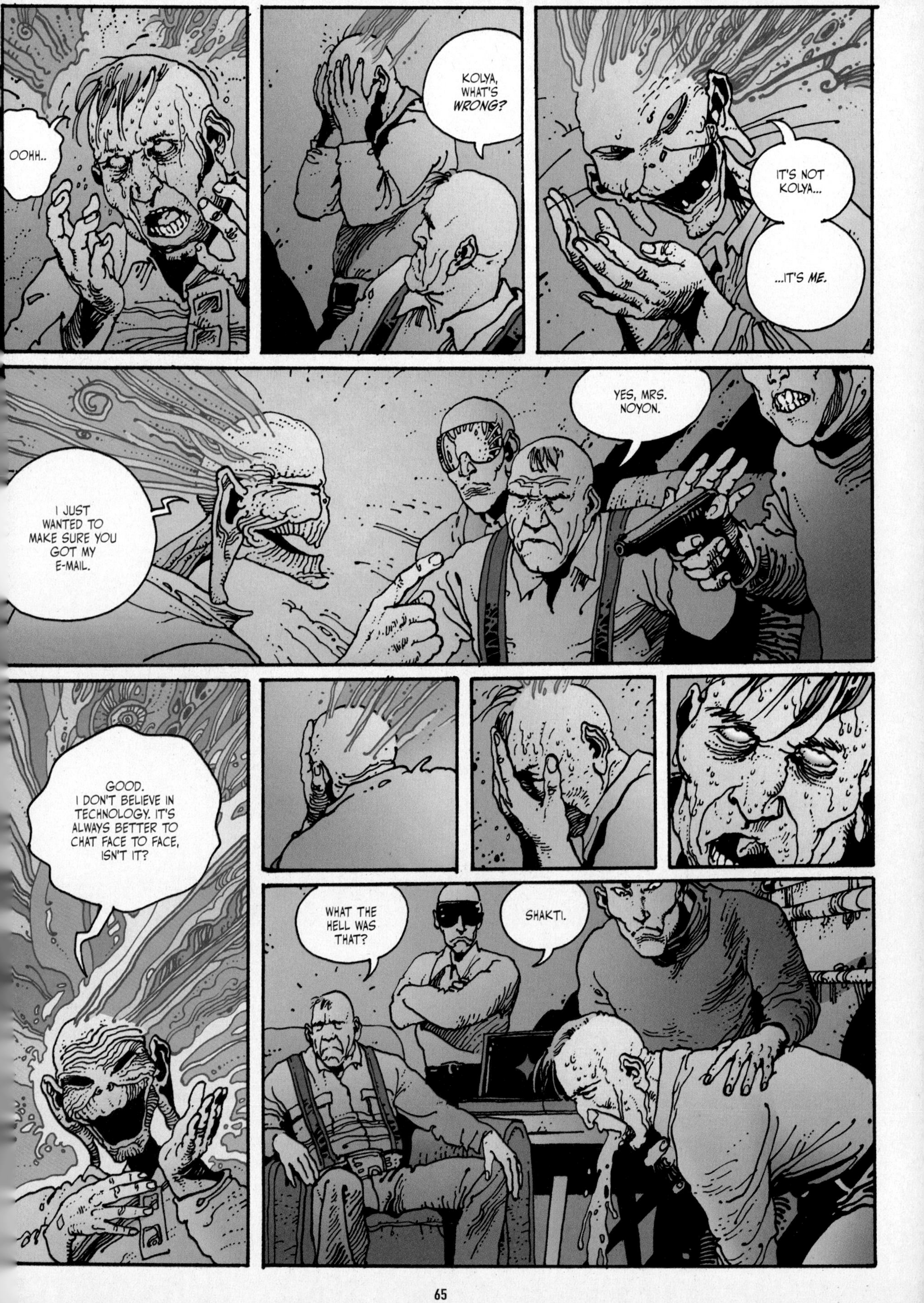
OOHH..
KOLYA, WHAT'S *WRONG?*
IT'S NOT KOLYA...
...IT'S *ME.*
I JUST WANTED TO MAKE SURE YOU GOT MY E-MAIL.
YES, MRS. NOYON.
GOOD. I DON'T BELIEVE IN TECHNOLOGY. IT'S ALWAYS BETTER TO CHAT FACE TO FACE, ISN'T IT?
WHAT THE HELL WAS THAT?
SHAKTI.

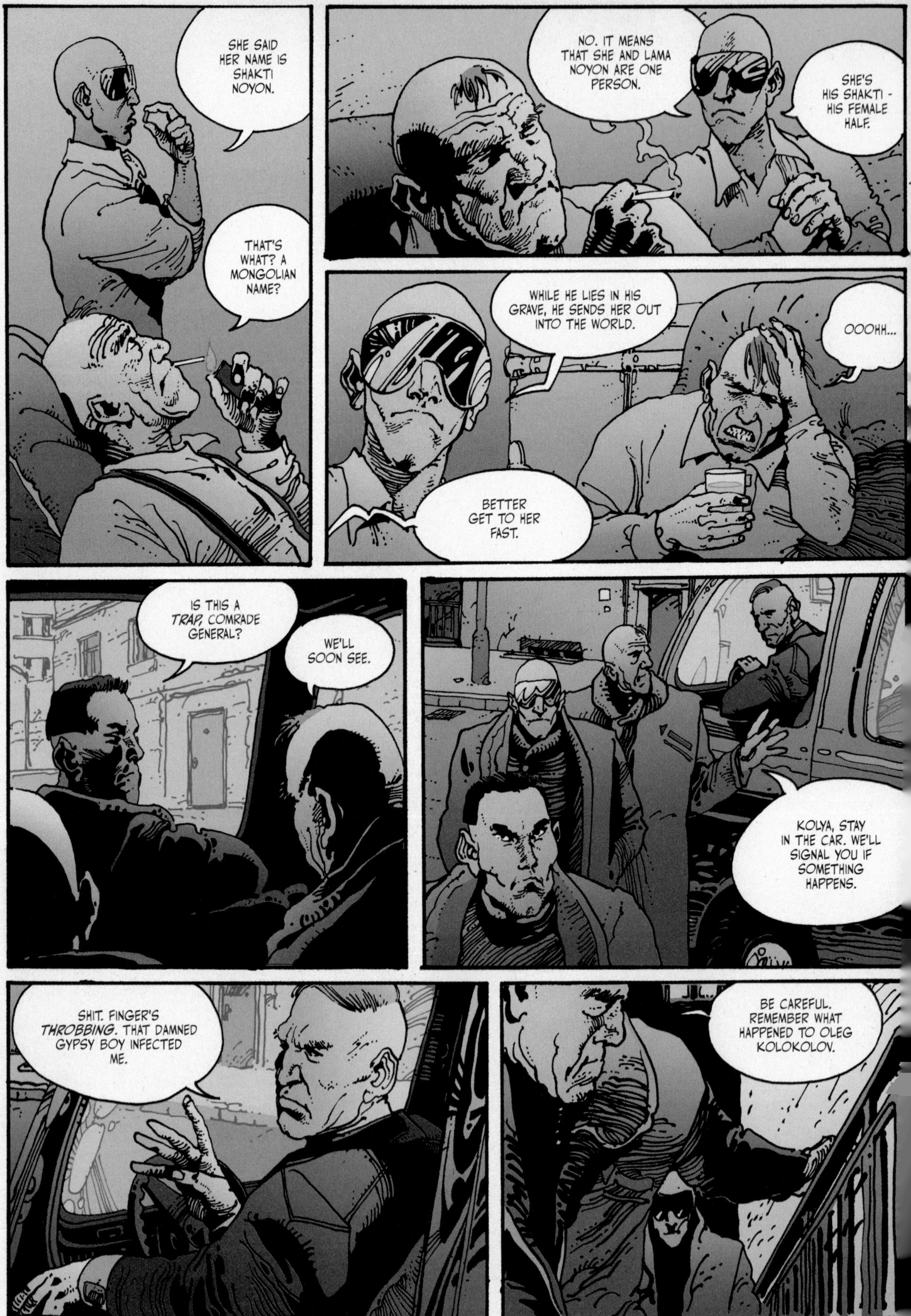

SHE SAID HER NAME IS SHAKTI NOYON.
THAT'S WHAT? A MONGOLIAN NAME?
NO. IT MEANS THAT SHE AND LAMA NOYON ARE ONE PERSON.
SHE'S HIS SHAKTI - HIS FEMALE HALF.
WHILE HE LIES IN HIS GRAVE, HE SENDS HER OUT INTO THE WORLD.
OOOHH...
BETTER GET TO HER FAST.
IS THIS A *TRAP,* COMRADE GENERAL?
WE'LL SOON SEE.
KOLYA, STAY IN THE CAR. WE'LL SIGNAL YOU IF SOMETHING HAPPENS.
SHIT. FINGER'S *THROBBING*. THAT DAMNED GYPSY BOY INFECTED ME.
BE CAREFUL. REMEMBER WHAT HAPPENED TO OLEG KOLOKOLOV.

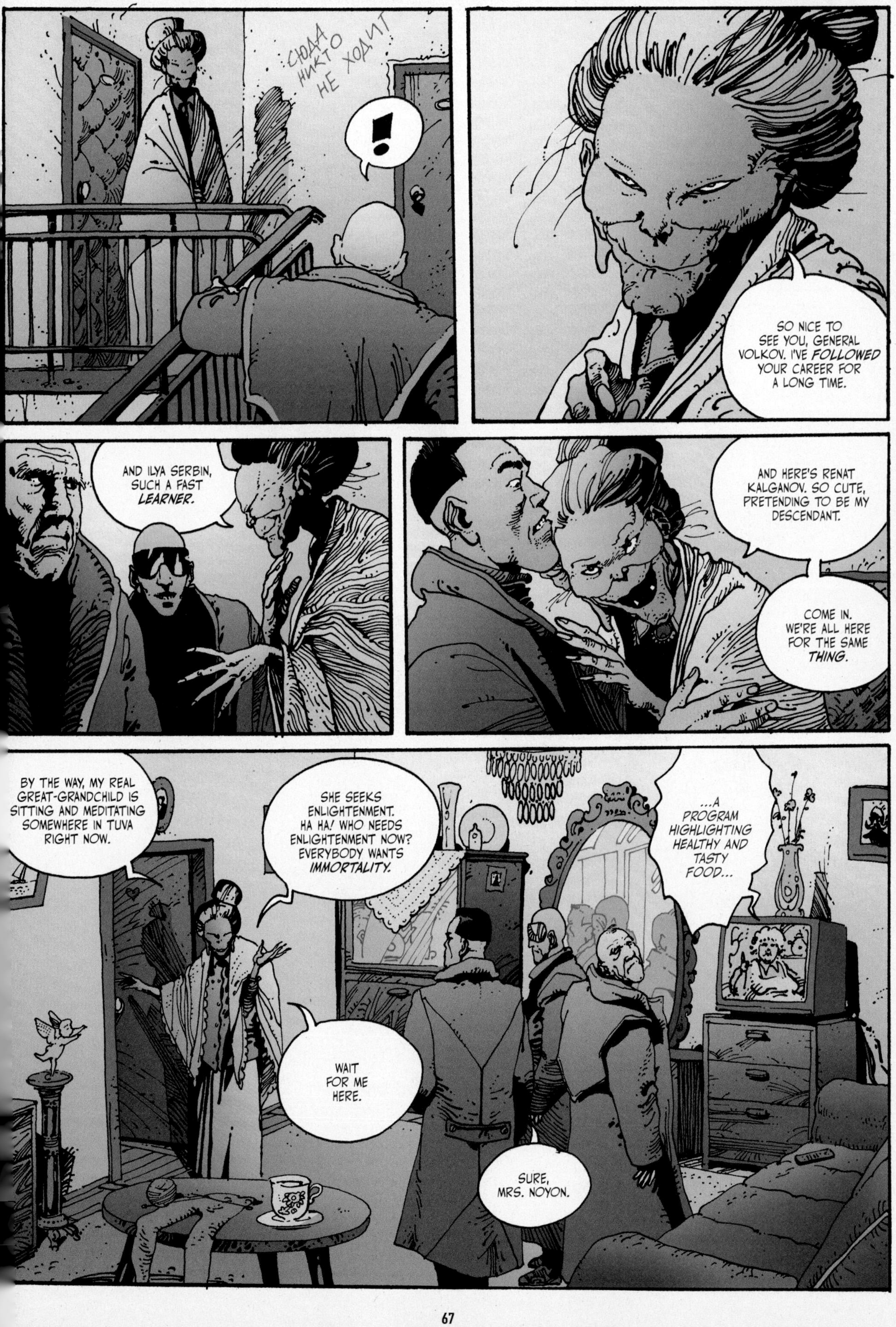
СЮДА НИКТО НЕ ХОДИТ
!
SO NICE TO SEE YOU, GENERAL VOLKOV. I'VE *FOLLOWED* YOUR CAREER FOR A LONG TIME.
AND ILYA SERBIN, SUCH A FAST *LEARNER.*
AND HERE'S RENAT KALGANOV. SO CUTE, PRETENDING TO BE MY DESCENDANT.
COME IN. WE'RE ALL HERE FOR THE SAME *THING.*
BY THE WAY, MY REAL GREAT-GRANDCHILD IS SITTING AND MEDITATING SOMEWHERE IN TUVA RIGHT NOW.
SHE SEEKS ENLIGHTENMENT. HA HA! WHO NEEDS ENLIGHTENMENT NOW? EVERYBODY WANTS *IMMORTALITY.*
...A PROGRAM HIGHLIGHTING HEALTHY AND TASTY FOOD...
WAIT FOR ME HERE.
SURE, MRS. NOYON.

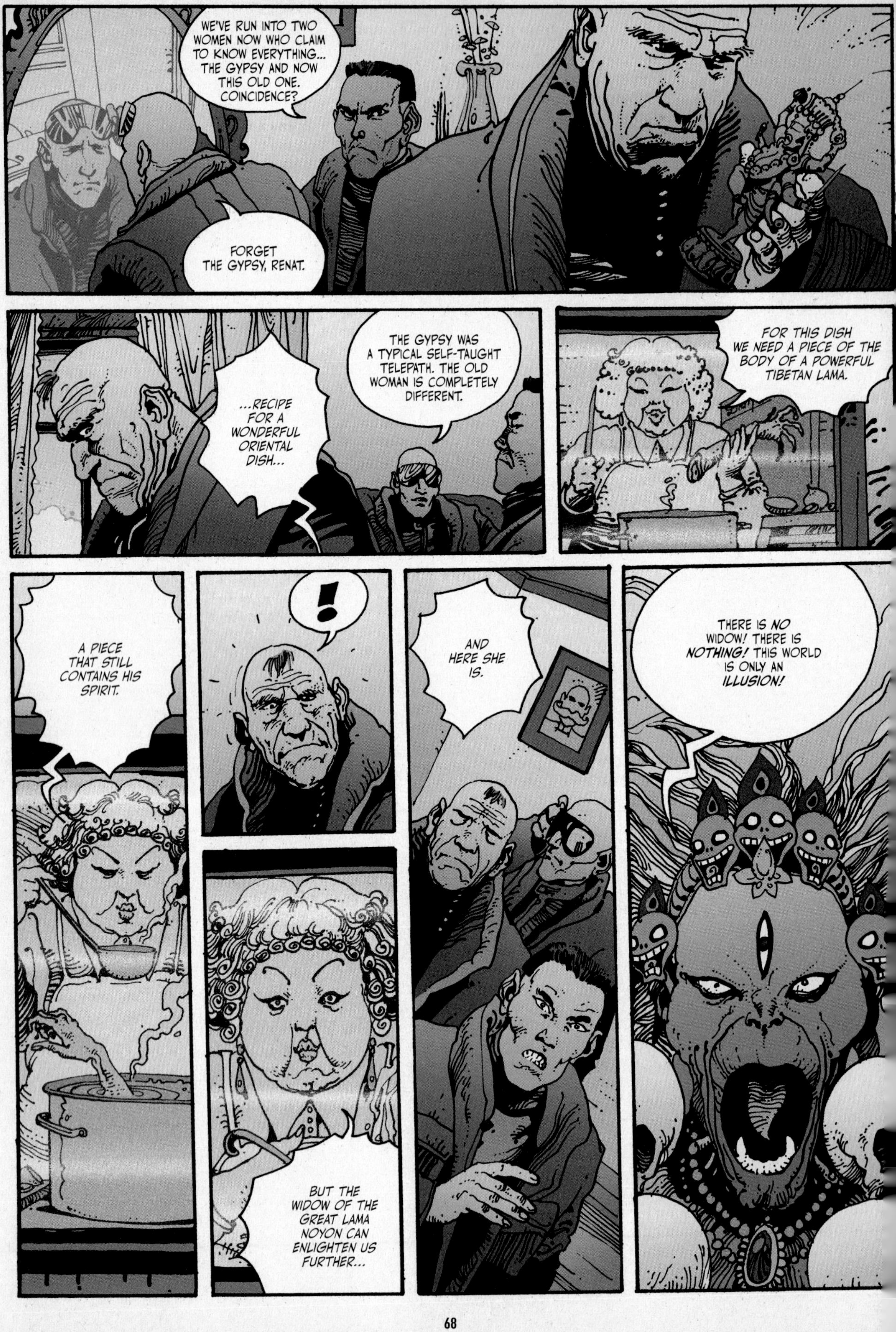
WE'VE RUN INTO TWO WOMEN NOW WHO CLAIM TO KNOW EVERYTHING... THE GYPSY AND NOW THIS OLD ONE. COINCIDENCE?
FORGET THE GYPSY, RENAT.
...RECIPE FOR A WONDERFUL ORIENTAL DISH...
THE GYPSY WAS A TYPICAL SELF-TAUGHT TELEPATH. THE OLD WOMAN IS COMPLETELY DIFFERENT.
FOR THIS DISH WE NEED A PIECE OF THE BODY OF A POWERFUL TIBETAN LAMA.
A PIECE THAT STILL CONTAINS HIS SPIRIT.
!
BUT THE WIDOW OF THE GREAT LAMA NOYON CAN ENLIGHTEN US FURTHER...
AND HERE SHE IS.
THERE IS NO WIDOW! THERE IS NOTHING! THIS WORLD IS ONLY AN ILLUSION!

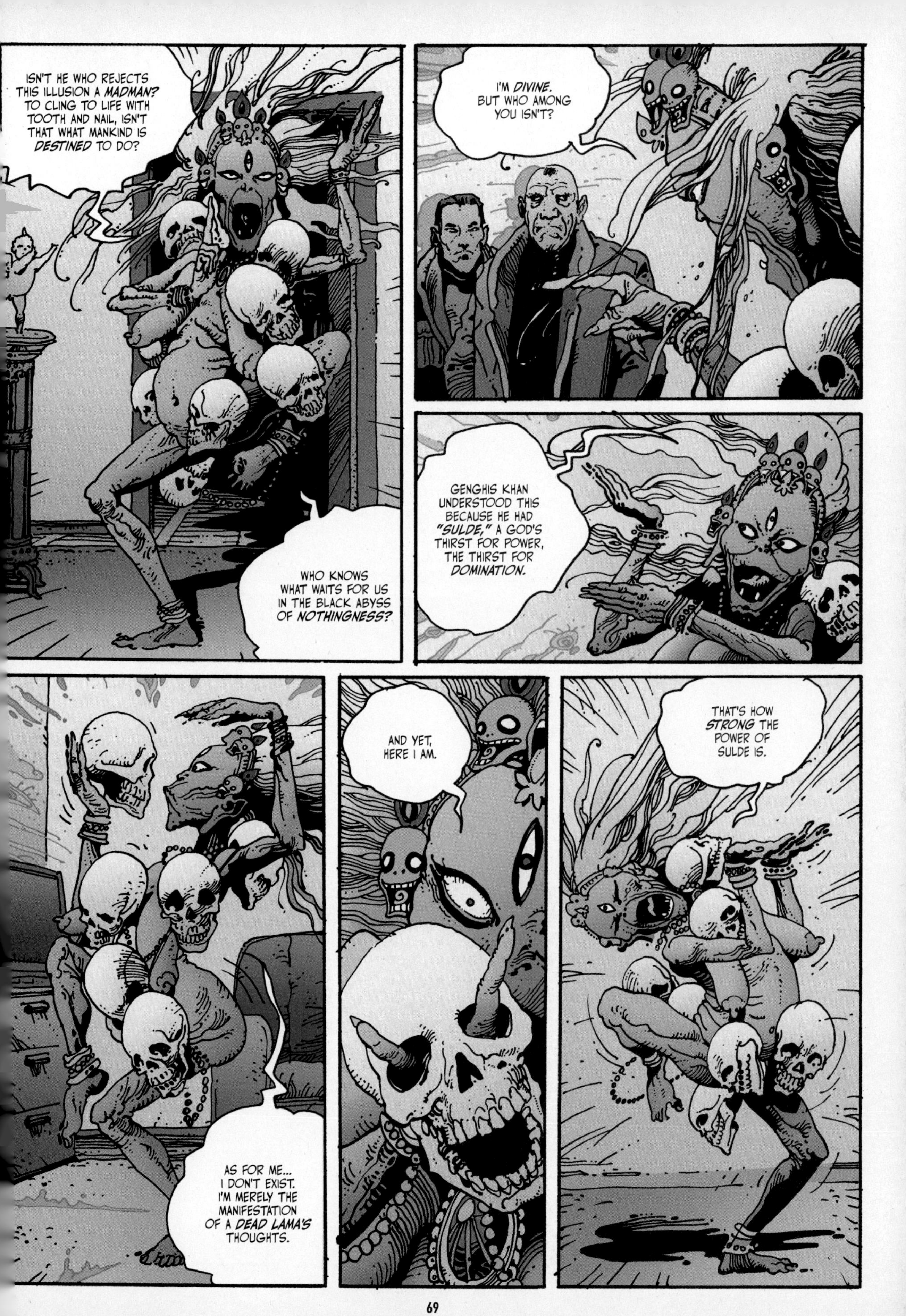
ISN'T HE WHO REJECTS THIS ILLUSION A *MADMAN?* TO CLING TO LIFE WITH TOOTH AND NAIL, ISN'T THAT WHAT MANKIND IS *DESTINED* TO DO?
WHO KNOWS WHAT WAITS FOR US IN THE BLACK ABYSS OF *NOTHINGNESS?*
I'M *DIVINE.* BUT WHO AMONG YOU ISN'T?
GENGHIS KHAN UNDERSTOOD THIS BECAUSE HE HAD *"SULDE,"* A GOD'S THIRST FOR POWER, THE THIRST FOR *DOMINATION.*
AS FOR ME... I DON'T EXIST. I'M MERELY THE MANIFESTATION OF A *DEAD LAMA'S* THOUGHTS.
AND YET, HERE I AM.
THAT'S HOW *STRONG* THE POWER OF SULDE IS.

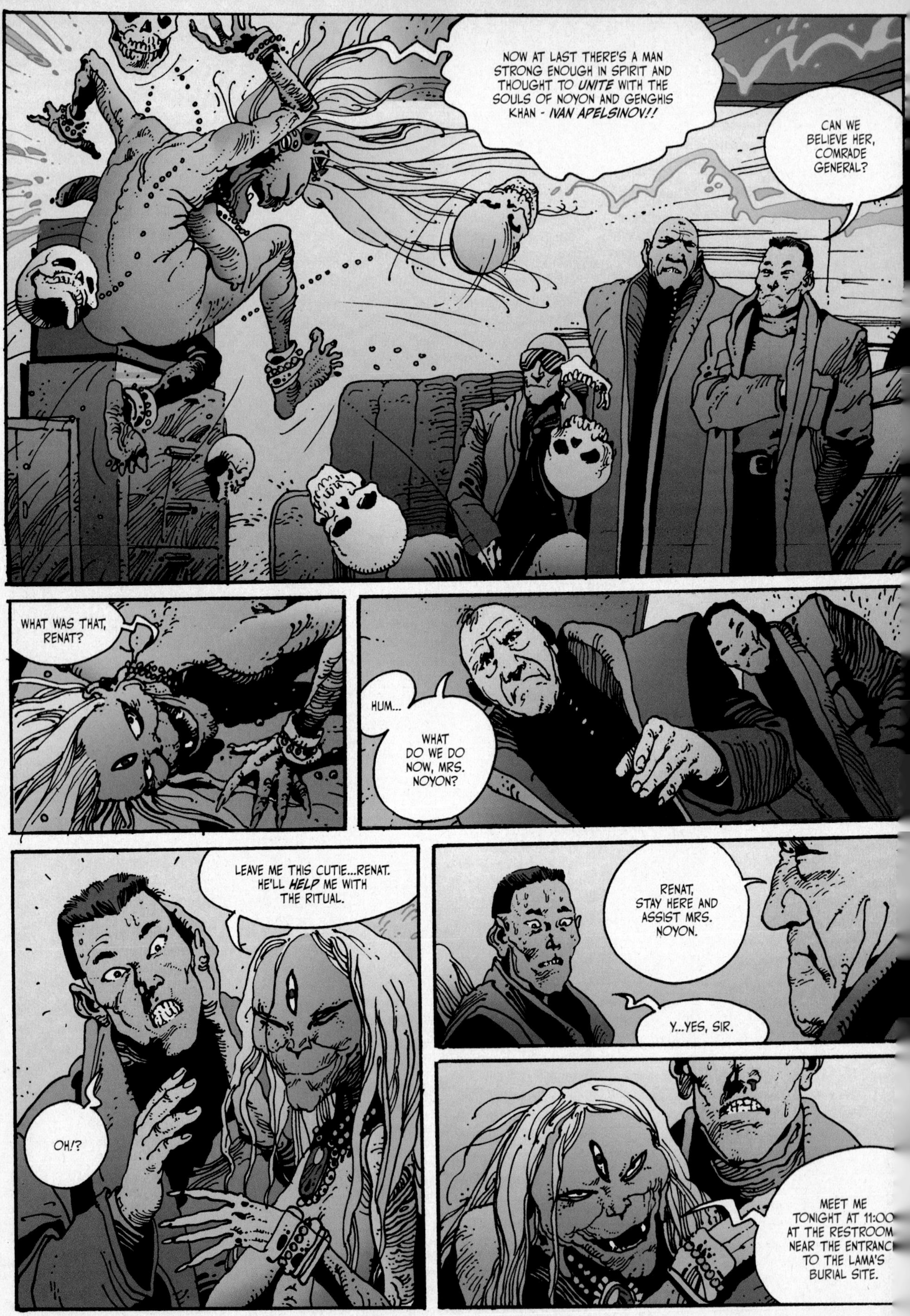
NOW AT LAST THERE'S A MAN STRONG ENOUGH IN SPIRIT AND THOUGHT TO *UNITE* WITH THE SOULS OF NOYON AND GENGHIS KHAN - *IVAN APELSINOV!!*
CAN WE BELIEVE HER, COMRADE GENERAL?
WHAT WAS THAT, RENAT?
HUM...
WHAT DO WE DO NOW, MRS. NOYON?
LEAVE ME THIS CUTIE...RENAT. HE'LL *HELP* ME WITH THE RITUAL.
OH!?
RENAT, STAY HERE AND ASSIST MRS. NOYON.
Y...YES, SIR.
MEET ME TONIGHT AT 11:00 AT THE RESTROOM NEAR THE ENTRANC TO THE LAMA'S BURIAL SITE.

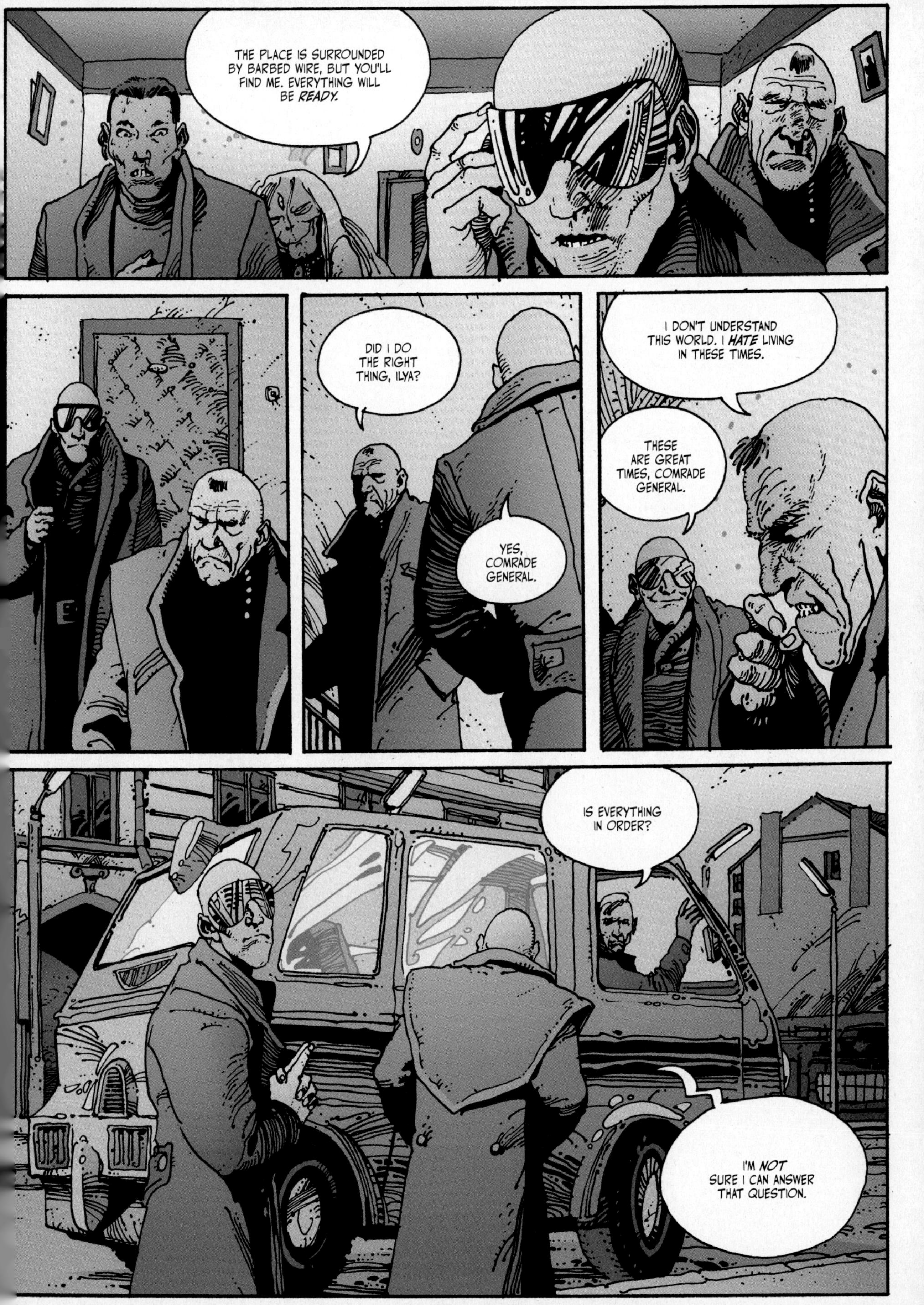
THE PLACE IS SURROUNDED BY BARBED WIRE, BUT YOU'LL FIND ME. EVERYTHING WILL BE *READY.*
DID I DO THE RIGHT THING, ILYA?
YES, COMRADE GENERAL.
I DON'T UNDERSTAND THIS WORLD. I *HATE* LIVING IN THESE TIMES.
THESE ARE GREAT TIMES, COMRADE GENERAL.
IS EVERYTHING IN ORDER?
I'M *NOT* SURE I CAN ANSWER THAT QUESTION.

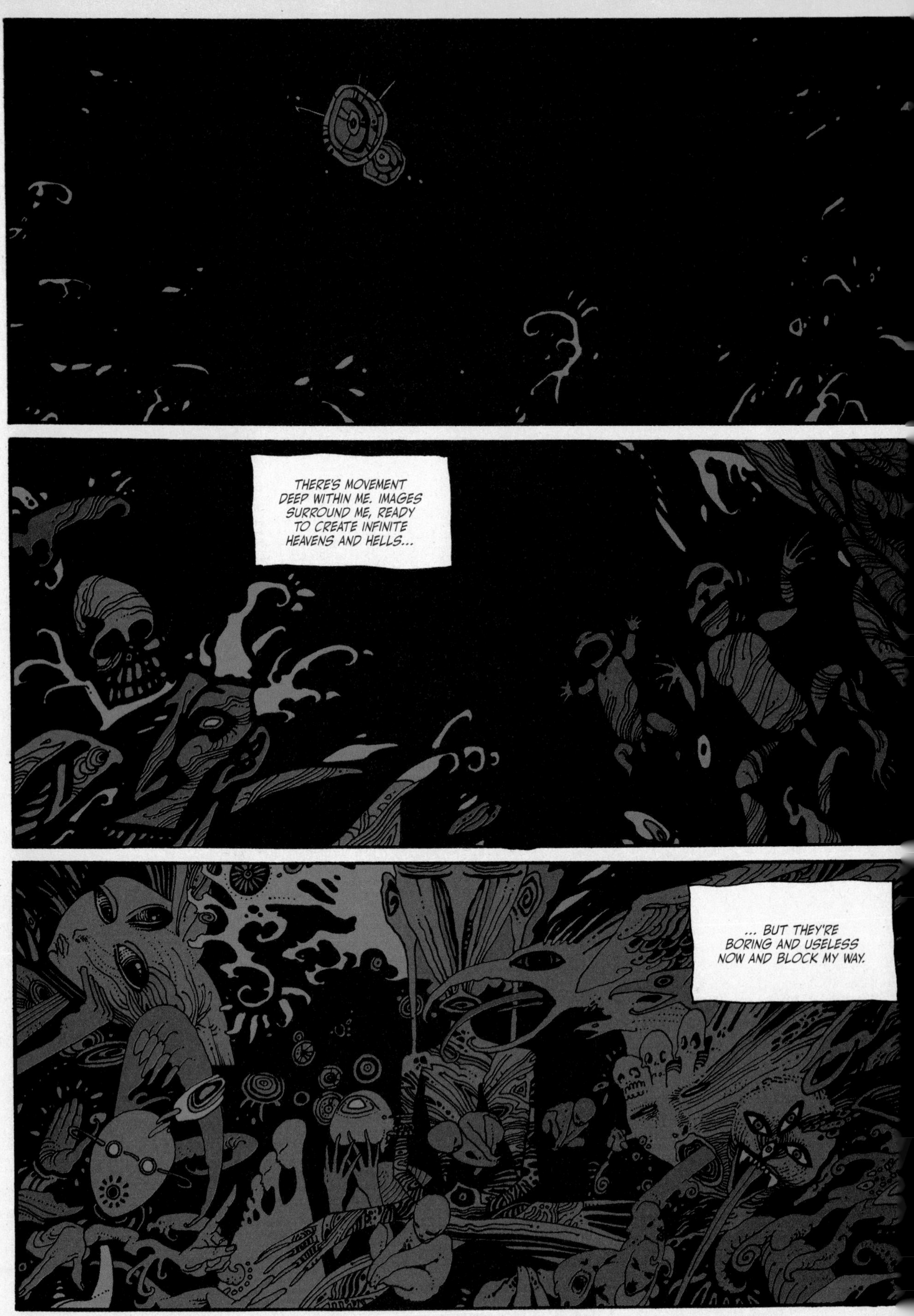
THERE'S MOVEMENT DEEP WITHIN ME. IMAGES SURROUND ME, READY TO CREATE INFINITE HEAVENS AND HELLS...
... BUT THEY'RE BORING AND USELESS NOW AND BLOCK MY WAY.

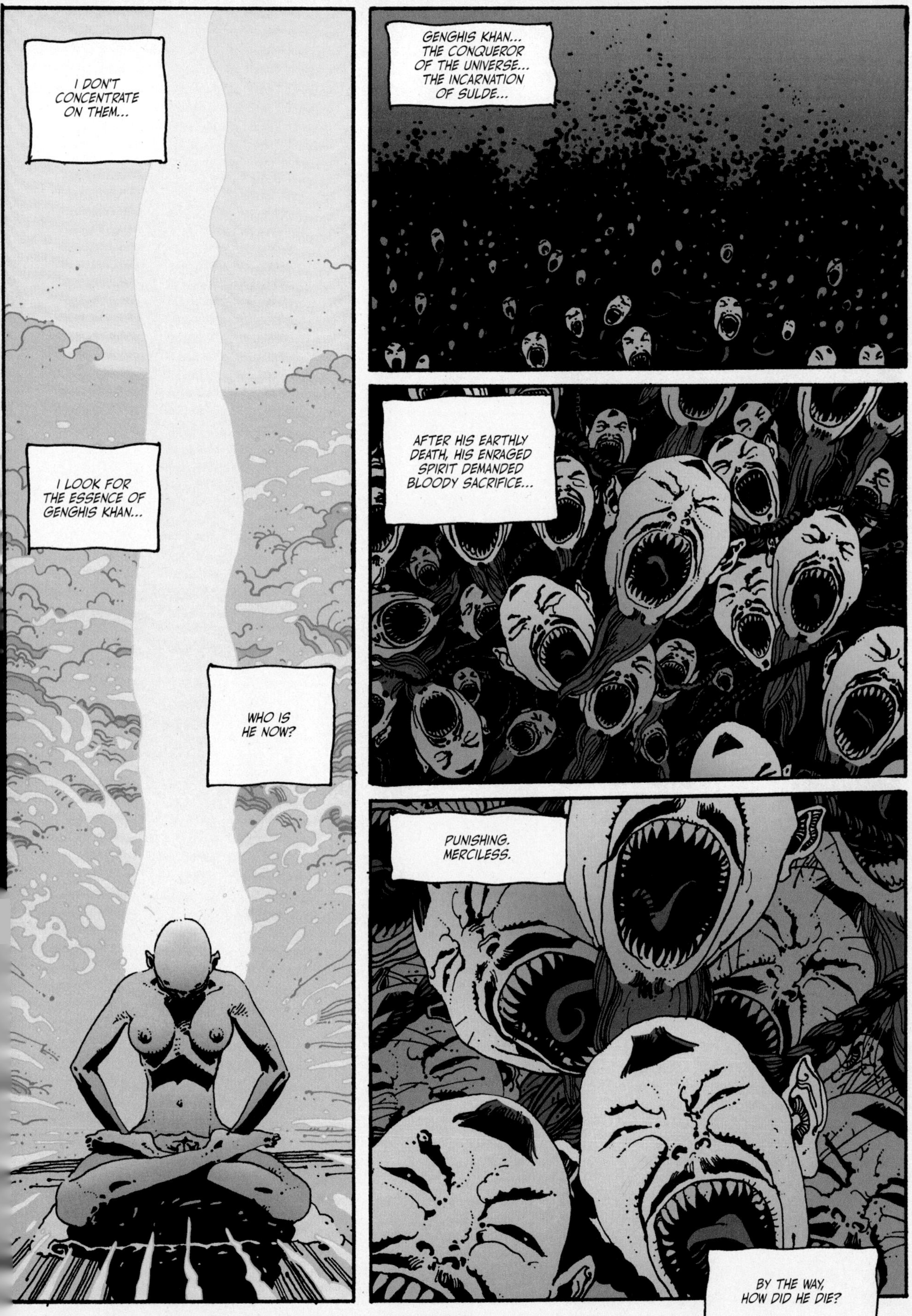
I DON'T CONCENTRATE ON THEM...
I LOOK FOR THE ESSENCE OF GENGHIS KHAN...
WHO IS HE NOW?
GENGHIS KHAN... THE CONQUEROR OF THE UNIVERSE... THE INCARNATION OF SULDE...
AFTER HIS EARTHLY DEATH, HIS ENRAGED SPIRIT DEMANDED BLOODY SACRIFICE...
PUNISHING. MERCILESS.
BY THE WAY, HOW DID HE DIE?

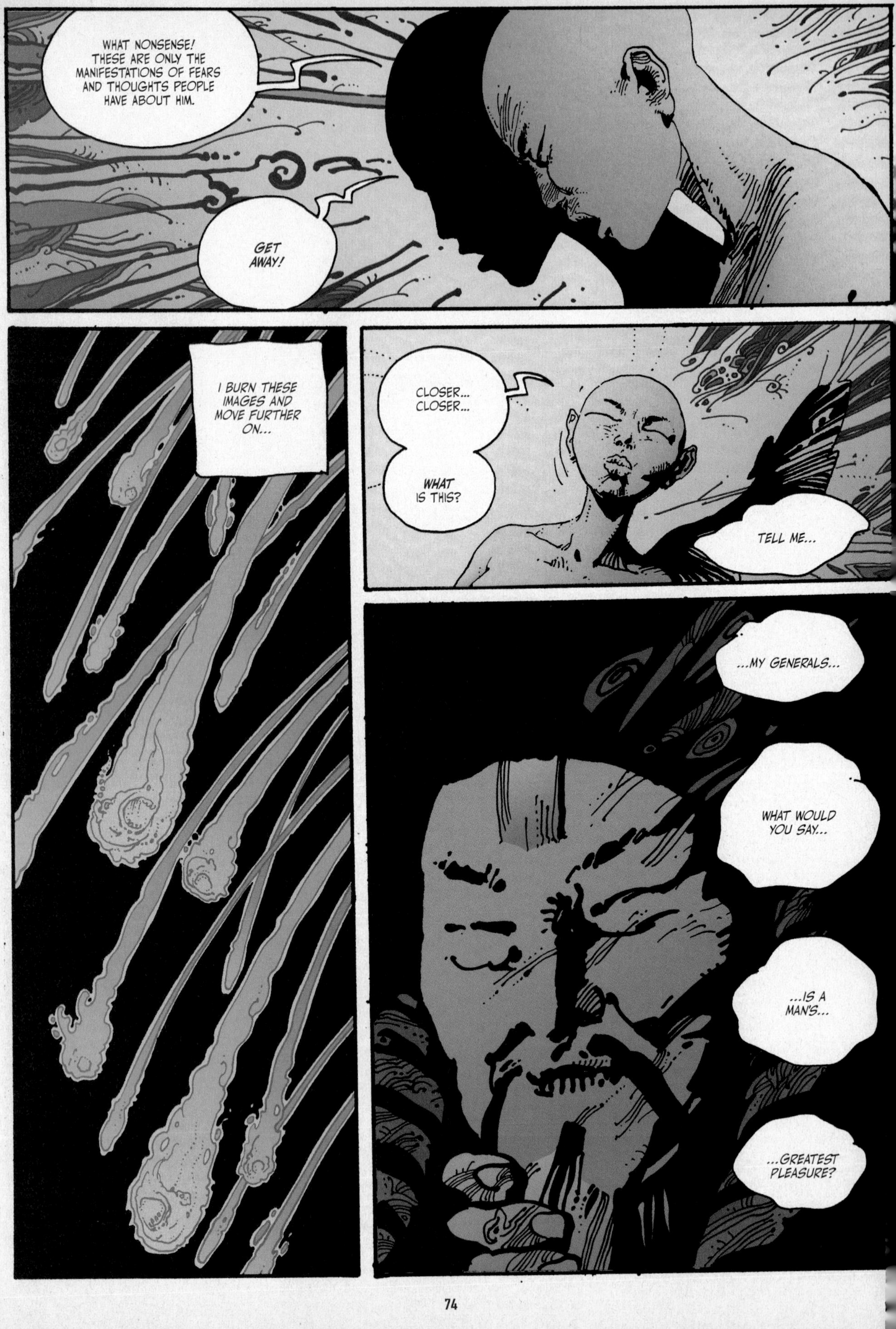
WHAT NONSENSE! THESE ARE ONLY THE MANIFESTATIONS OF FEARS AND THOUGHTS PEOPLE HAVE ABOUT HIM.
GET AWAY!
I BURN THESE IMAGES AND MOVE FURTHER ON...
CLOSER... CLOSER...
WHAT IS THIS?
TELL ME...
...MY GENERALS...
WHAT WOULD YOU SAY...
...IS A MAN'S...
...GREATEST PLEASURE?

YOU, BOGURTCHI. ANSWER ME **FIRST!**

THE HIGHEST PLEASURE, O GREAT WARRIOR, IS TO STRADDLE A FINE HORSE IN THE EARLY SPRING WITH A FALCON ON YOUR ARM AS YOU RIDE TO THE HUNT.

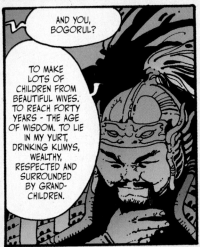

AND YOU, BOGORUL?

TO MAKE LOTS OF CHILDREN FROM BEAUTIFUL WIVES. TO REACH FORTY YEARS - THE AGE OF WISDOM. TO LIE IN MY YURT, DRINKING KUMYS, WEALTHY, RESPECTED AND SURROUNDED BY GRAND-CHILDREN.

YOU, SUBUDAY-BAHATUR?

TO FALL IN LOVE FOR THE FIRST TIME AT THE AGE OF FIFTEEN WITH A BEAUTIFUL GIRL, TAKE HER UPON MY HORSE AND GALLOP FAR TO THE STEPPES.

ENOUGH!

THIS IS THE DIFFERENCE BETWEEN BEING GREAT AND BEING **INSIGNIFICANT.**

THE GREATEST PLEASURE IS TO **SUPPRESS** THE REBEL. TO DRIVE HIM BEFORE YOUR HORSE, TO TAKE **EVERYTHING** HE POSSESSES. TO SEE THE FACES OF THOSE DEAR TO HIM AWASH IN **TEARS.** IF I THOUGHT LIKE YOU, WHERE WOULD THE MONGOLS BE? WHO WOULD **EVER** HAVE HEARD OF US?

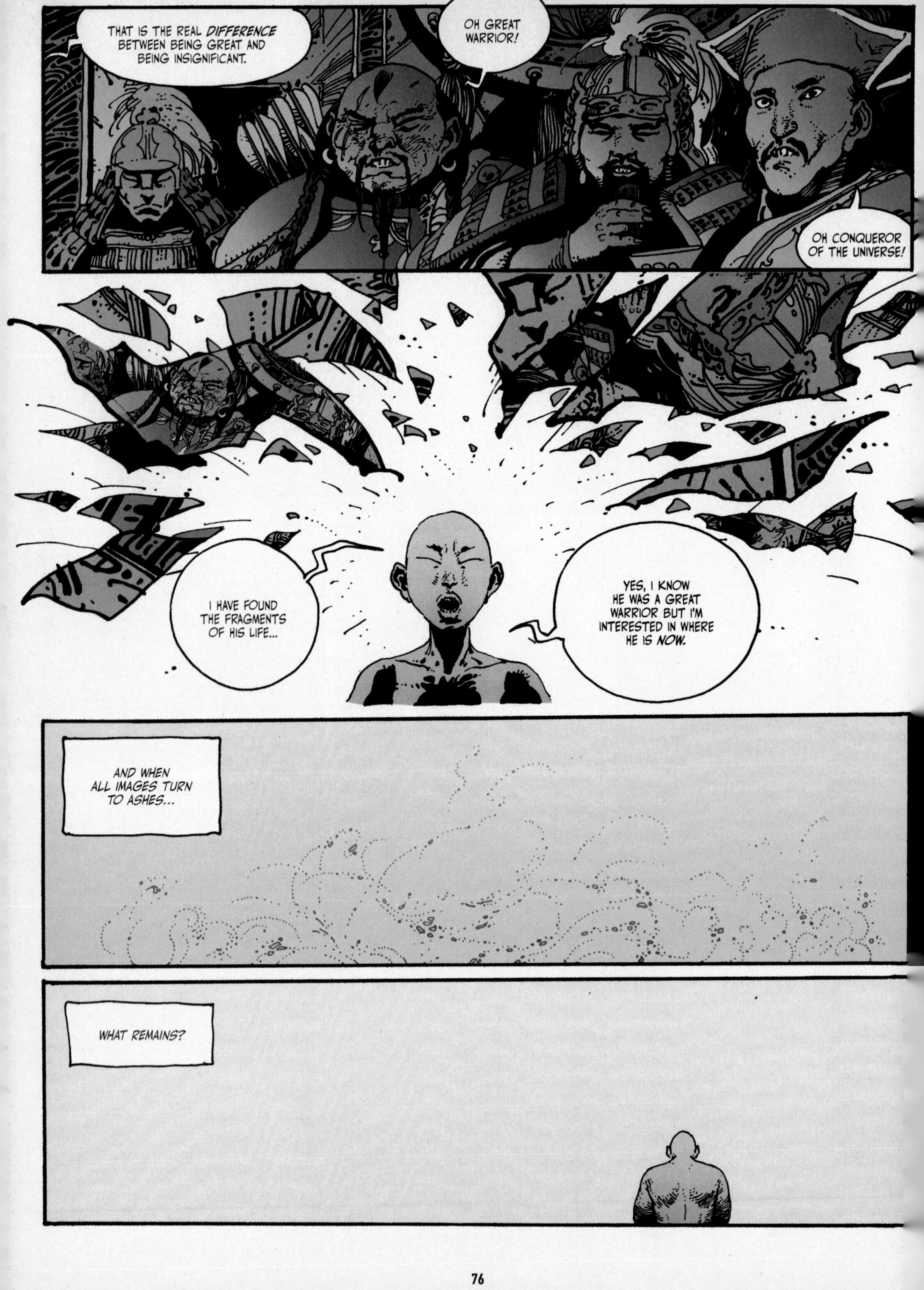
THAT IS THE REAL *DIFFERENCE* BETWEEN BEING GREAT AND BEING INSIGNIFICANT.
OH GREAT WARRIOR!
OH CONQUEROR OF THE UNIVERSE!
I HAVE FOUND THE FRAGMENTS OF HIS LIFE...
YES, I KNOW HE WAS A GREAT WARRIOR BUT I'M INTERESTED IN WHERE HE IS *NOW.*
AND WHEN ALL IMAGES TURN TO ASHES...
WHAT REMAINS?

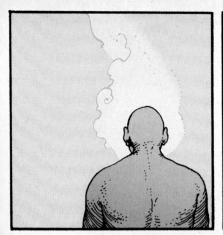
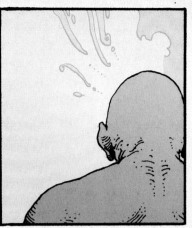

FINALLY. I'VE BEEN EXPECTING YOU.

WHO ARE YOU?

I AM GENGHIS KHAN. DON'T YOU RECOGNIZE ME?

HAVE WE MET BEFORE?

YES. SIT BESIDE ME.

AND TRY TO REMEMBER.

TO REMEMBER... YOU?

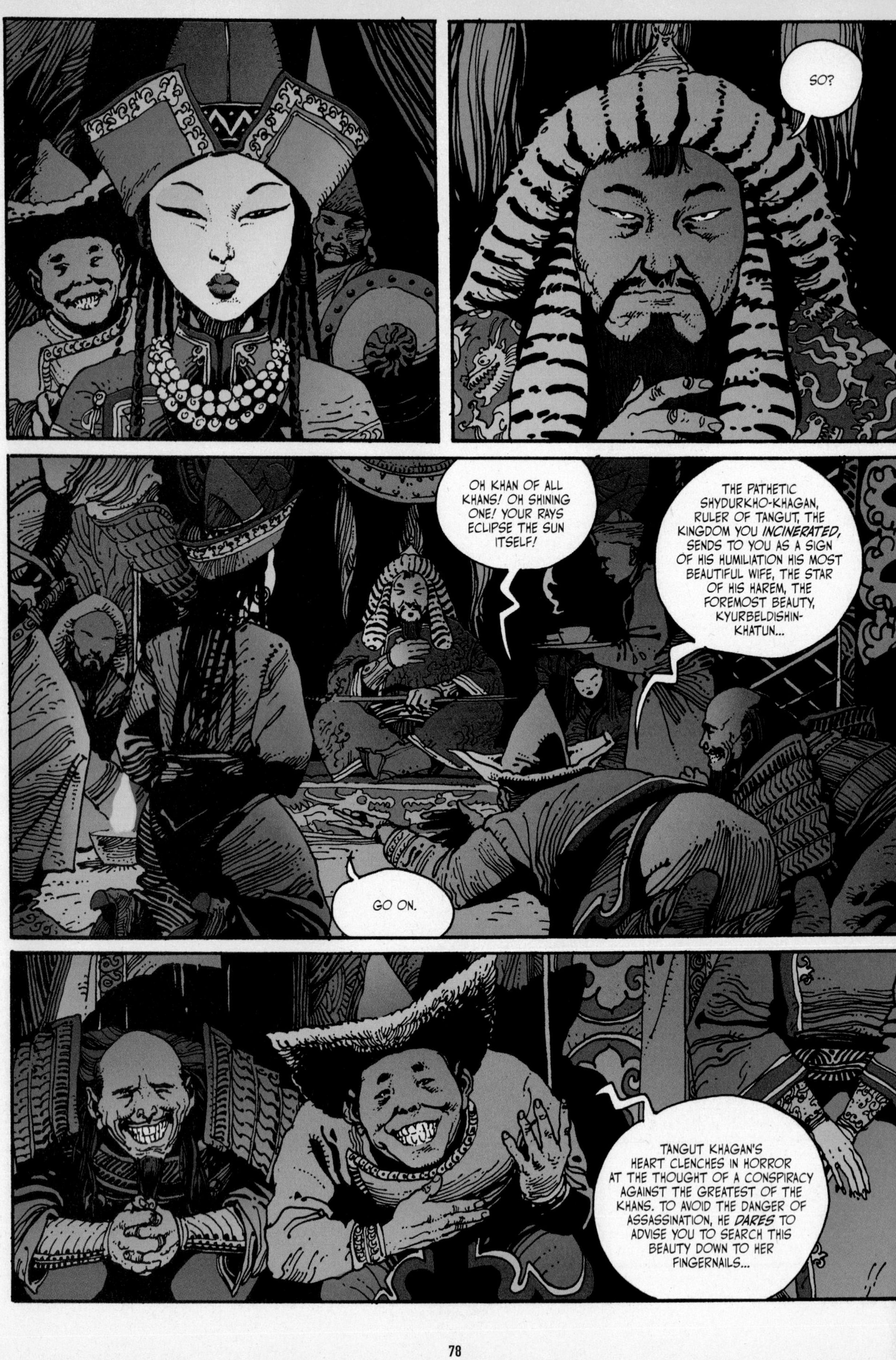
SO?
OH KHAN OF ALL KHANS! OH SHINING ONE! YOUR RAYS ECLIPSE THE SUN ITSELF!
THE PATHETIC SHYDURKHO-KHAGAN, RULER OF TANGUT, THE KINGDOM YOU *INCINERATED*, SENDS TO YOU AS A SIGN OF HIS HUMILIATION HIS MOST BEAUTIFUL WIFE, THE STAR OF HIS HAREM, THE FOREMOST BEAUTY, KYURBELDISHIN-KHATUN...
GO ON.
TANGUT KHAGAN'S HEART CLENCHES IN HORROR AT THE THOUGHT OF A CONSPIRACY AGAINST THE GREATEST OF THE KHANS. TO AVOID THE DANGER OF ASSASSINATION, HE *DARES* TO ADVISE YOU TO SEARCH THIS BEAUTY DOWN TO HER FINGERNAILS...

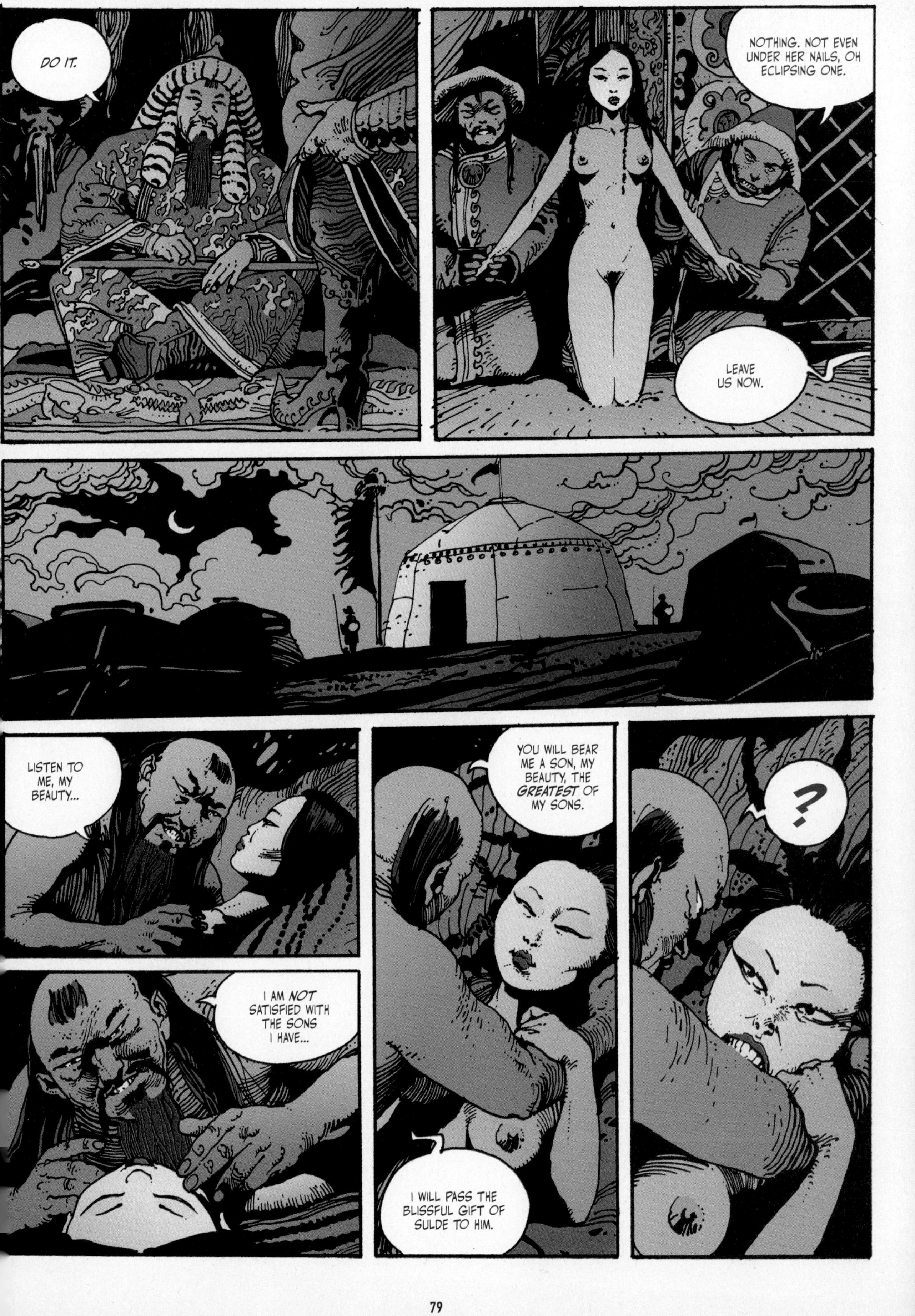
DO IT.
NOTHING. NOT EVEN UNDER HER NAILS, OH ECLIPSING ONE.
LEAVE US NOW.
LISTEN TO ME, MY BEAUTY...
I AM NOT SATISFIED WITH THE SONS I HAVE...
YOU WILL BEAR ME A SON, MY BEAUTY, THE GREATEST OF MY SONS.
I WILL PASS THE BLISSFUL GIFT OF SULDE TO HIM.
?

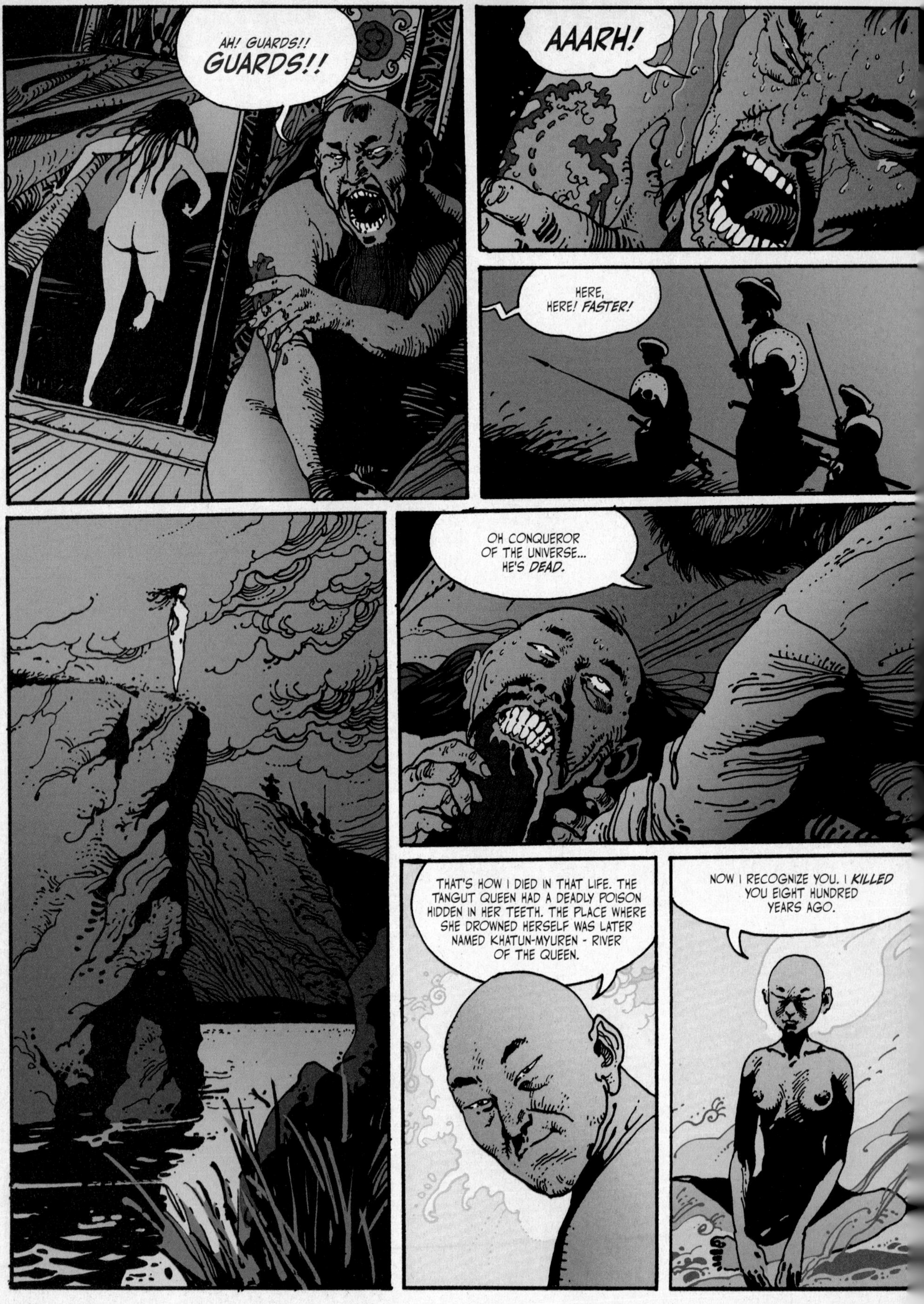
AH! GUARDS!! GUARDS!!
AAARH!
HERE, HERE! FASTER!
OH CONQUEROR OF THE UNIVERSE... HE'S DEAD.
THAT'S HOW I DIED IN THAT LIFE. THE TANGUT QUEEN HAD A DEADLY POISON HIDDEN IN HER TEETH. THE PLACE WHERE SHE DROWNED HERSELF WAS LATER NAMED KHATUN-MYUREN - RIVER OF THE QUEEN.
NOW I RECOGNIZE YOU. I KILLED YOU EIGHT HUNDRED YEARS AGO.

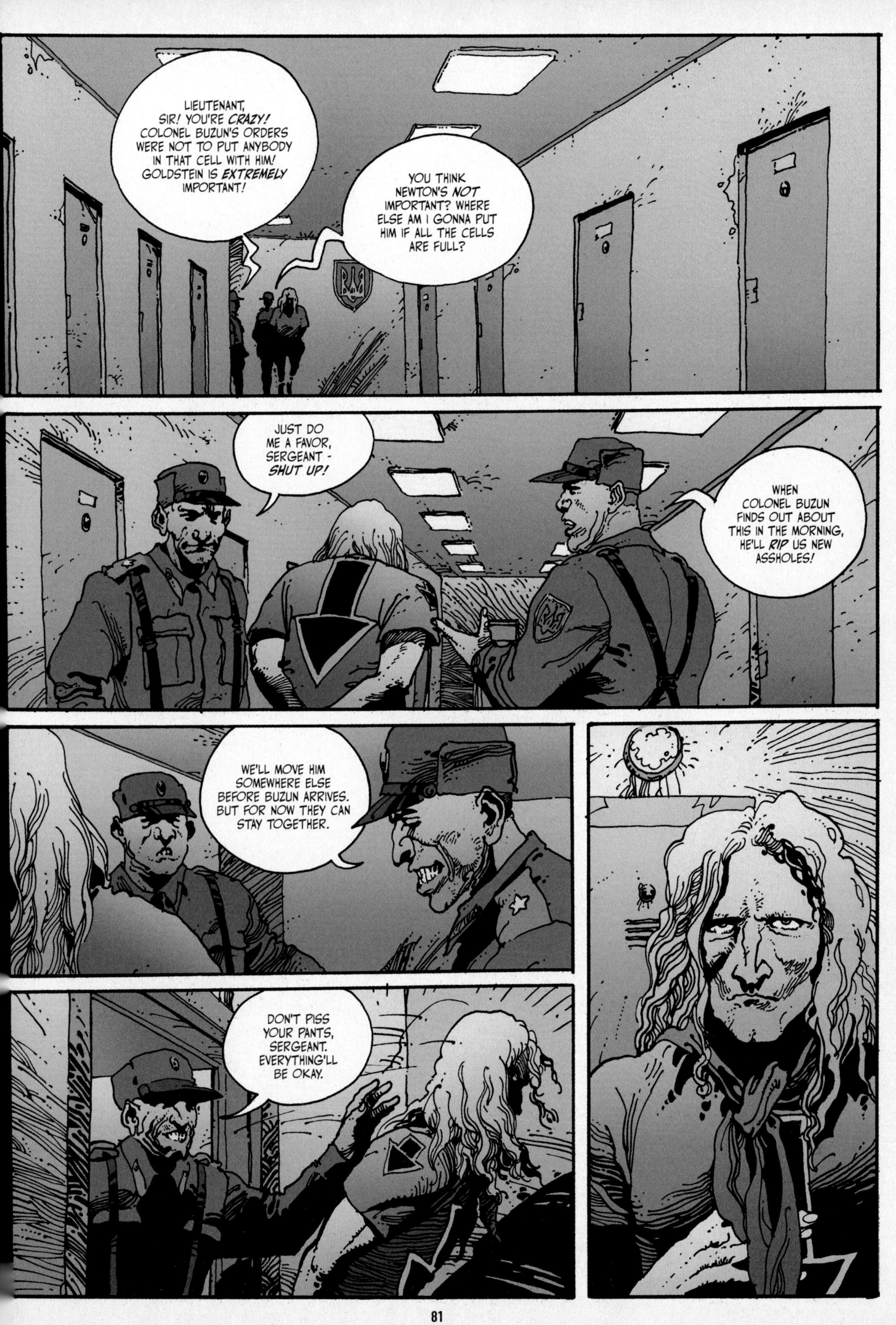
LIEUTENANT, SIR! YOU'RE CRAZY! COLONEL BUZUN'S ORDERS WERE NOT TO PUT ANYBODY IN THAT CELL WITH HIM! GOLDSTEIN IS EXTREMELY IMPORTANT!
YOU THINK NEWTON'S NOT IMPORTANT? WHERE ELSE AM I GONNA PUT HIM IF ALL THE CELLS ARE FULL?
JUST DO ME A FAVOR, SERGEANT - SHUT UP!
WHEN COLONEL BUZUN FINDS OUT ABOUT THIS IN THE MORNING, HE'LL RIP US NEW ASSHOLES!
WE'LL MOVE HIM SOMEWHERE ELSE BEFORE BUZUN ARRIVES. BUT FOR NOW THEY CAN STAY TOGETHER.
DON'T PISS YOUR PANTS, SERGEANT. EVERYTHING'LL BE OKAY.

DO YOU KNOW *WHO* I AM?

DO YOU KNOW WHY THE WORLD IS SUCH A VIOLENT PLACE?

NO.

NO.

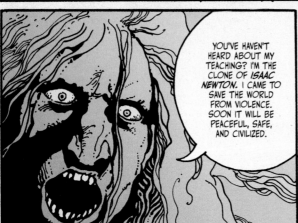

YOU'VE HAVEN'T HEARD ABOUT MY TEACHING? I'M THE CLONE OF *ISAAC NEWTON.* I CAME TO SAVE THE WORLD FROM VIOLENCE. SOON IT WILL BE PEACEFUL, SAFE, AND CIVILIZED.

ALL HUMAN VIOLENCE SPRINGS FROM NATURE. MEN SELDOM THINK WITH THEIR HEADS, THEY USUALLY THINK WITH THEIR *BALLS.* BUT ONE LITTLE OPERATION AND YOU'RE ON THE NEXT LEVEL OF *EVOLUTION.*

HOW'S THAT?

A MAN *WITHOUT GENITALS* IS CAPABLE OF PURE REASON. REASON PROPELS US TOWARD SAFETY AND LOGIC. THE *DARK AGES* INSPIRED BY MYSTICISM WILL BE GONE AND THEN...

THANKS ANYWAY, BUT MY FOUR WIVES ARE STILL *WAITING* FOR ME IN HEAVENLY CHECHNYA.

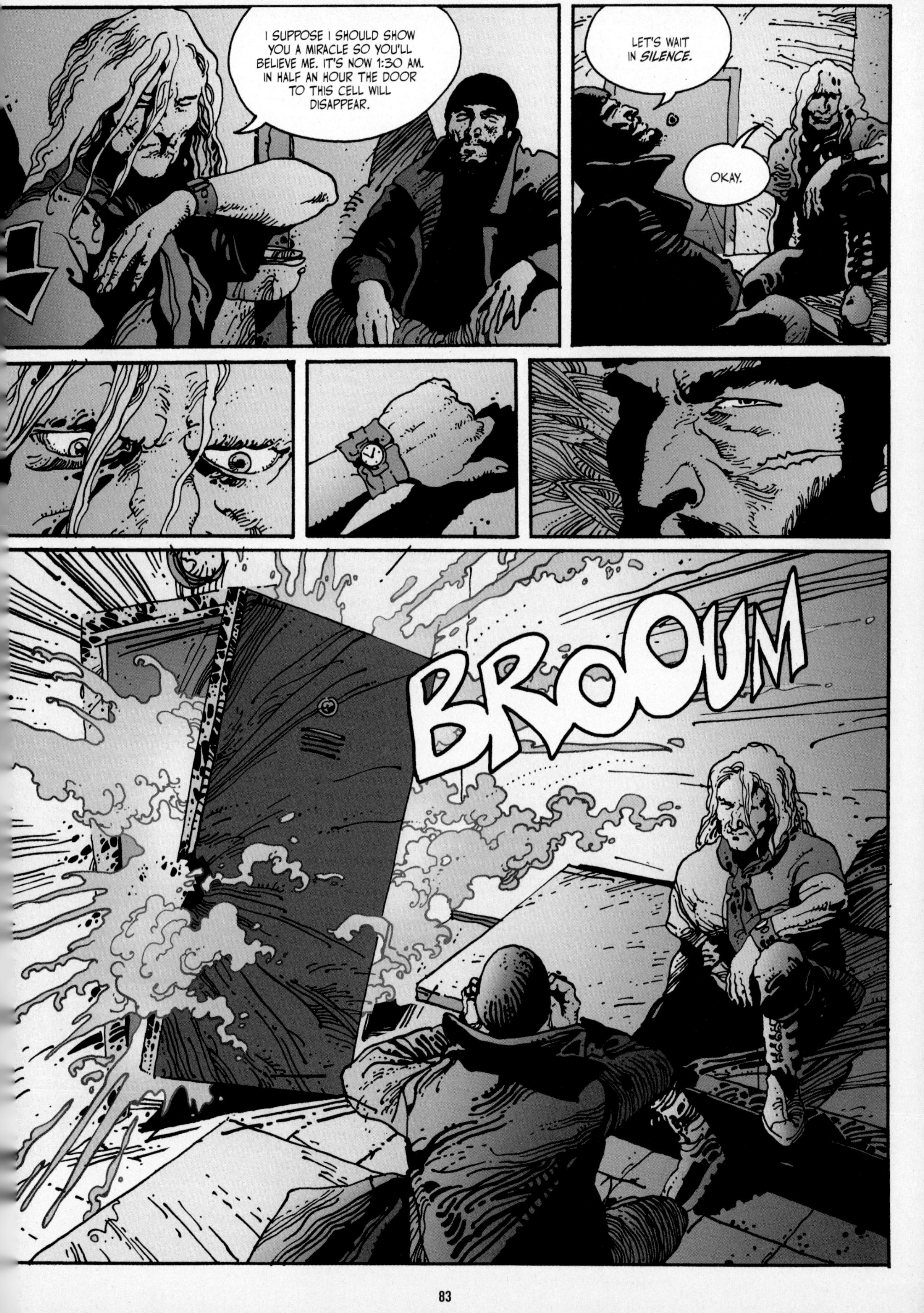
I SUPPOSE I SHOULD SHOW YOU A MIRACLE SO YOU'LL BELIEVE ME. IT'S NOW 1:30 AM. IN HALF AN HOUR THE DOOR TO THIS CELL WILL DISAPPEAR.
LET'S WAIT IN *SILENCE*.
OKAY.
BROOOUM

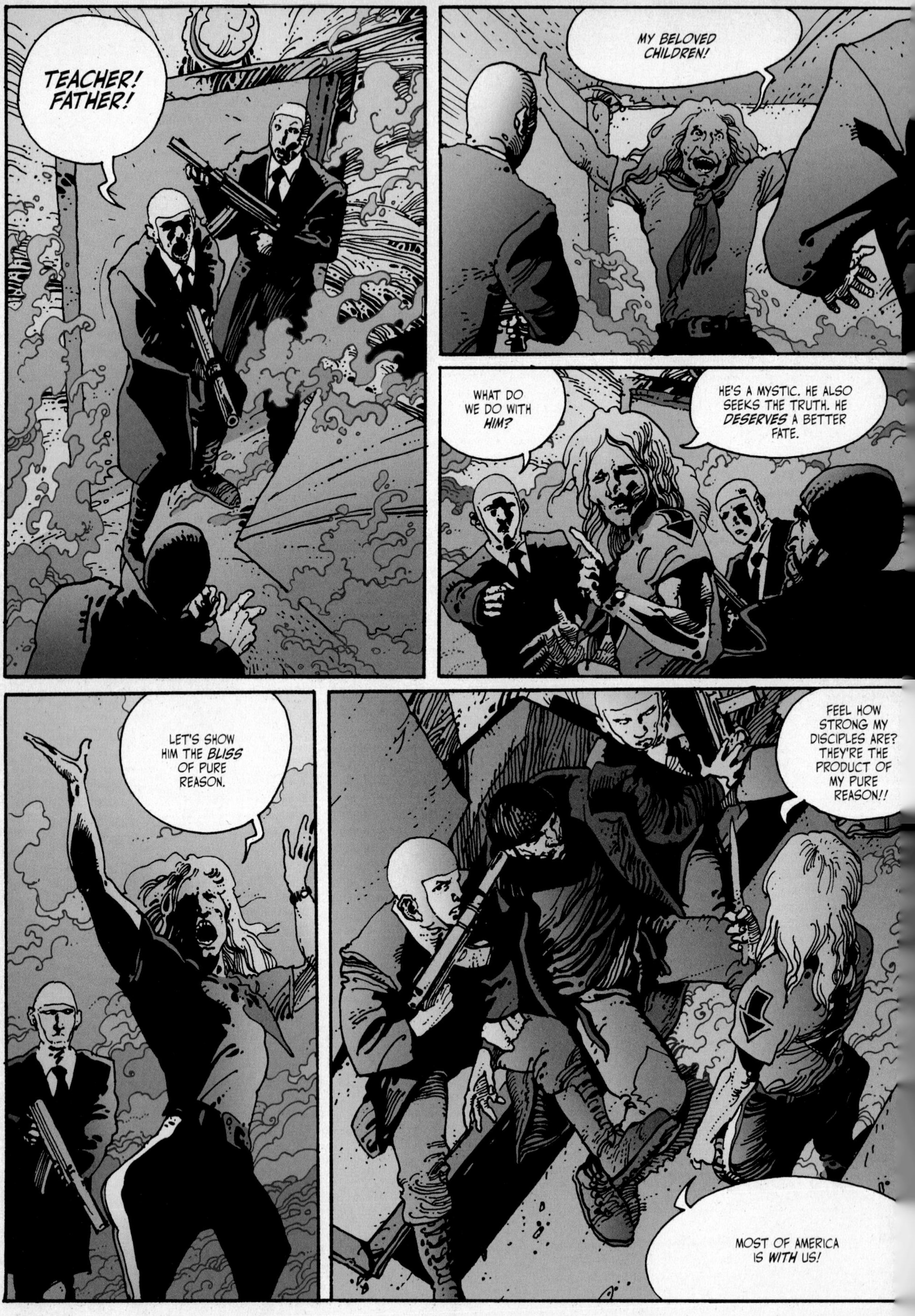
TEACHER! FATHER!
MY BELOVED CHILDREN!
WHAT DO WE DO WITH HIM?
HE'S A MYSTIC. HE ALSO SEEKS THE TRUTH. HE DESERVES A BETTER FATE.
LET'S SHOW HIM THE BLISS OF PURE REASON.
FEEL HOW STRONG MY DISCIPLES ARE? THEY'RE THE PRODUCT OF MY PURE REASON!!
MOST OF AMERICA IS WITH US!

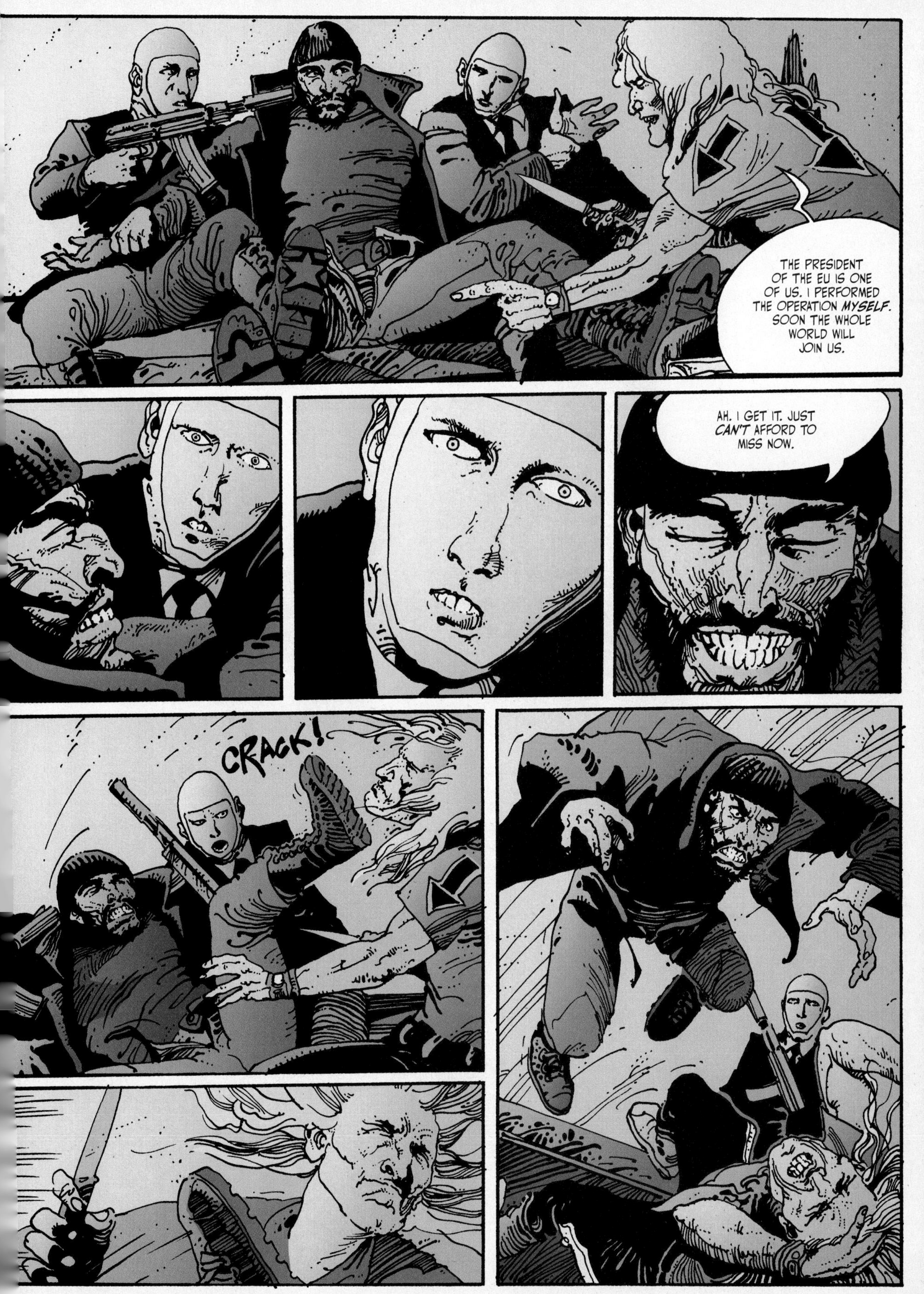
THE PRESIDENT OF THE EU IS ONE OF US. I PERFORMED THE OPERATION MYSELF. SOON THE WHOLE WORLD WILL JOIN US.
AH. I GET IT. JUST CAN'T AFFORD TO MISS NOW.
CRACK!

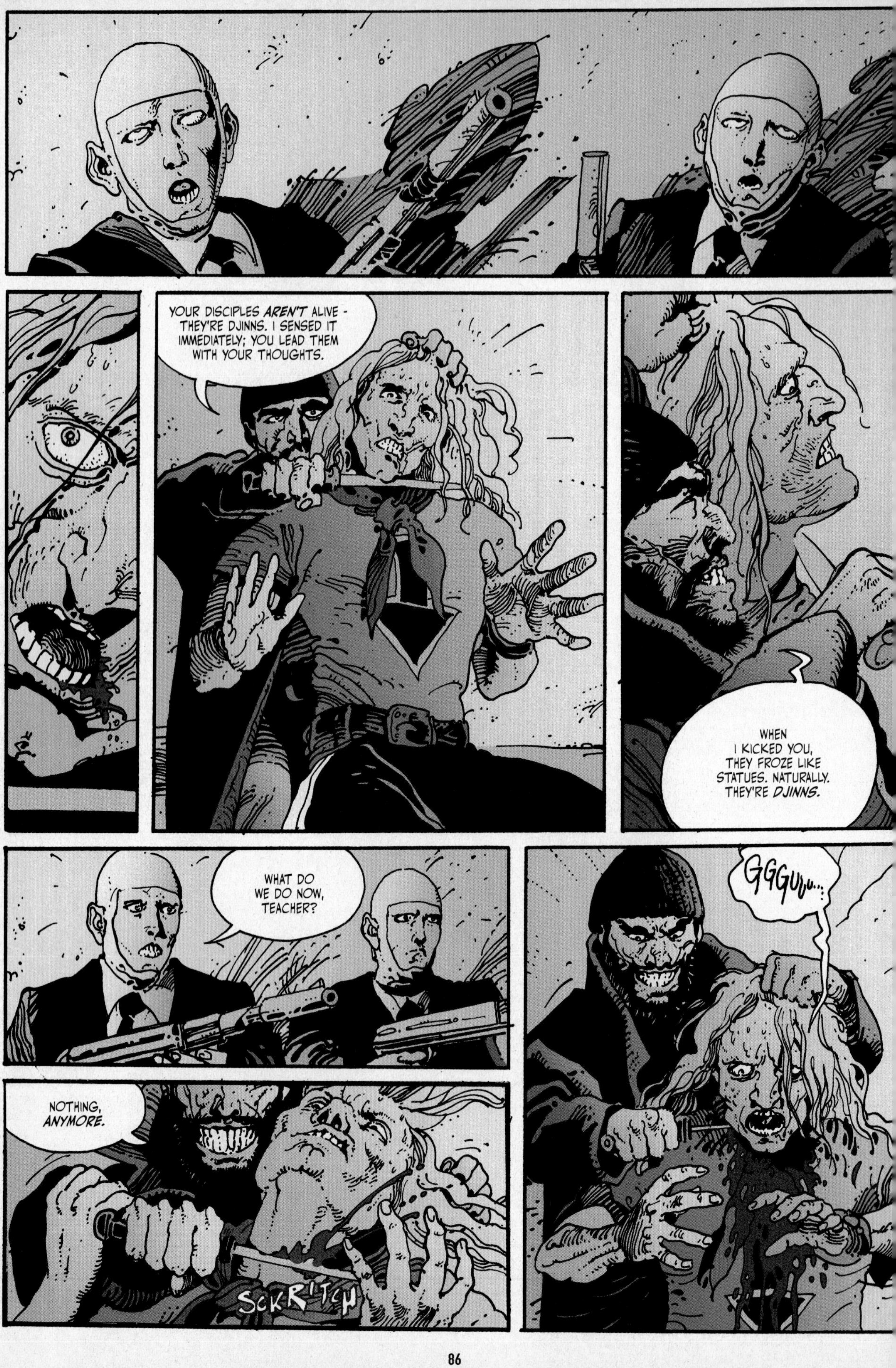

YOUR DISCIPLES *AREN'T* ALIVE - THEY'RE DJINNS. I SENSED IT IMMEDIATELY; YOU LEAD THEM WITH YOUR THOUGHTS.
WHEN I KICKED YOU, THEY FROZE LIKE STATUES. NATURALLY. THEY'RE *DJINNS.*
WHAT DO WE DO NOW, TEACHER?
GGGUU...
NOTHING, *ANYMORE.*
SCKRITCH

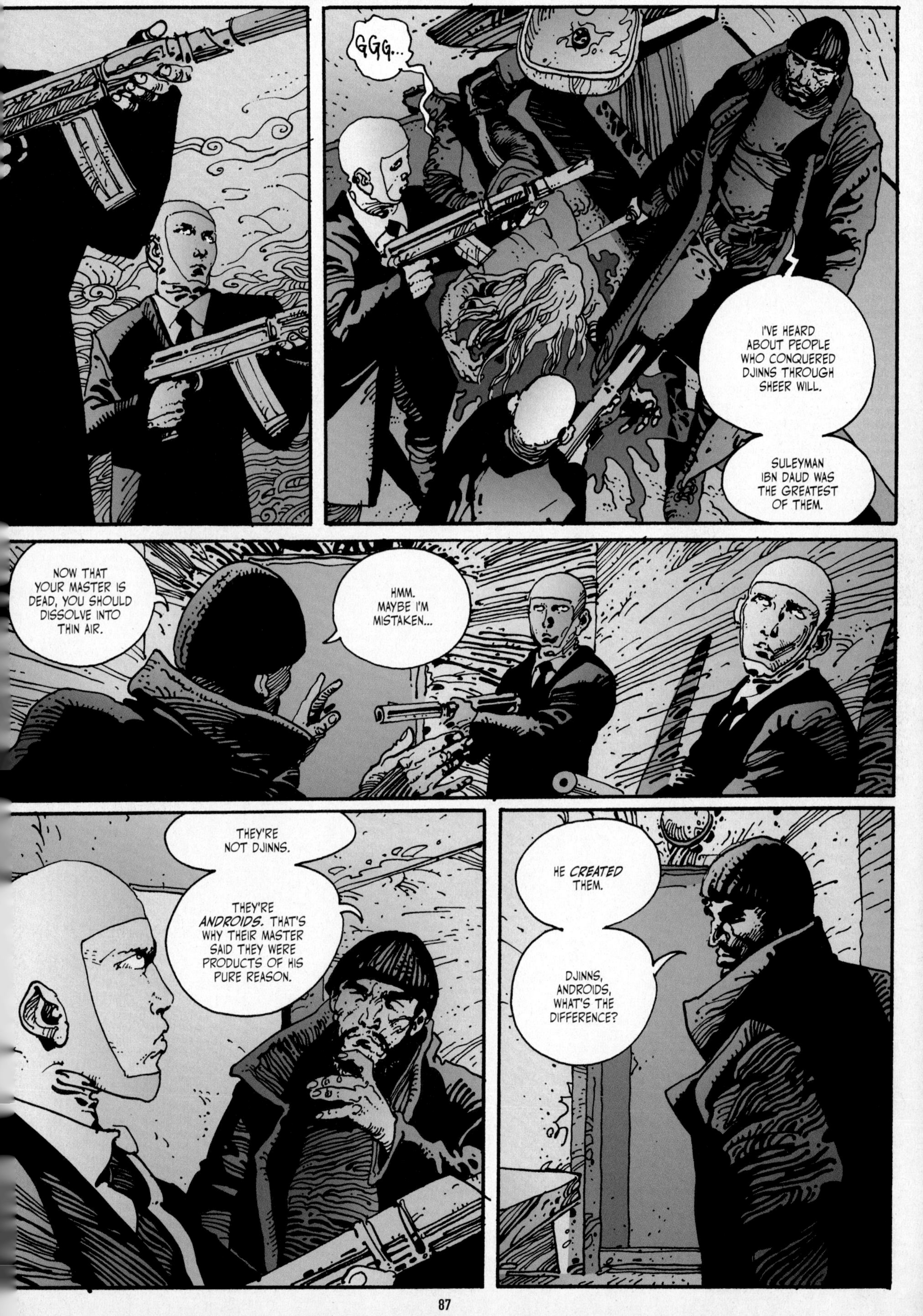
GGG...
I'VE HEARD ABOUT PEOPLE WHO CONQUERED DJINNS THROUGH SHEER WILL.
SULEYMAN IBN DAUD WAS THE GREATEST OF THEM.
NOW THAT YOUR MASTER IS DEAD, YOU SHOULD DISSOLVE INTO THIN AIR.
HMM. MAYBE I'M MISTAKEN...
THEY'RE NOT DJINNS.
THEY'RE *ANDROIDS.* THAT'S WHY THEIR MASTER SAID THEY WERE PRODUCTS OF HIS PURE REASON.
HE *CREATED* THEM.
DJINNS, ANDROIDS, WHAT'S THE DIFFERENCE?

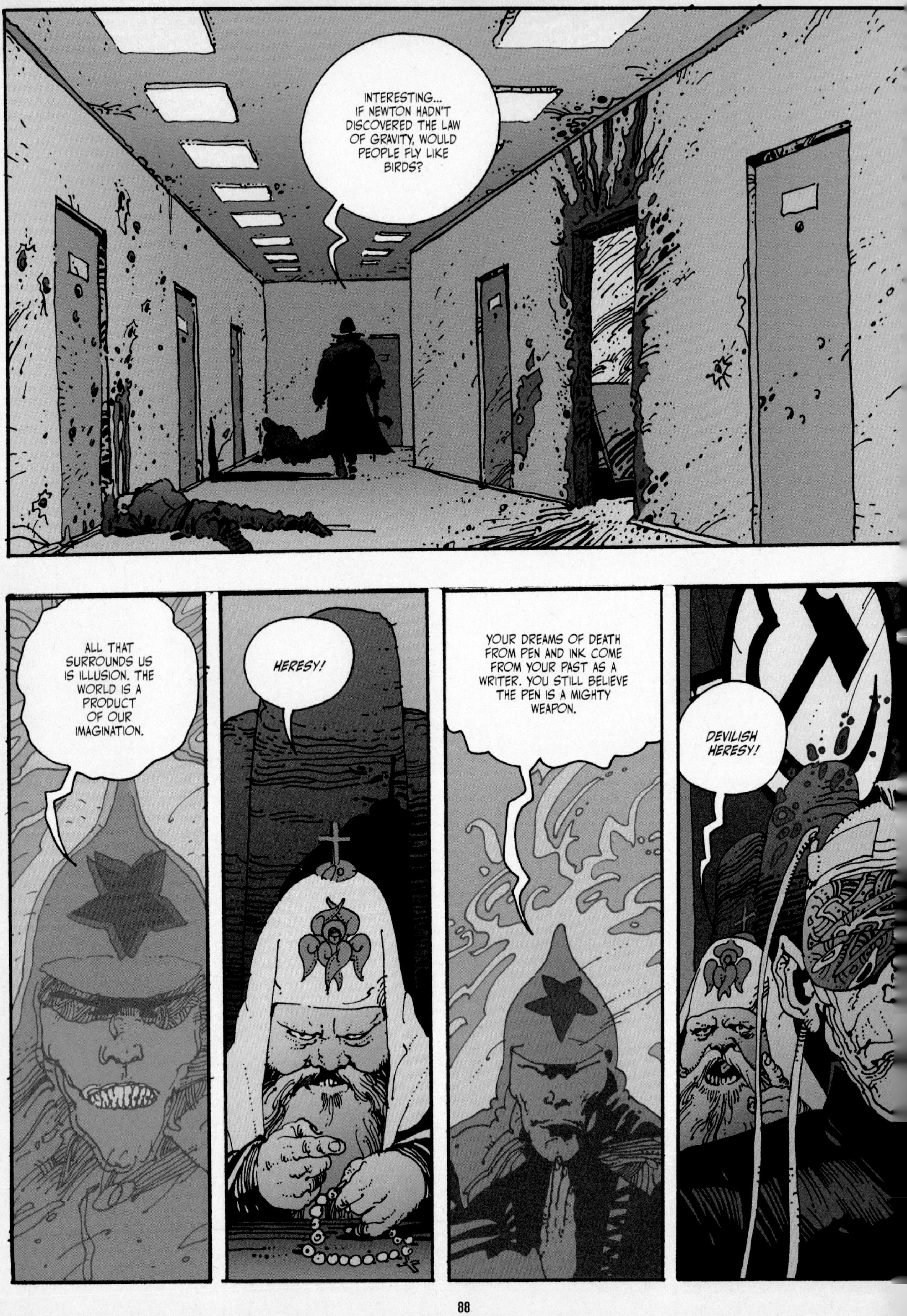
INTERESTING... IF NEWTON HADN'T DISCOVERED THE LAW OF GRAVITY, WOULD PEOPLE FLY LIKE BIRDS?
ALL THAT SURROUNDS US IS ILLUSION. THE WORLD IS A PRODUCT OF OUR IMAGINATION.
HERESY!
YOUR DREAMS OF DEATH FROM PEN AND INK COME FROM YOUR PAST AS A WRITER. YOU STILL BELIEVE THE PEN IS A MIGHTY WEAPON.
DEVILISH HERESY!

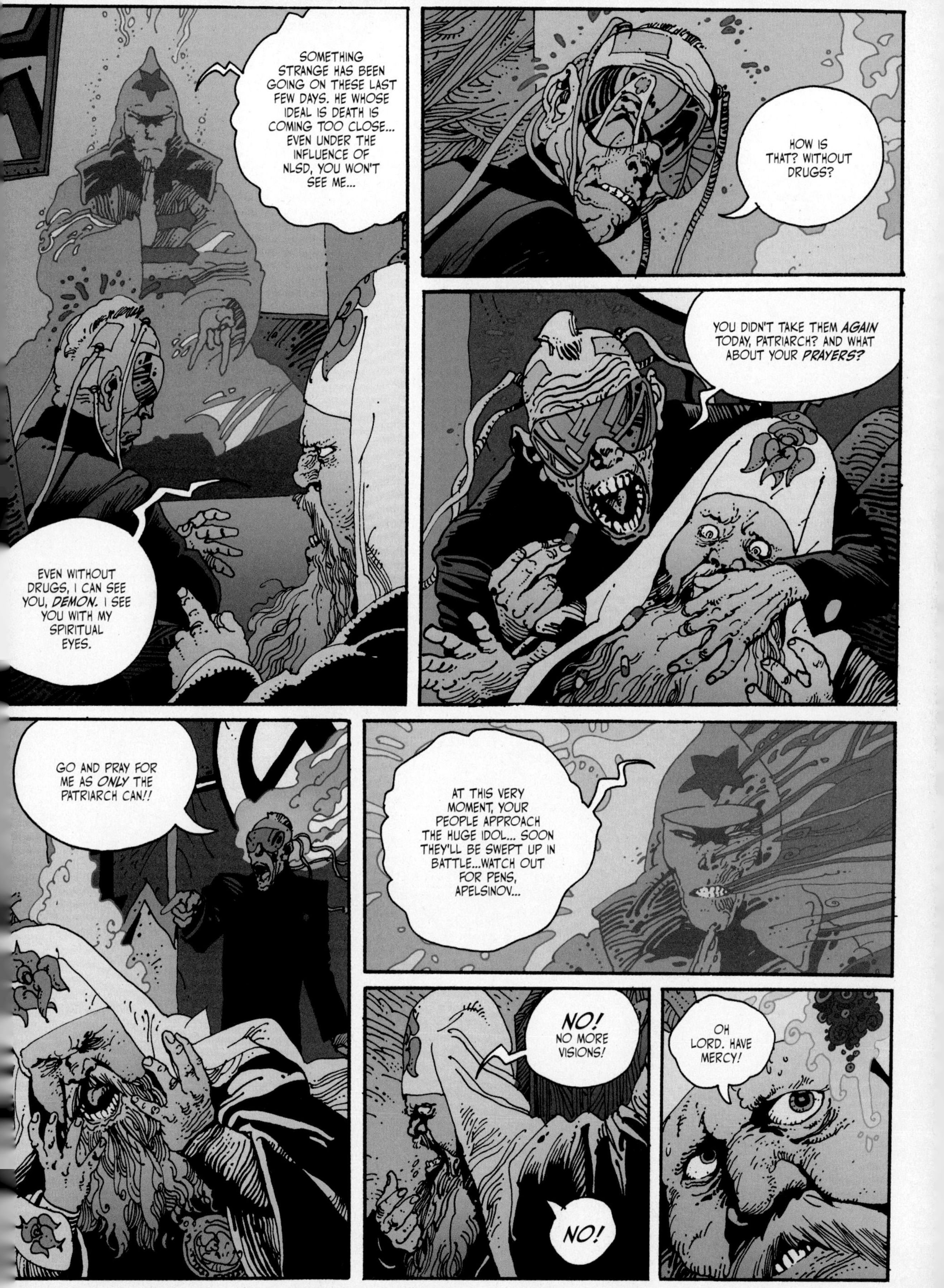
SOMETHING STRANGE HAS BEEN GOING ON THESE LAST FEW DAYS. HE WHOSE IDEAL IS DEATH IS COMING TOO CLOSE... EVEN UNDER THE INFLUENCE OF NLSD, YOU WON'T SEE ME...
EVEN WITHOUT DRUGS, I CAN SEE YOU, *DEMON*. I SEE YOU WITH MY SPIRITUAL EYES.
HOW IS THAT? WITHOUT DRUGS?
YOU DIDN'T TAKE THEM *AGAIN* TODAY, PATRIARCH? AND WHAT ABOUT YOUR *PRAYERS?*
GO AND PRAY FOR ME AS *ONLY* THE PATRIARCH CAN*!!*
AT THIS VERY MOMENT, YOUR PEOPLE APPROACH THE HUGE IDOL... SOON THEY'LL BE SWEPT UP IN BATTLE...WATCH OUT FOR PENS, APELSINOV...
NO! NO MORE VISIONS!
NO!
OH LORD. HAVE MERCY!

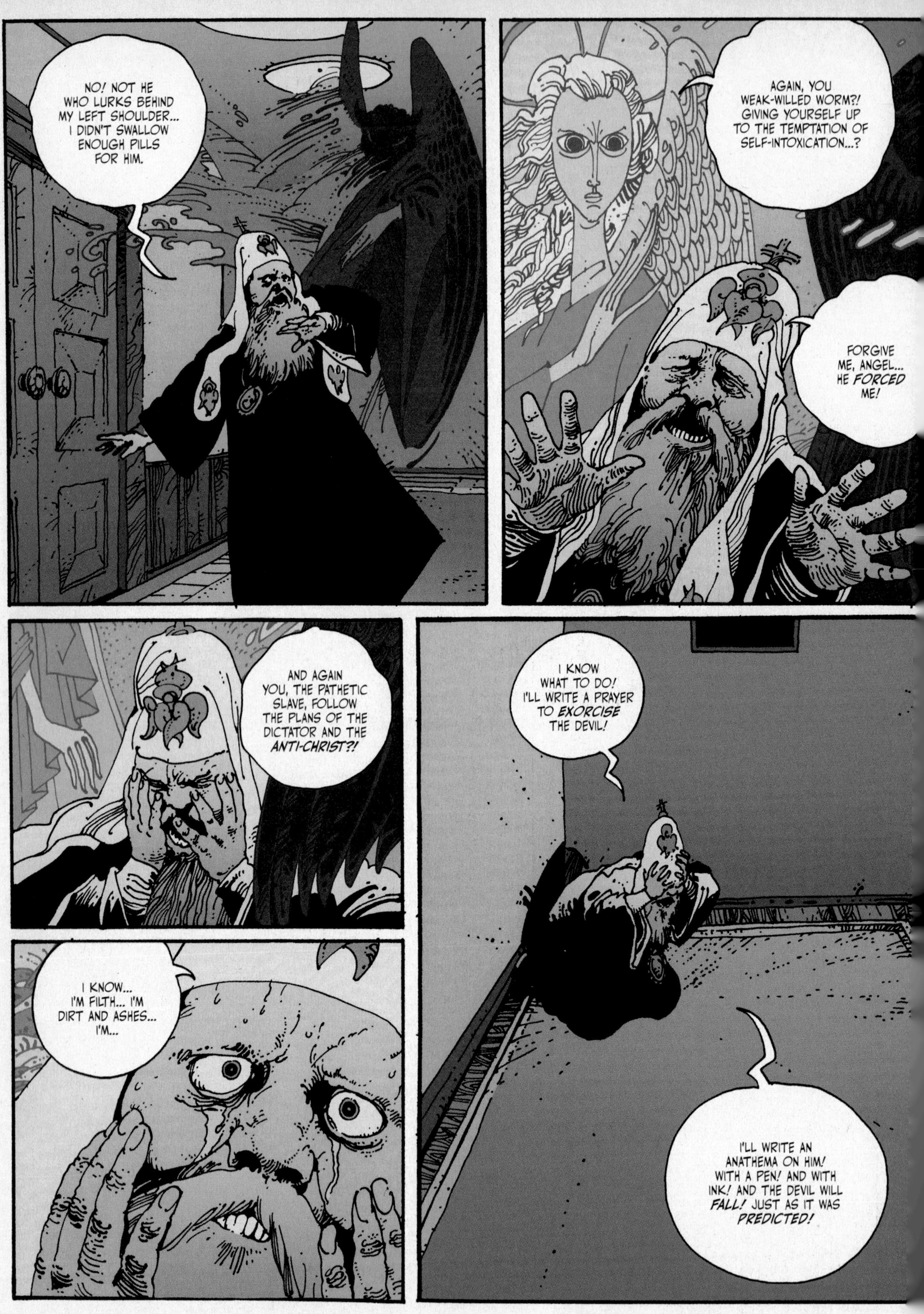
NO! NOT HE WHO LURKS BEHIND MY LEFT SHOULDER... I DIDN'T SWALLOW ENOUGH PILLS FOR HIM.
AGAIN, YOU WEAK-WILLED WORM?! GIVING YOURSELF UP TO THE TEMPTATION OF SELF-INTOXICATION...?
FORGIVE ME, ANGEL... HE *FORCED* ME!
AND AGAIN YOU, THE PATHETIC SLAVE, FOLLOW THE PLANS OF THE DICTATOR AND THE *ANTI-CHRIST?!*
I KNOW... I'M FILTH... I'M DIRT AND ASHES... I'M...
I KNOW WHAT TO DO! I'LL WRITE A PRAYER TO *EXORCISE* THE DEVIL!
I'LL WRITE AN ANATHEMA ON HIM! WITH A PEN! AND WITH INK! AND THE DEVIL WILL *FALL!* JUST AS IT WAS *PREDICTED!*

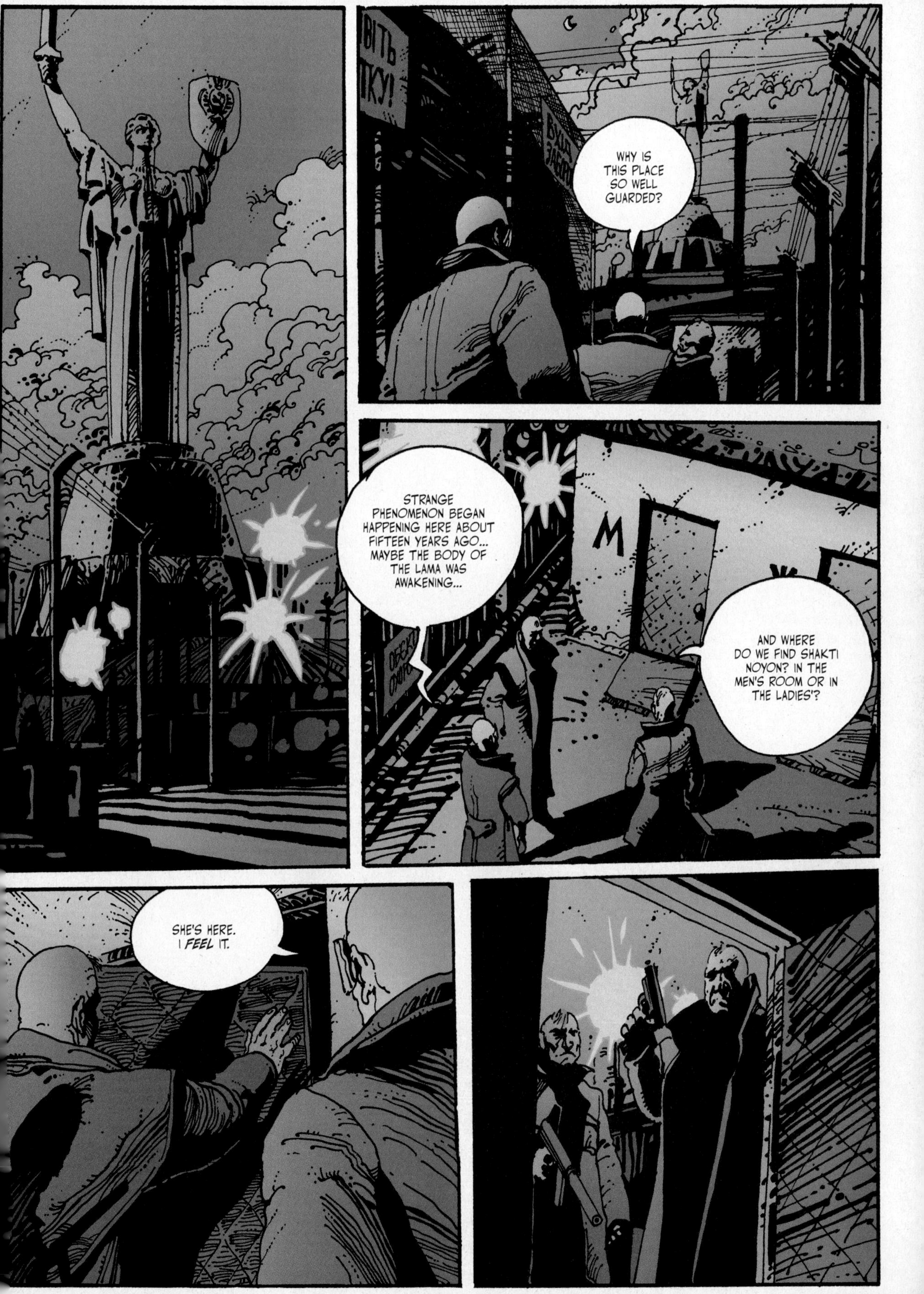
WHY IS THIS PLACE SO WELL GUARDED?
STRANGE PHENOMENON BEGAN HAPPENING HERE ABOUT FIFTEEN YEARS AGO... MAYBE THE BODY OF THE LAMA WAS AWAKENING...
AND WHERE DO WE FIND SHAKTI NOYON? IN THE MEN'S ROOM OR IN THE LADIES'?
SHE'S HERE. I *FEEL* IT.

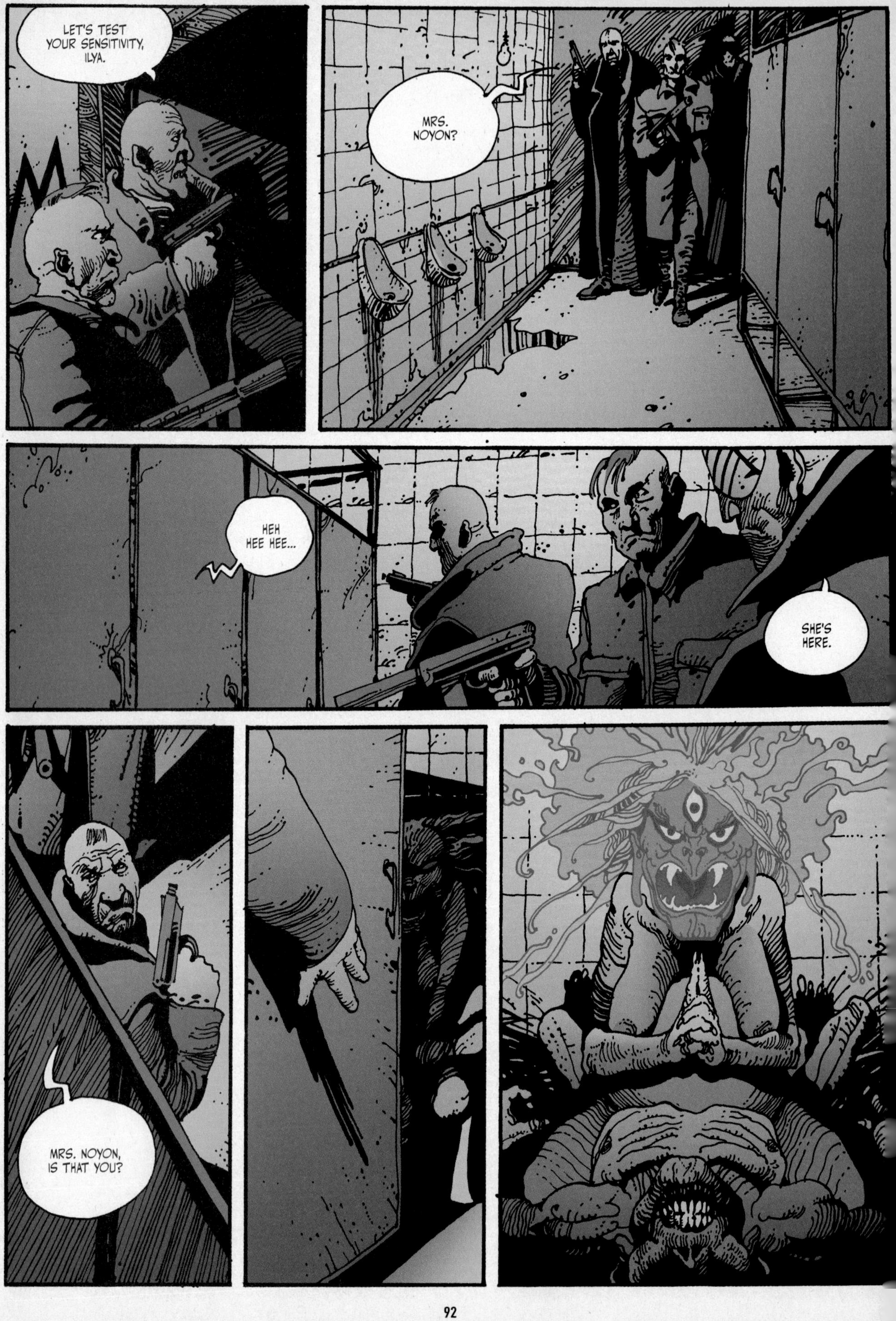
LET'S TEST YOUR SENSITIVITY, ILYA.
MRS. NOYON?
HEH HEE HEE...
SHE'S HERE.
MRS. NOYON, IS THAT YOU?

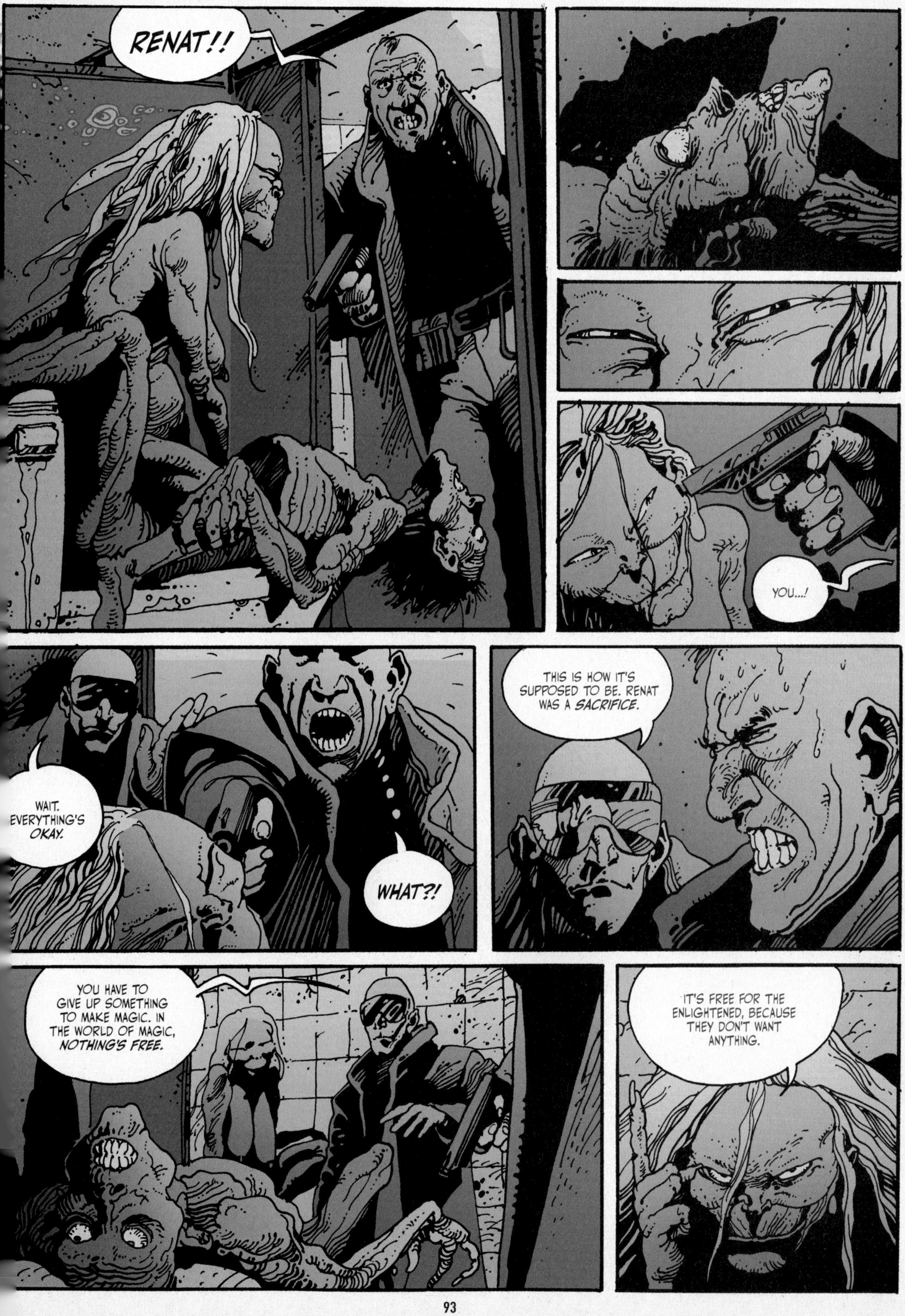
RENAT!!
YOU...!
WAIT. EVERYTHING'S OKAY.
WHAT?!
THIS IS HOW IT'S SUPPOSED TO BE. RENAT WAS A SACRIFICE.
YOU HAVE TO GIVE UP SOMETHING TO MAKE MAGIC. IN THE WORLD OF MAGIC, NOTHING'S FREE.
IT'S FREE FOR THE ENLIGHTENED, BECAUSE THEY DON'T WANT ANYTHING.

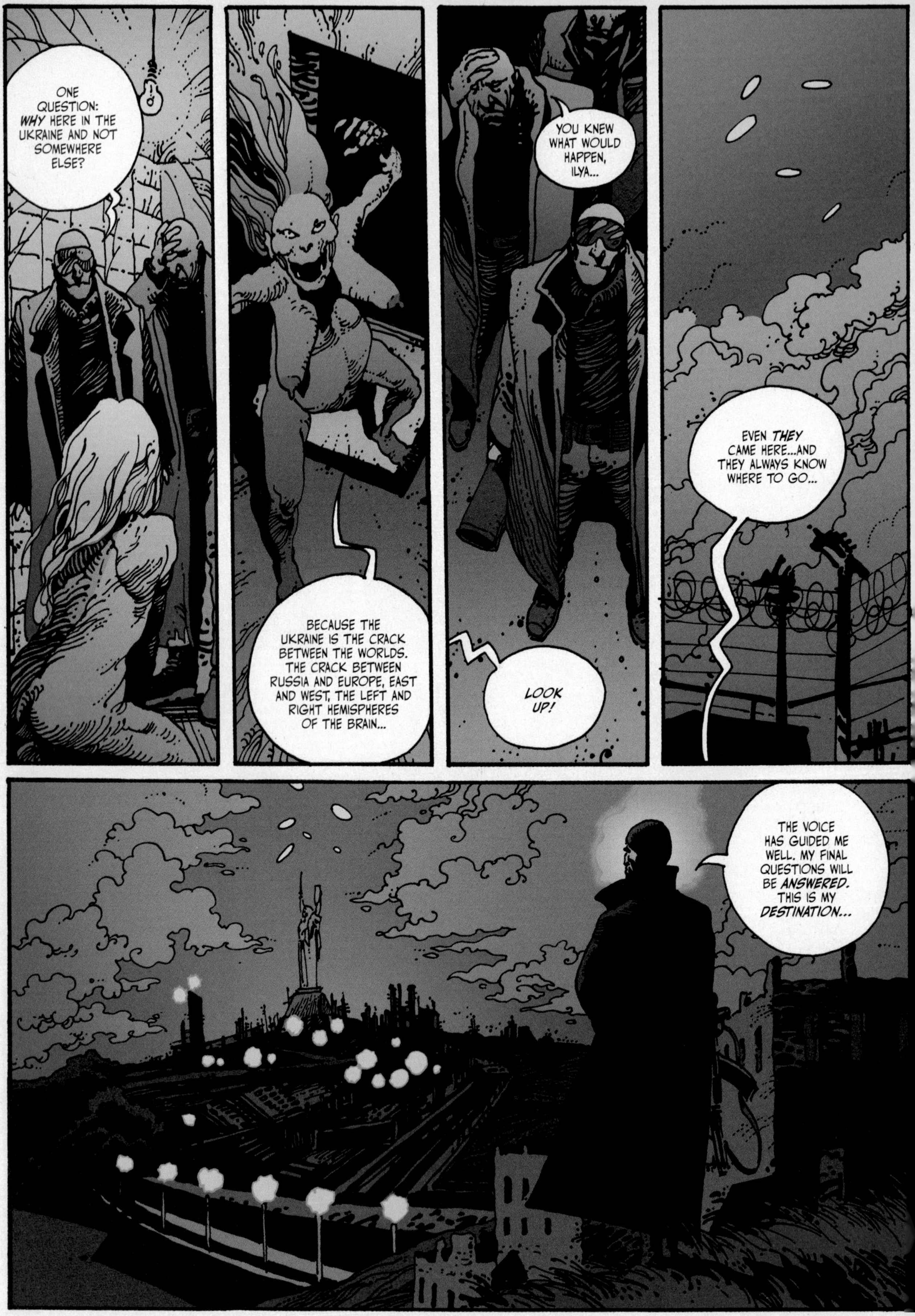
ONE QUESTION: WHY HERE IN THE UKRAINE AND NOT SOMEWHERE ELSE?
BECAUSE THE UKRAINE IS THE CRACK BETWEEN THE WORLDS. THE CRACK BETWEEN RUSSIA AND EUROPE, EAST AND WEST, THE LEFT AND RIGHT HEMISPHERES OF THE BRAIN...
YOU KNEW WHAT WOULD HAPPEN, ILYA...
LOOK UP!
EVEN THEY CAME HERE...AND THEY ALWAYS KNOW WHERE TO GO...
THE VOICE HAS GUIDED ME WELL. MY FINAL QUESTIONS WILL BE ANSWERED. THIS IS MY DESTINATION...

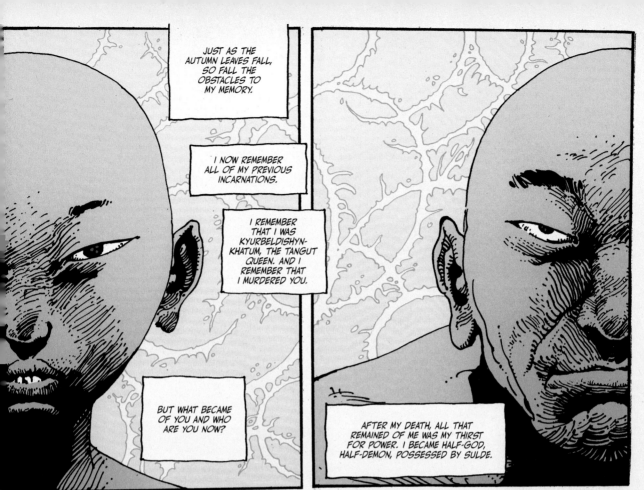

JUST AS THE AUTUMN LEAVES FALL, SO FALL THE OBSTACLES TO MY MEMORY.

I NOW REMEMBER ALL OF MY PREVIOUS INCARNATIONS.

I REMEMBER THAT I WAS KYURBELDISHYN-KHATUM, THE TANGUT QUEEN. AND I REMEMBER THAT I MURDERED YOU.

BUT WHAT BECAME OF YOU AND WHO ARE YOU NOW?

AFTER MY DEATH, ALL THAT REMAINED OF ME WAS MY THIRST FOR POWER. I BECAME HALF-GOD, HALF-DEMON, POSSESSED BY SULDE.

THE SHAMANS MADE SACRIFICES TO ME AT THE HOLY GROUND OF THE EIGHT WHITE YURTS.

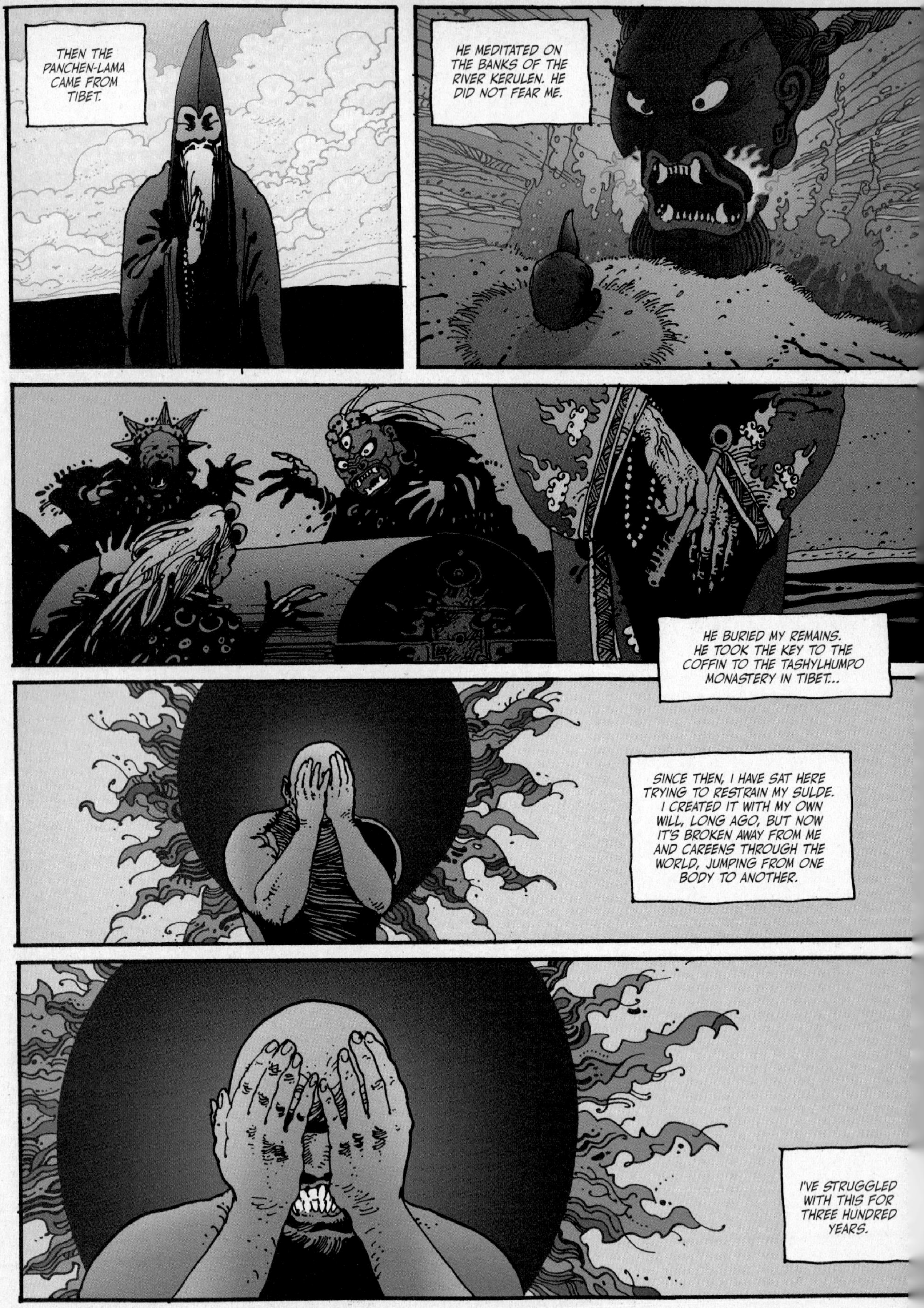
THEN THE PANCHEN-LAMA CAME FROM TIBET.
HE MEDITATED ON THE BANKS OF THE RIVER KERULEN. HE DID NOT FEAR ME.
HE BURIED MY REMAINS. HE TOOK THE KEY TO THE COFFIN TO THE TASHYLHUMPO MONASTERY IN TIBET...
SINCE THEN, I HAVE SAT HERE TRYING TO RESTRAIN MY SULDE. I CREATED IT WITH MY OWN WILL, LONG AGO, BUT NOW IT'S BROKEN AWAY FROM ME AND CAREENS THROUGH THE WORLD, JUMPING FROM ONE BODY TO ANOTHER.
I'VE STRUGGLED WITH THIS FOR THREE HUNDRED YEARS.

LAMA NOYON WAS ONE OF THE STRONGEST INCARNATIONS OF SULDE.

HE USED THE PAINTER ROERICH TO PENETRATE RUSSIA.

THE RUSSIAN DICTATOR IS HIS LATEST PERSONIFICATION...

AND I NO LONGER HAVE THE POWER TO STOP THIS SUCCESSION OF BIRTHS.

YOU *REJECTED* YOUR FEMALE HALF AND BECAME WEAK AND INSANE.

THE MALE HALF ALWAYS WANTS TO CONQUER AND DESTROY...

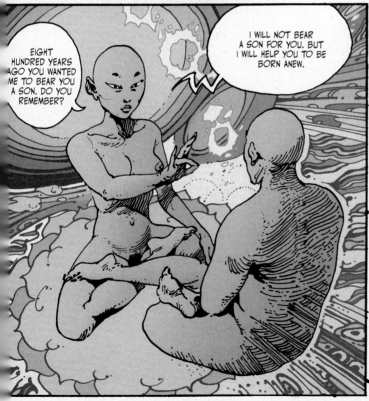

EIGHT HUNDRED YEARS AGO YOU WANTED ME TO BEAR YOU A SON. DO YOU REMEMBER?

I WILL NOT BEAR A SON FOR YOU. BUT I WILL HELP YOU TO BE BORN ANEW.

DID YOUR PANCHEN-LAMA EVER TELL YOU ABOUT *TANTRAS?*

FORGET EVERYTHING YOU EVER KNEW...

97

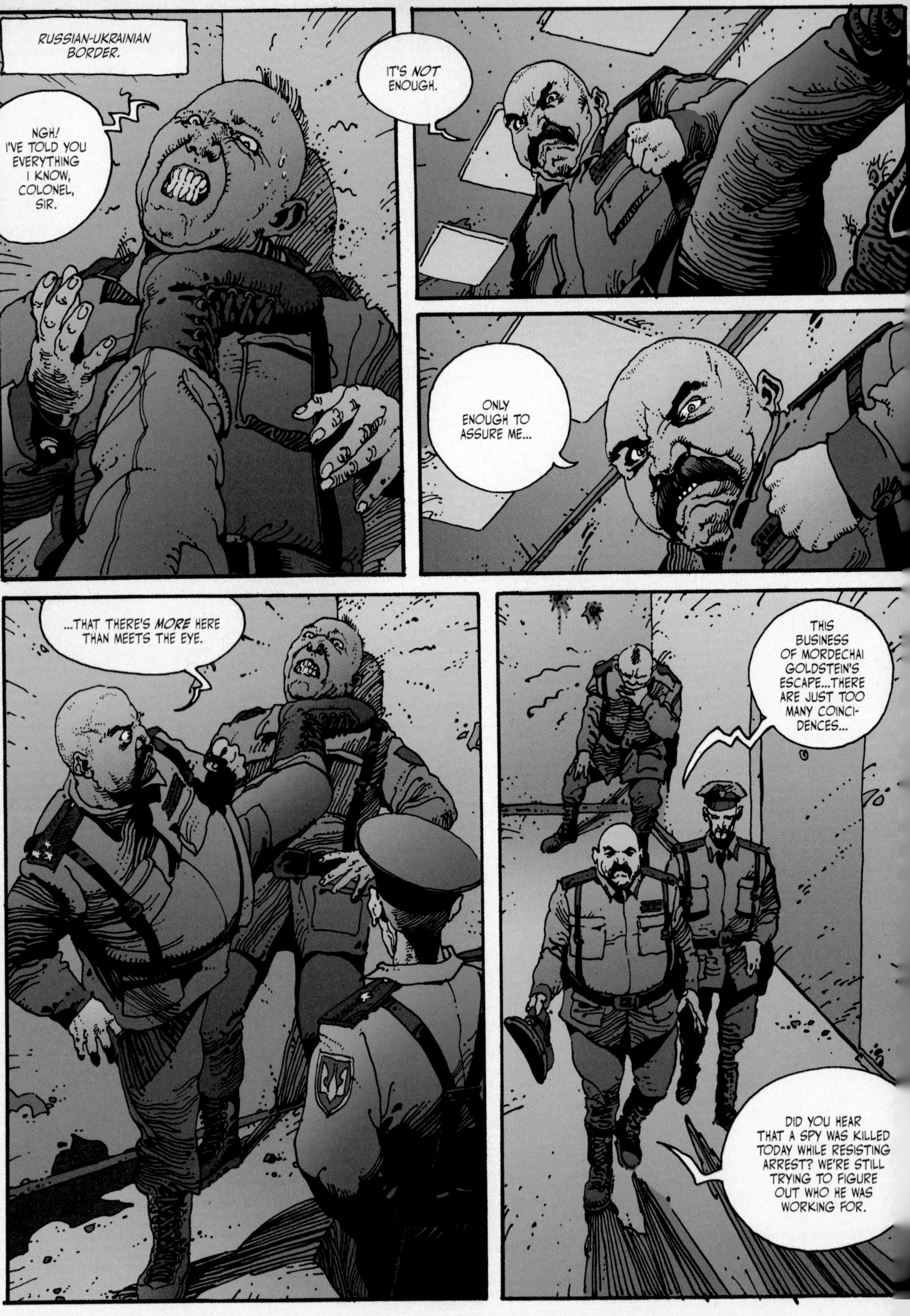
RUSSIAN-UKRAINIAN BORDER.
NGH! I'VE TOLD YOU EVERYTHING I KNOW, COLONEL, SIR.
IT'S NOT ENOUGH.
ONLY ENOUGH TO ASSURE ME...
...THAT THERE'S MORE HERE THAN MEETS THE EYE.
THIS BUSINESS OF MORDECHAI GOLDSTEIN'S ESCAPE...THERE ARE JUST TOO MANY COINCI-DENCES...
DID YOU HEAR THAT A SPY WAS KILLED TODAY WHILE RESISTING ARREST? WE'RE STILL TRYING TO FIGURE OUT WHO HE WAS WORKING FOR.

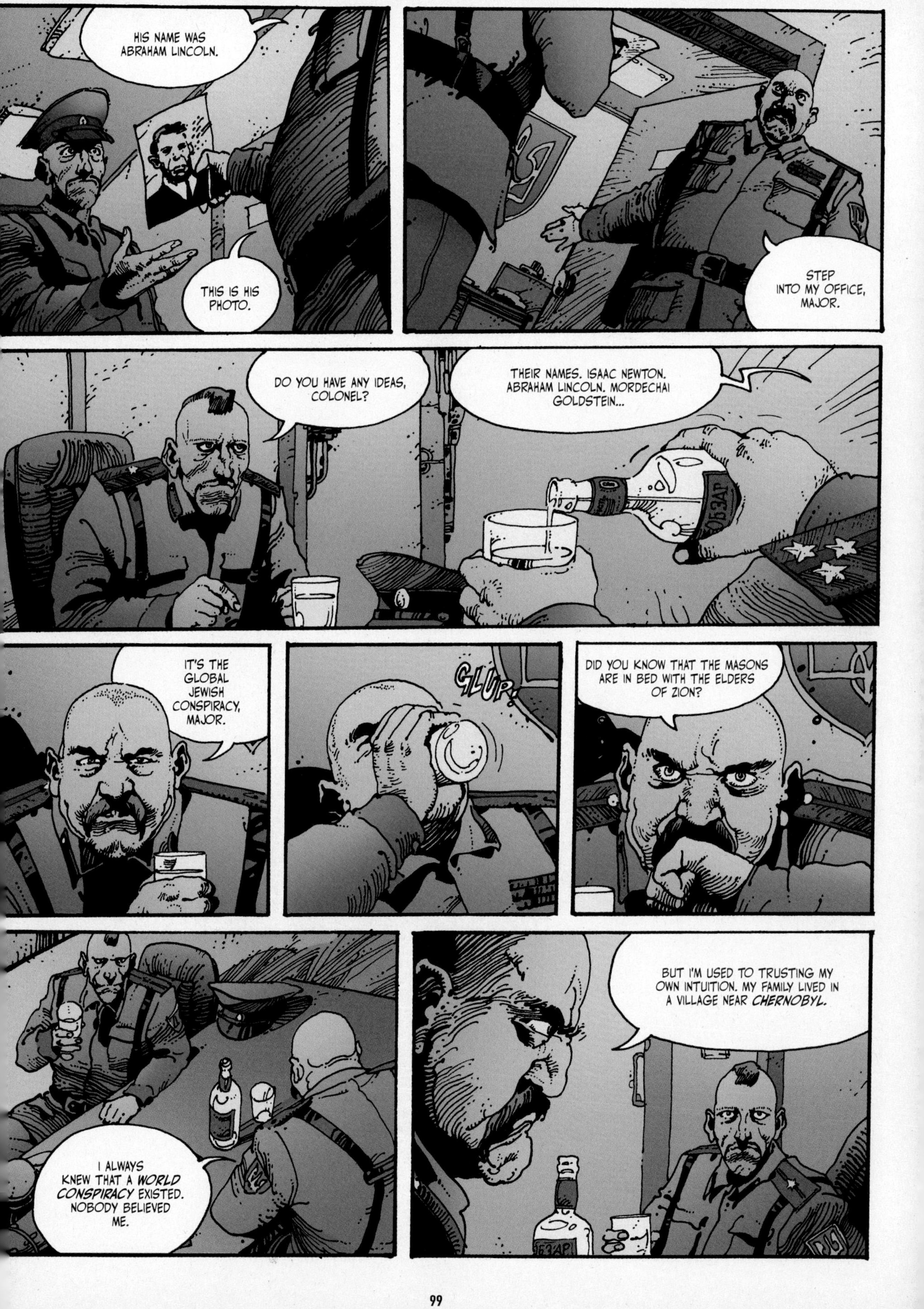
HIS NAME WAS ABRAHAM LINCOLN.
THIS IS HIS PHOTO.
STEP INTO MY OFFICE, MAJOR.
DO YOU HAVE ANY IDEAS, COLONEL?
THEIR NAMES. ISAAC NEWTON. ABRAHAM LINCOLN. MORDECHAI GOLDSTEIN...
IT'S THE GLOBAL JEWISH CONSPIRACY, MAJOR.
GLUP!
DID YOU KNOW THAT THE MASONS ARE IN BED WITH THE ELDERS OF ZION?
I ALWAYS KNEW THAT A *WORLD CONSPIRACY* EXISTED. NOBODY BELIEVED ME.
BUT I'M USED TO TRUSTING MY OWN INTUITION. MY FAMILY LIVED IN A VILLAGE NEAR *CHERNOBYL.*

IN 1987, THEY TOLD MY PARENTS THAT THEY COULDN'T STAY THERE ANYMORE. BUT MY MOTHER, A SIMPLE, HONEST WOMAN, KNEW THEY WERE CHEATING HER.

THEY HAD MADE UP SOME RIDICULOUS STORY TO GET THE LAND. SOMETHING ABOUT AN ACCIDENT AND RADIATION THAT NOBODY COULD EVEN SEE.

MY PARENTS REFUSED TO LEAVE.

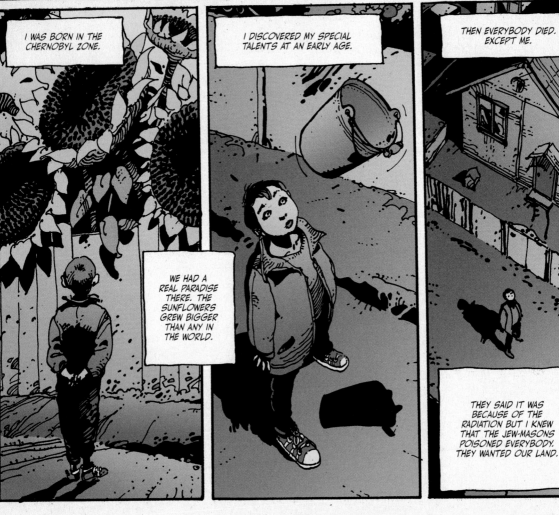

I WAS BORN IN THE CHERNOBYL ZONE.

WE HAD A REAL PARADISE THERE. THE SUNFLOWERS GREW BIGGER THAN ANY IN THE WORLD.

I DISCOVERED MY SPECIAL TALENTS AT AN EARLY AGE.

THEN EVERYBODY DIED. EXCEPT ME.

THEY SAID IT WAS BECAUSE OF THE RADIATION BUT I KNEW THAT THE JEW-MASONS POISONED EVERYBODY. THEY WANTED OUR LAND.

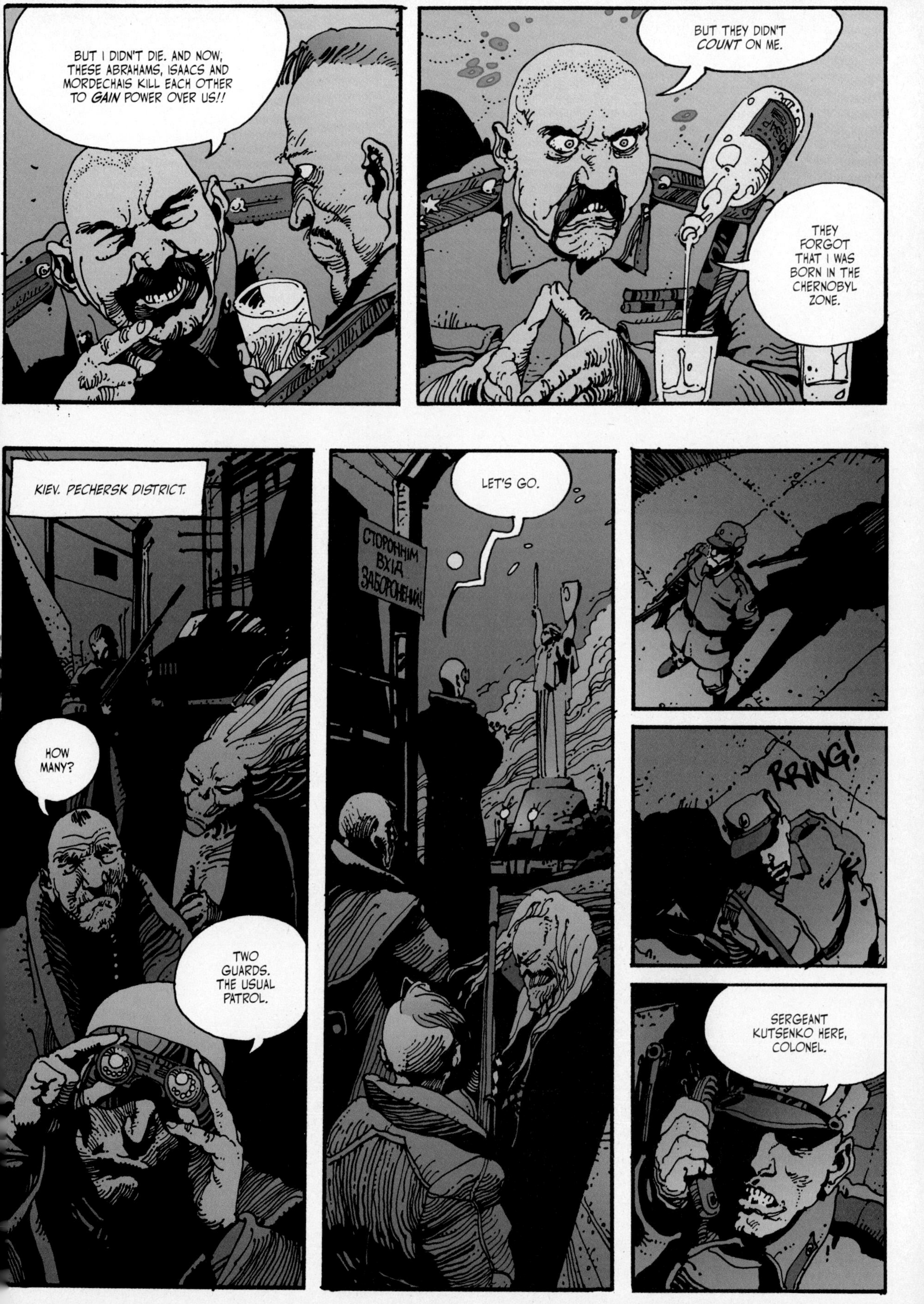
BUT I DIDN'T DIE. AND NOW, THESE ABRAHAMS, ISAACS AND MORDECHAIS KILL EACH OTHER TO GAIN POWER OVER US!!
BUT THEY DIDN'T COUNT ON ME.
THEY FORGOT THAT I WAS BORN IN THE CHERNOBYL ZONE.
KIEV. PECHERSK DISTRICT.
HOW MANY?
TWO GUARDS. THE USUAL PATROL.
LET'S GO.
СТОРОННІМ ВХІД ЗАБОРОНЕНИЙ!
RRING!
SERGEANT KUTSENKO HERE, COLONEL.

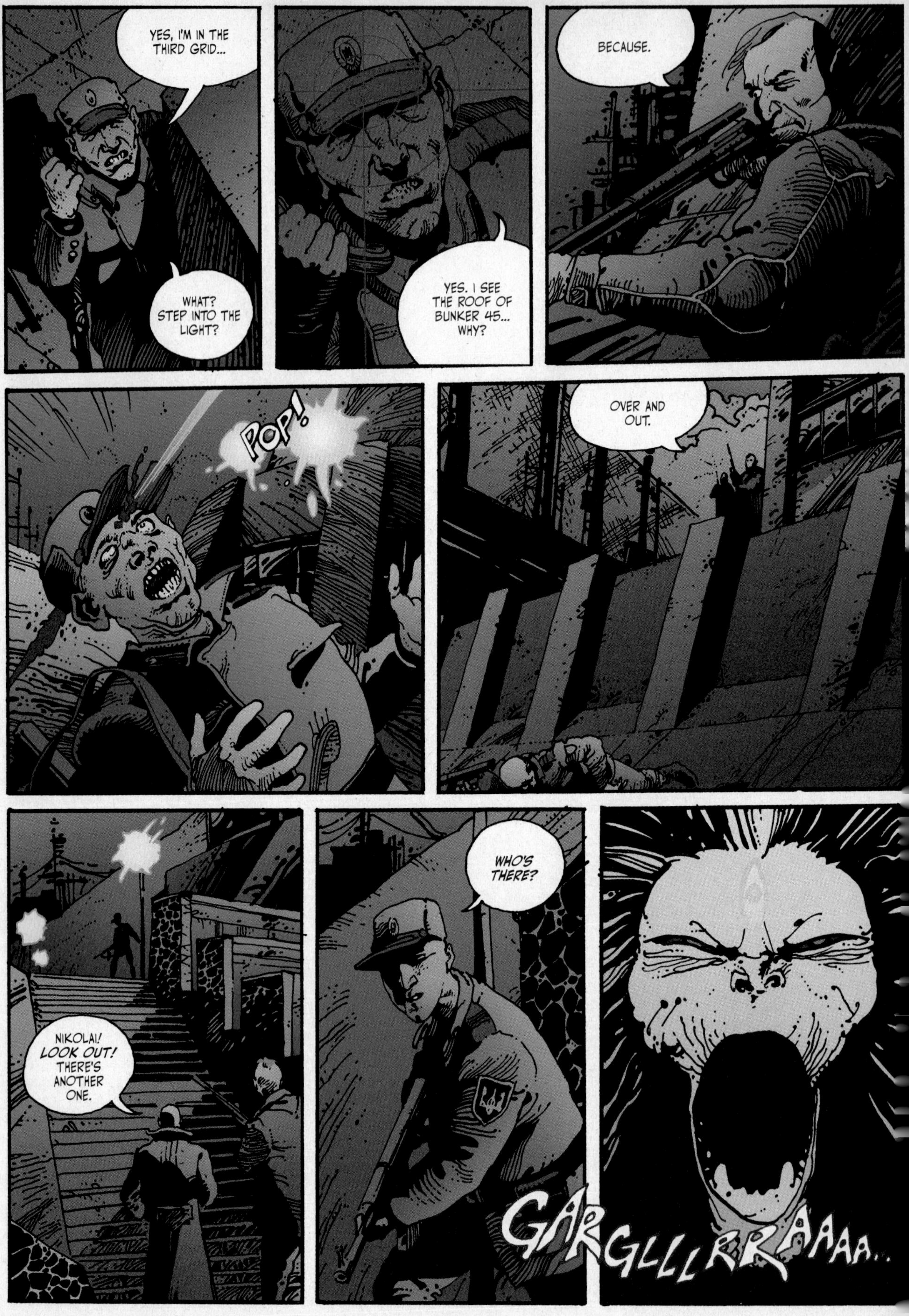
YES, I'M IN THE THIRD GRID...
WHAT? STEP INTO THE LIGHT?
YES. I SEE THE ROOF OF BUNKER 45... WHY?
BECAUSE.
POP!
OVER AND OUT.
NIKOLAI! *LOOK OUT!* THERE'S ANOTHER ONE.
WHO'S THERE?
GARGLLLRRRAAAA...

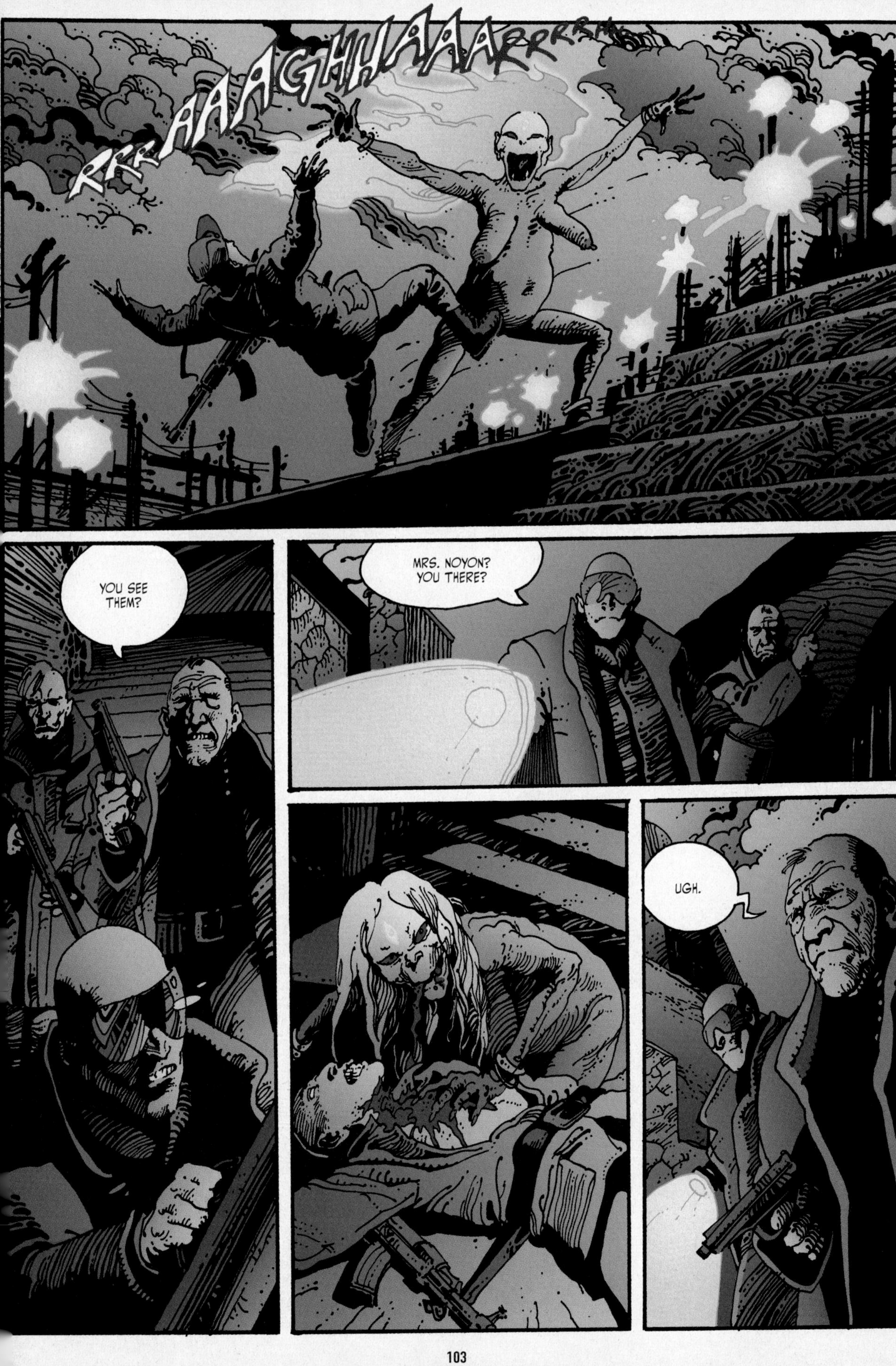
RRRAAAAGHHAAARRRRRHH
YOU SEE THEM?
MRS. NOYON? YOU THERE?
UGH.

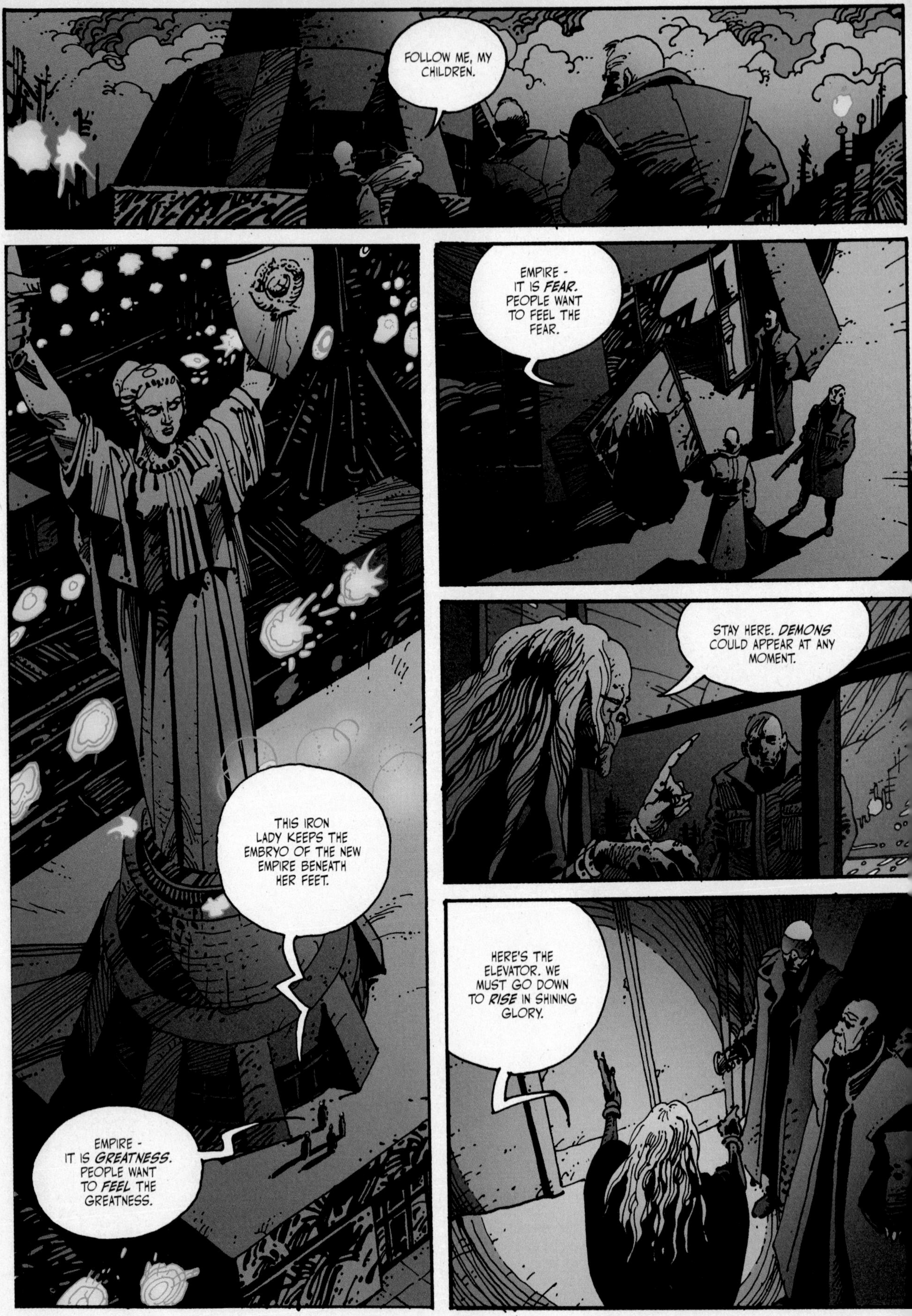
FOLLOW ME, MY CHILDREN.
THIS IRON LADY KEEPS THE EMBRYO OF THE NEW EMPIRE BENEATH HER FEET.
EMPIRE - IT IS GREATNESS. PEOPLE WANT TO FEEL THE GREATNESS.
EMPIRE - IT IS FEAR. PEOPLE WANT TO FEEL THE FEAR.
STAY HERE. DEMONS COULD APPEAR AT ANY MOMENT.
HERE'S THE ELEVATOR. WE MUST GO DOWN TO RISE IN SHINING GLORY.

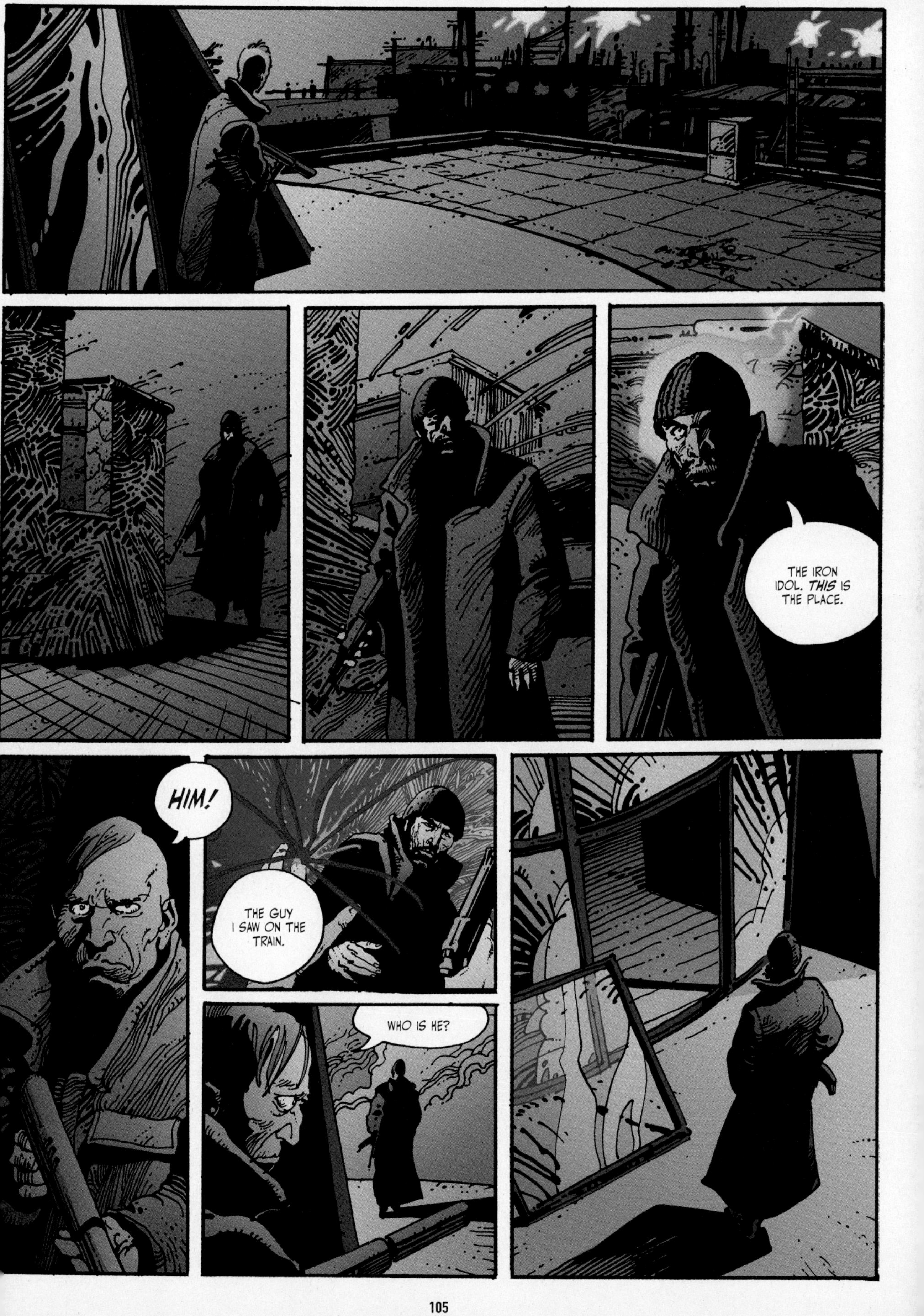
THE IRON IDOL. THIS IS THE PLACE.
HIM!
THE GUY I SAW ON THE TRAIN.
WHO IS HE?

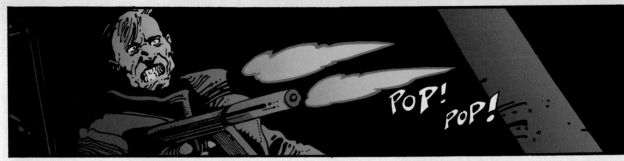

POP! POP!

I *KNOW* YOU. FROM THE TRAIN. I HAD A *STRANGE* VISION.

ONLY *ALLAH* KNOWS FOR CERTAIN WHAT OUR VISIONS MEAN.

I KNEW I'D SEE YOU AGAIN... IN THESE DAYS, THIS AGE OF *MYSTICISM* AND *SORCERY*, AMAZING THINGS ARE ALL AROUND US.

I THINK THAT VISION WAS A SIGN OF *DEATH*.

?!

AAH!

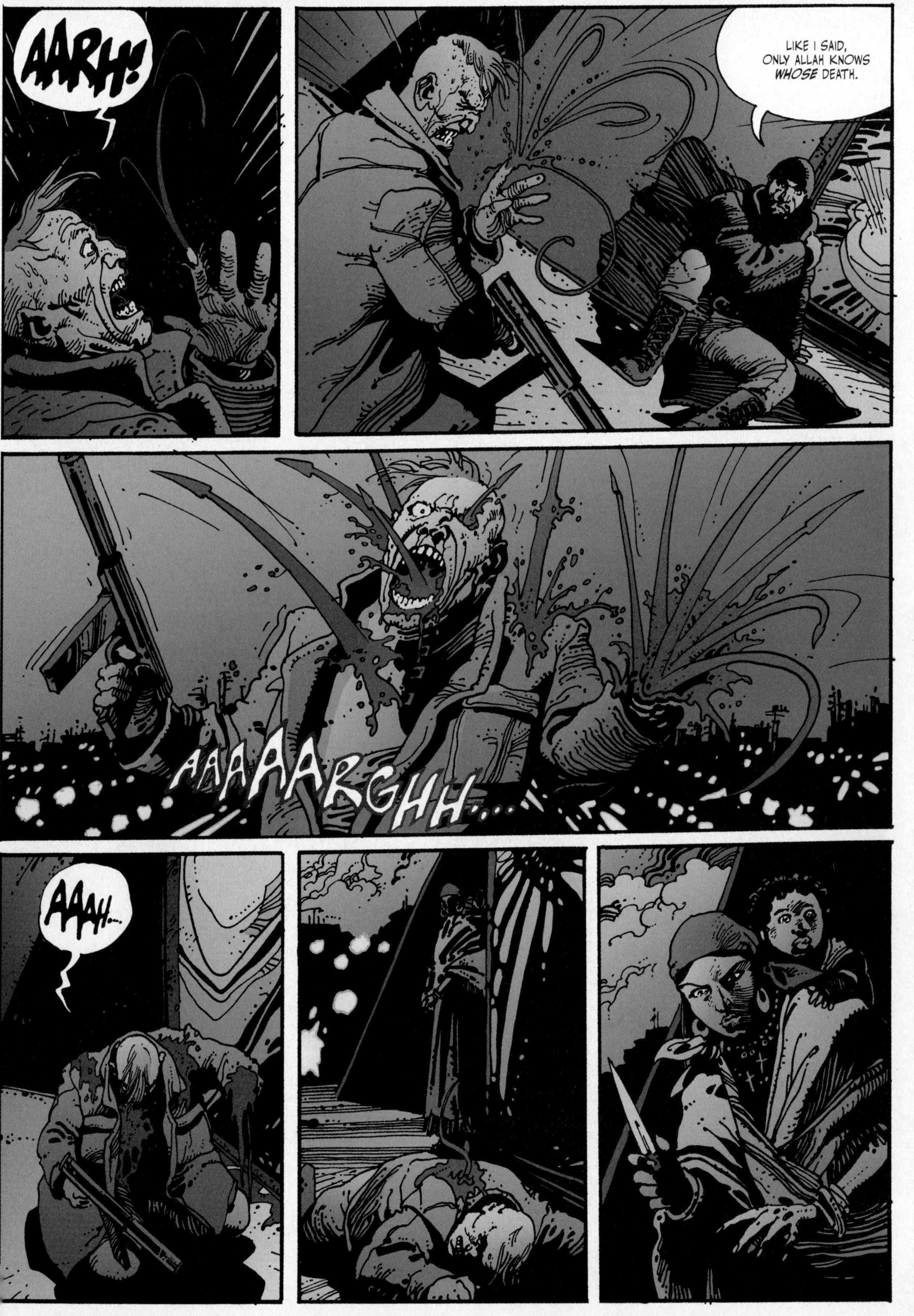
AARH!
LIKE I SAID, ONLY ALLAH KNOWS WHOSE DEATH.
AAAAARGHH...
AAAH...

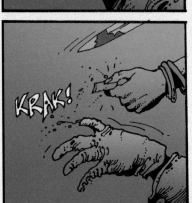

KRAK!

OKAY. SO MAYBE IT WASN'T SO SMART OF ME TO WASTE THE RED TENTACLES OF MAHAKHALI ON THE FIRST SON OF A BITCH WE RAN INTO.

WHEN YOU MEET *GOD*, PUT IN A GOOD WORD FOR DAMNED SOULS LIKE US.

YOU GOT IT.

WE ARE ALL JUST LETTERS IN THE BOOK OF ALLAH... TELL ME, MY GUIDING VOICE, WHAT AWAITS ME ON THE *FINAL PAGE?*

MOSCOW.

I TOOK A PEN AND WROTE THE ANATHEMA, OH MY LORD... I READ IT AGAIN AND AGAIN... I PRAYED AND CRIED...

YET YOU DIDN'T ANSWER ME, OH LORD!

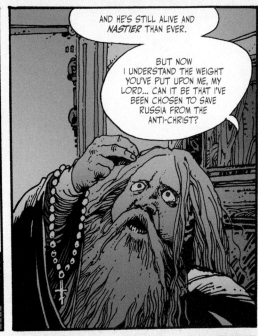

AND HE'S STILL ALIVE AND NASTIER THAN EVER.

BUT NOW I UNDERSTAND THE WEIGHT YOU'VE PUT UPON ME, MY LORD... CAN IT BE THAT I'VE BEEN CHOSEN TO SAVE RUSSIA FROM THE ANTI-CHRIST?

ST. GEORGE KILLED THE EVIL DRAGON... CAN I?

I AM WEAK.

O LORD, HELP ME.

YOUR HOLINESS, THE DICTATOR WILL MEET WITH YOU NOW, AS YOU REQUESTED.

TANTRA...
THIS IS WHEN
PASSION IGNITES
AND LUST BECOMES
POWER.

OUR BODIES
ARE MADE OF
LIGHT.

THE WORLD
DRAGON LIVES IN
YOUR LOINS.

IT SLIDES
UP YOUR
SPINE...

AND
PENETRATES
YOUR HEAD AS
LIGHT.

IT WILL
GIVE YOU NEW
SIGHT...

... AND
KNOWLEDGE OF
YOURSELF.

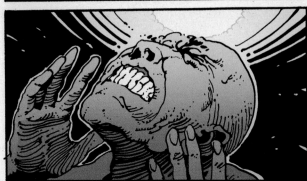

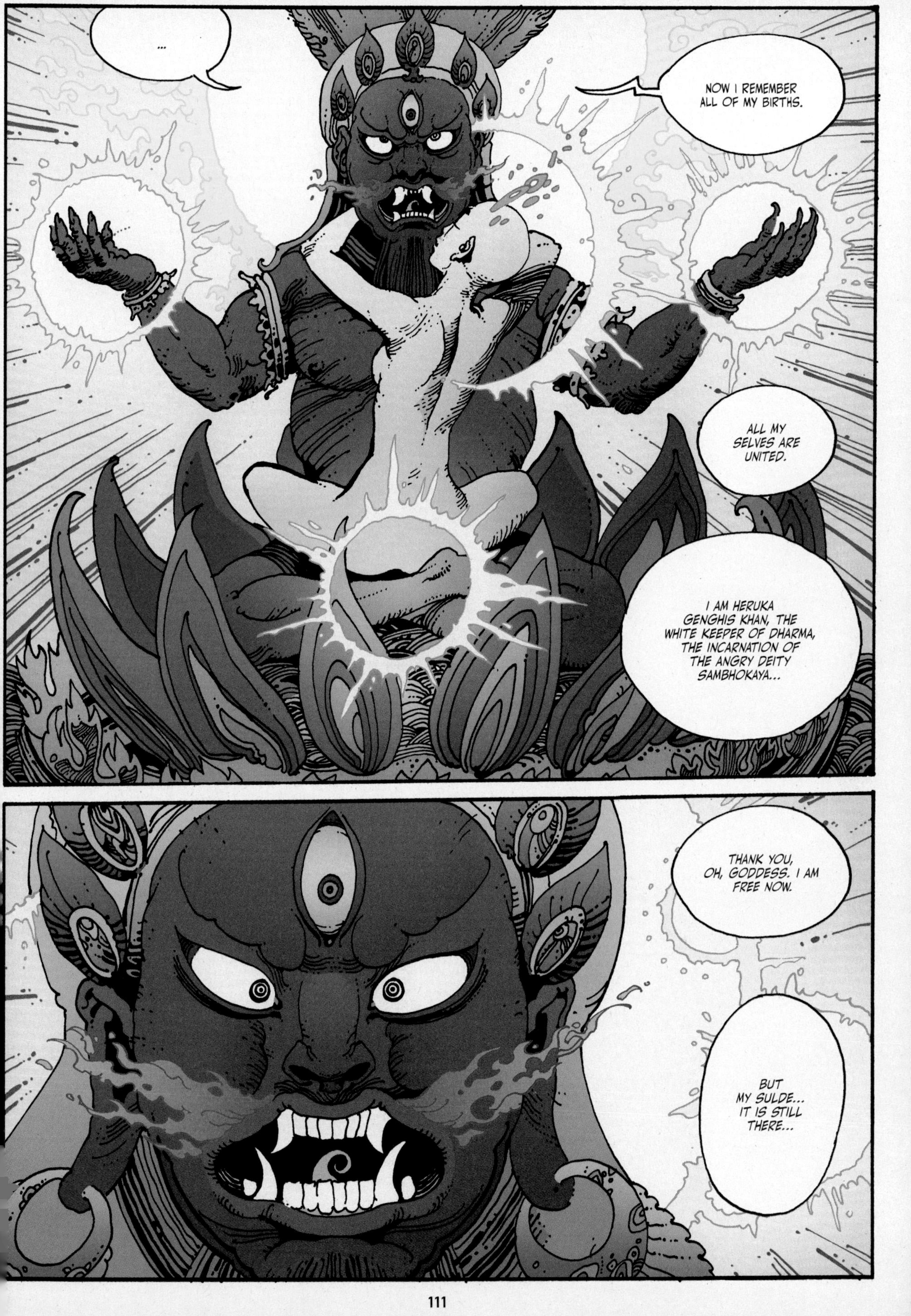
...
NOW I REMEMBER ALL OF MY BIRTHS.
ALL MY SELVES ARE UNITED.
I AM HERUKA GENGHIS KHAN, THE WHITE KEEPER OF DHARMA, THE INCARNATION OF THE ANGRY DEITY SAMBHOKAYA...
THANK YOU, OH, GODDESS. I AM FREE NOW.
BUT MY SULDE... IT IS STILL THERE...

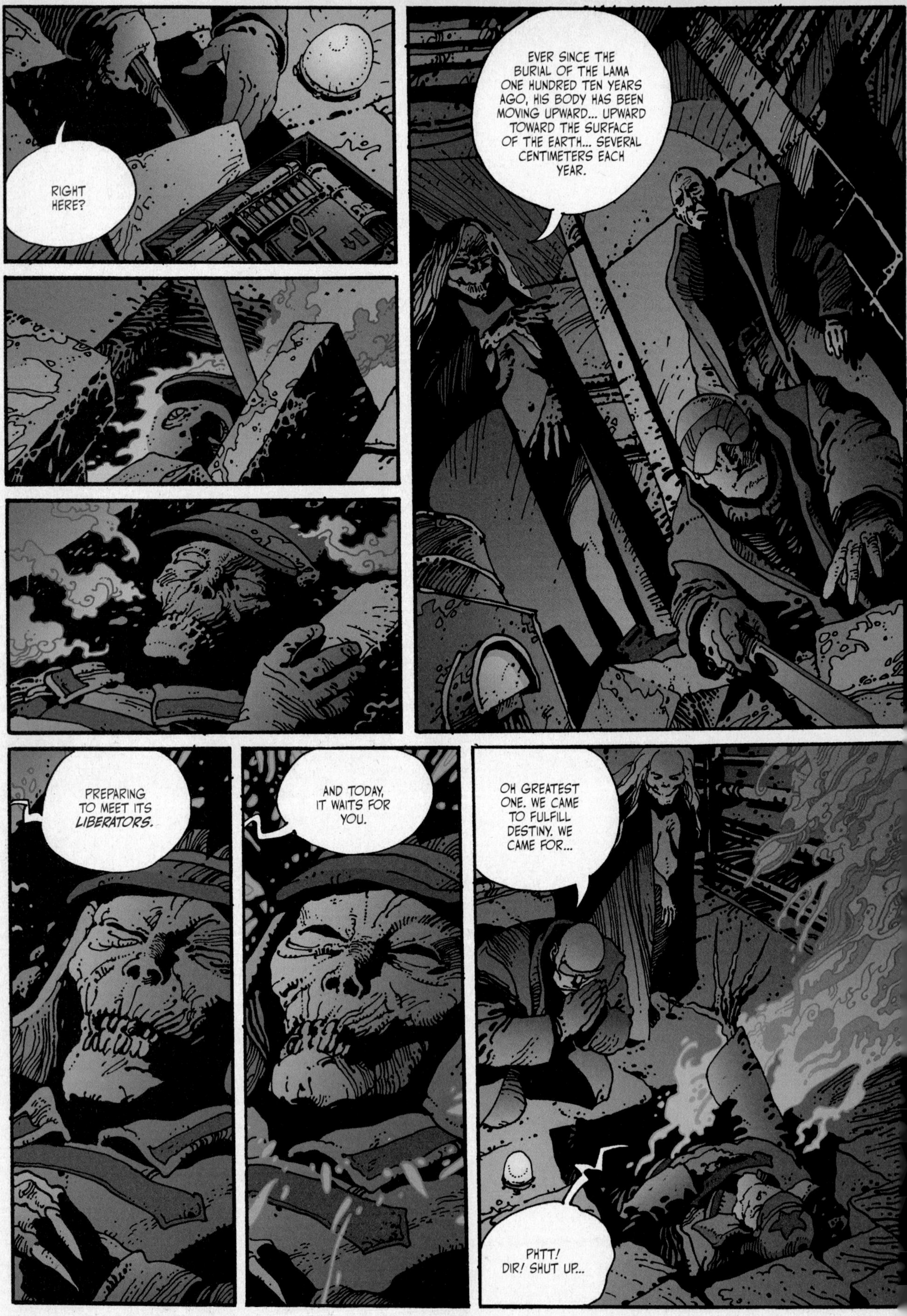
RIGHT HERE?
EVER SINCE THE BURIAL OF THE LAMA ONE HUNDRED TEN YEARS AGO, HIS BODY HAS BEEN MOVING UPWARD... UPWARD TOWARD THE SURFACE OF THE EARTH... SEVERAL CENTIMETERS EACH YEAR.
PREPARING TO MEET ITS *LIBERATORS*.
AND TODAY, IT WAITS FOR YOU.
OH GREATEST ONE. WE CAME TO FULFILL DESTINY. WE CAME FOR...
PHTT! DIR! SHUT UP...

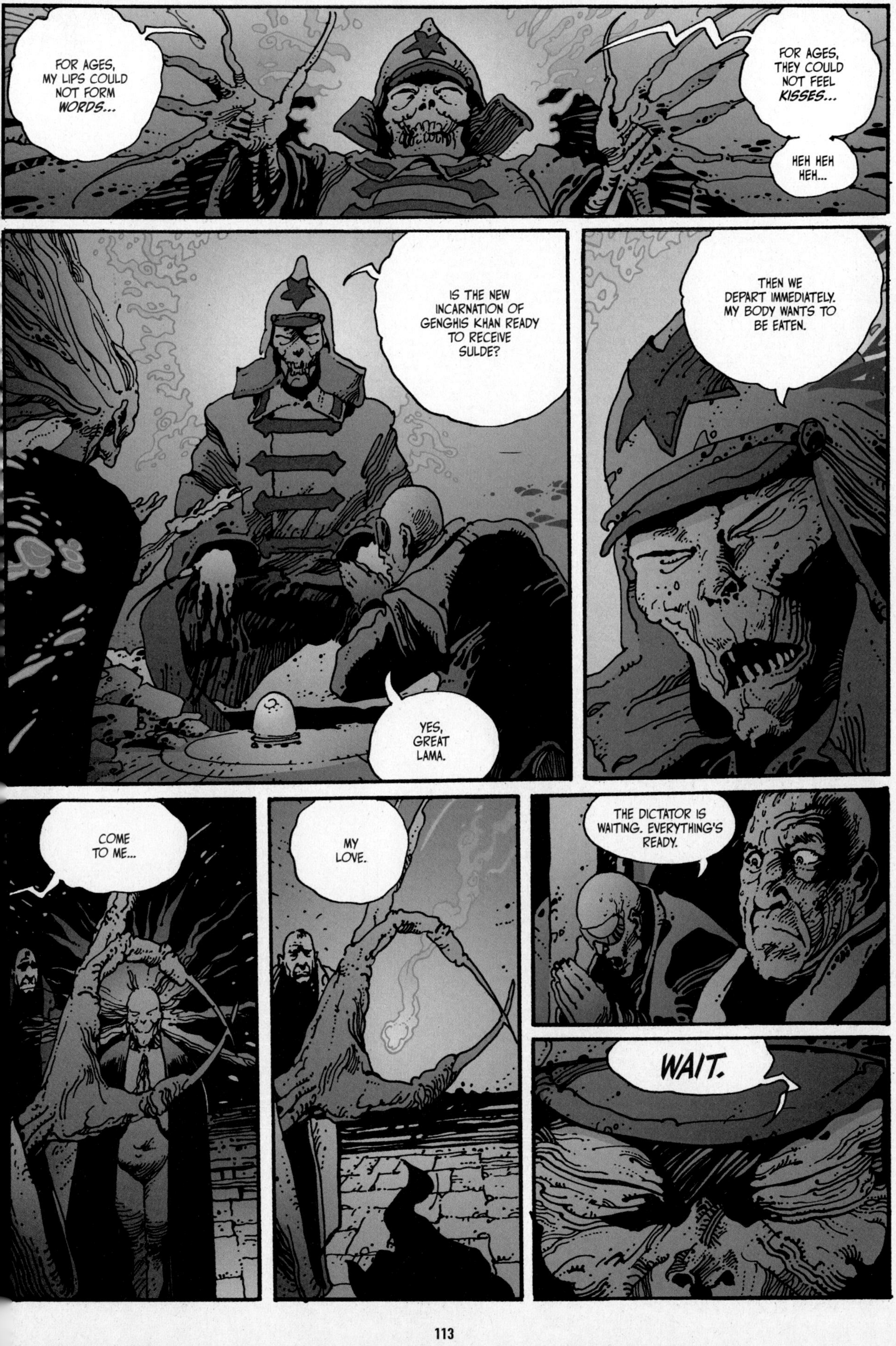
FOR AGES, MY LIPS COULD NOT FORM *WORDS...*
FOR AGES, THEY COULD NOT FEEL *KISSES...*
HEH HEH HEH...
IS THE NEW INCARNATION OF GENGHIS KHAN READY TO RECEIVE SULDE?
YES, GREAT LAMA.
THEN WE DEPART IMMEDIATELY. MY BODY WANTS TO BE EATEN.
COME TO ME...
MY LOVE.
THE DICTATOR IS WAITING. EVERYTHING'S READY.
WAIT.

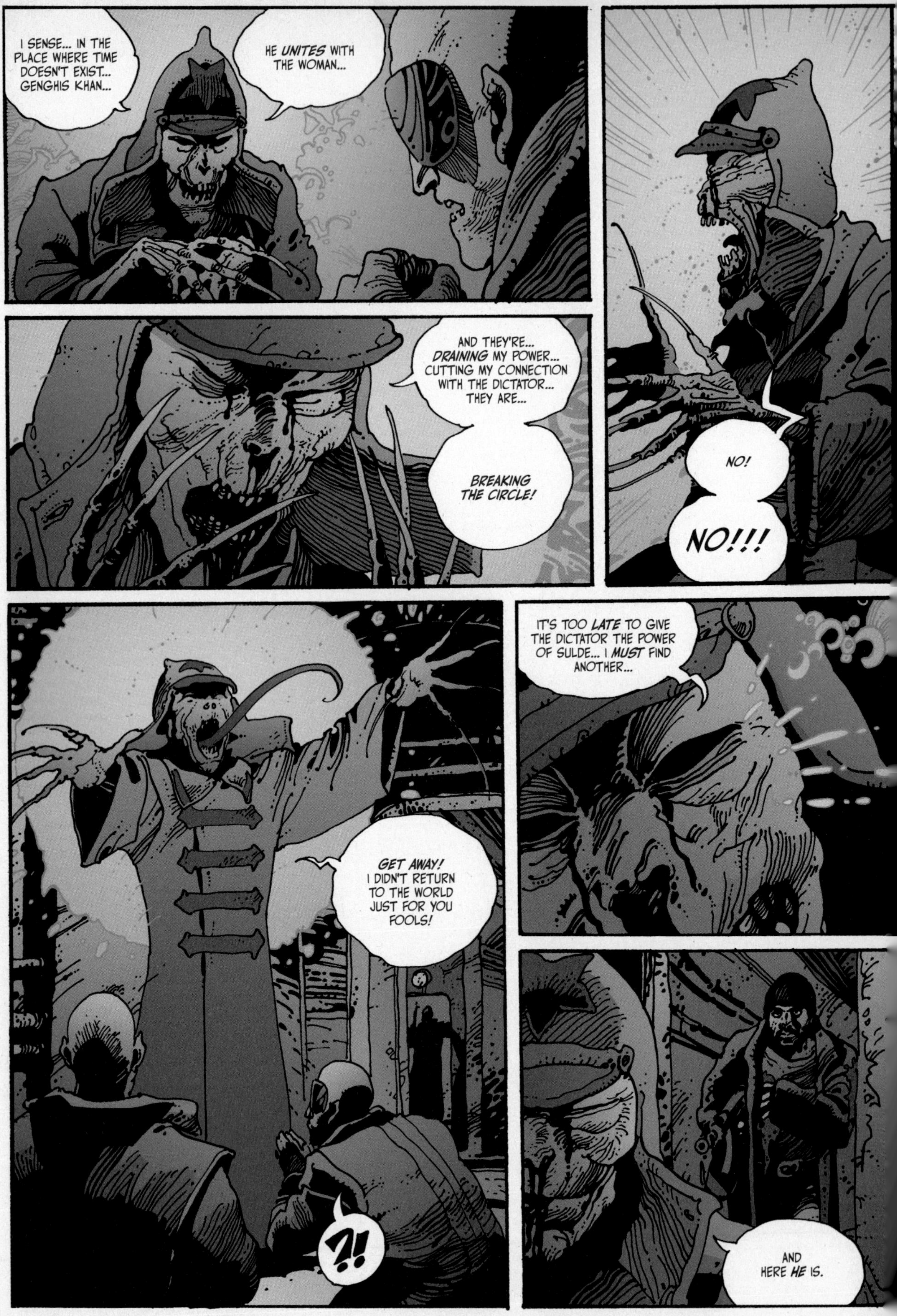

I SENSE... IN THE PLACE WHERE TIME DOESN'T EXIST... GENGHIS KHAN...
HE *UNITES* WITH THE WOMAN...
AND THEY'RE... *DRAINING* MY POWER... CUTTING MY CONNECTION WITH THE DICTATOR... THEY ARE...
BREAKING THE CIRCLE!
NO!
NO!!!
GET AWAY! I DIDN'T RETURN TO THE WORLD JUST FOR YOU FOOLS!
?!
IT'S TOO *LATE* TO GIVE THE DICTATOR THE POWER OF SULDE... I *MUST* FIND ANOTHER...
AND HERE *HE* IS.

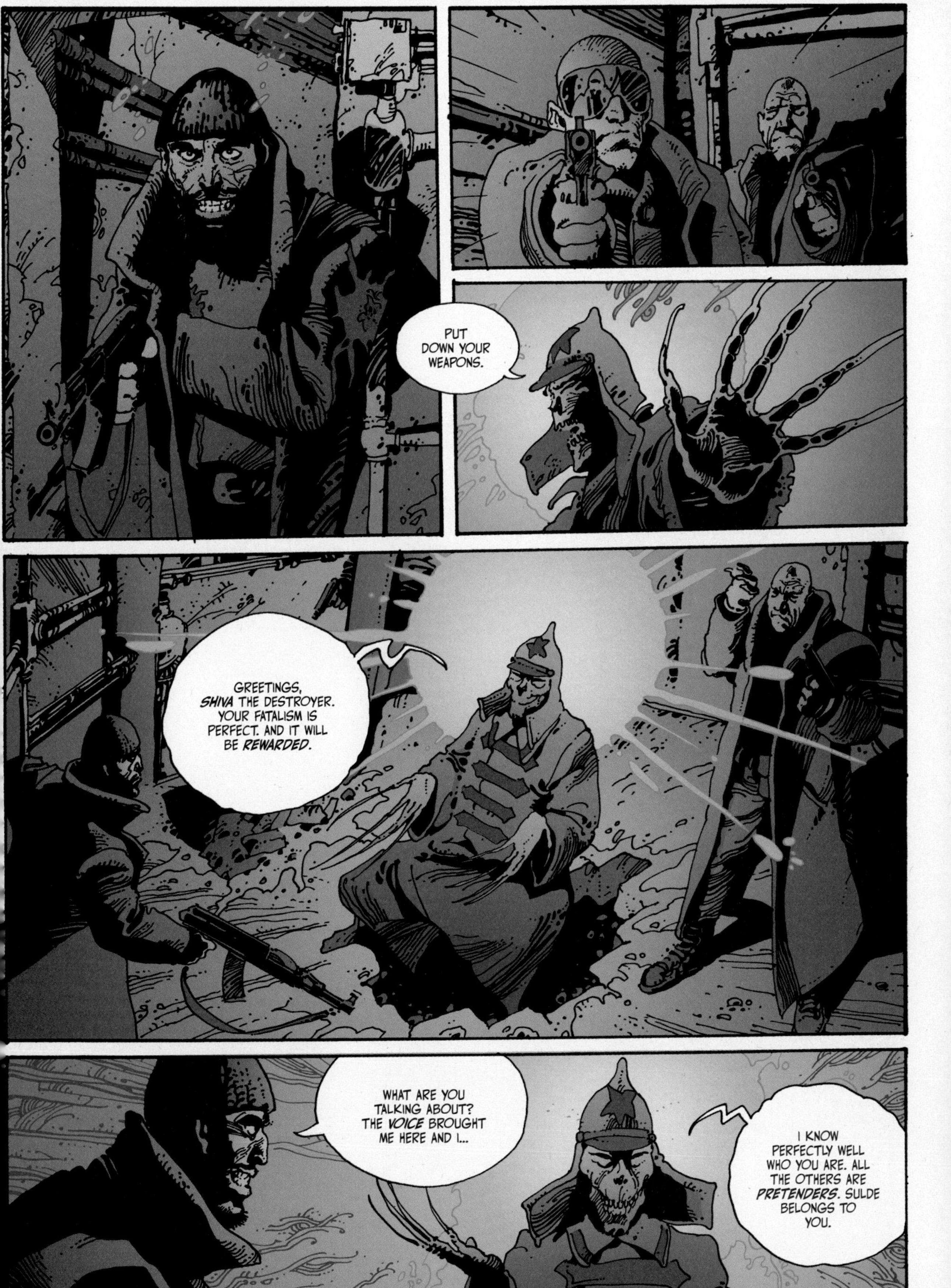
PUT DOWN YOUR WEAPONS.
GREETINGS, SHIVA THE DESTROYER. YOUR FATALISM IS PERFECT. AND IT WILL BE REWARDED.
WHAT ARE YOU TALKING ABOUT? THE VOICE BROUGHT ME HERE AND I...
I KNOW PERFECTLY WELL WHO YOU ARE. ALL THE OTHERS ARE PRETENDERS. SULDE BELONGS TO YOU.

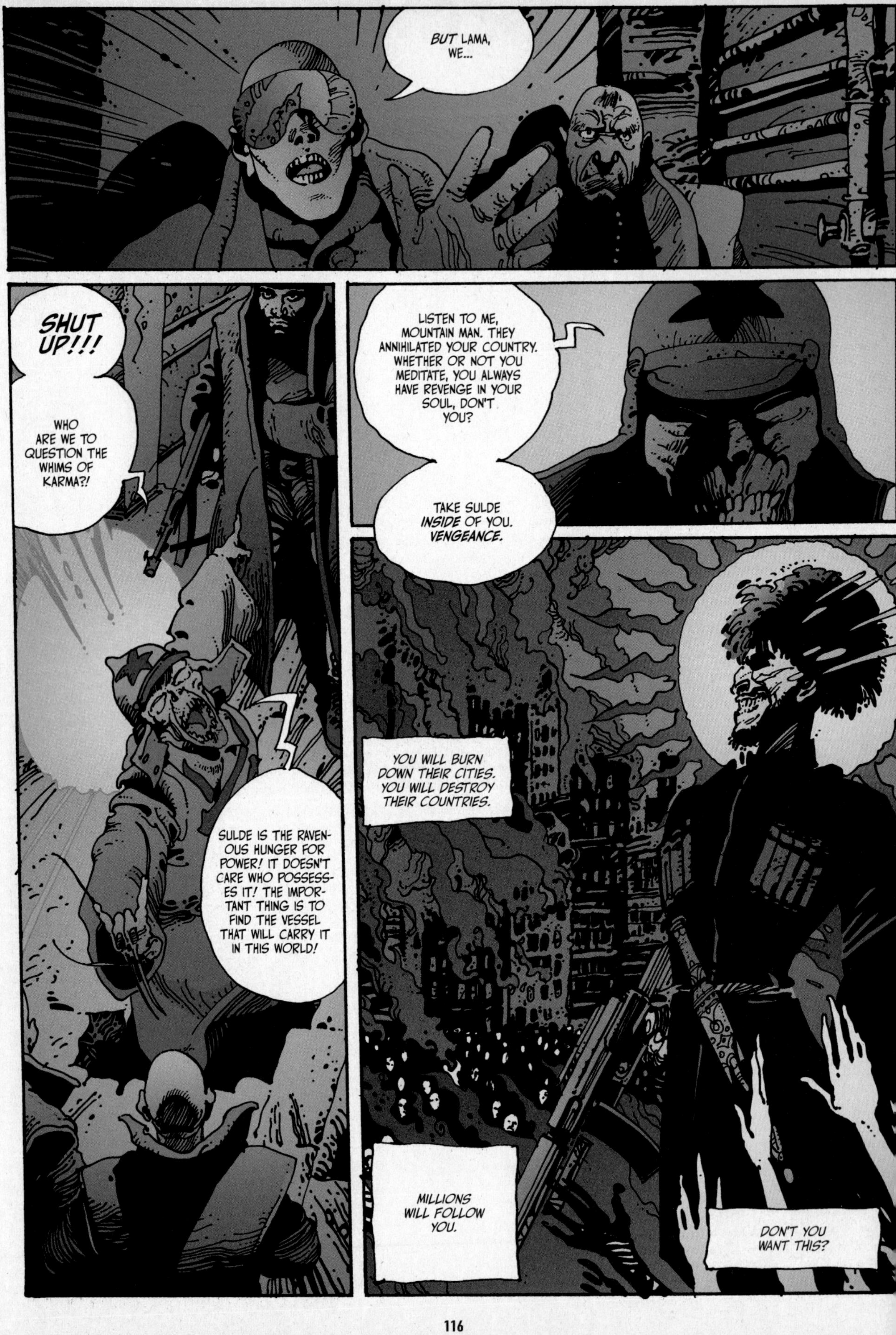
BUT LAMA, WE...
SHUT UP!!!
WHO ARE WE TO QUESTION THE WHIMS OF KARMA?!
LISTEN TO ME, MOUNTAIN MAN. THEY ANNIHILATED YOUR COUNTRY. WHETHER OR NOT YOU MEDITATE, YOU ALWAYS HAVE REVENGE IN YOUR SOUL, DON'T YOU?
TAKE SULDE INSIDE OF YOU. VENGEANCE.
SULDE IS THE RAVENOUS HUNGER FOR POWER! IT DOESN'T CARE WHO POSSESSES IT! THE IMPORTANT THING IS TO FIND THE VESSEL THAT WILL CARRY IT IN THIS WORLD!
YOU WILL BURN DOWN THEIR CITIES. YOU WILL DESTROY THEIR COUNTRIES.
MILLIONS WILL FOLLOW YOU.
DON'T YOU WANT THIS?

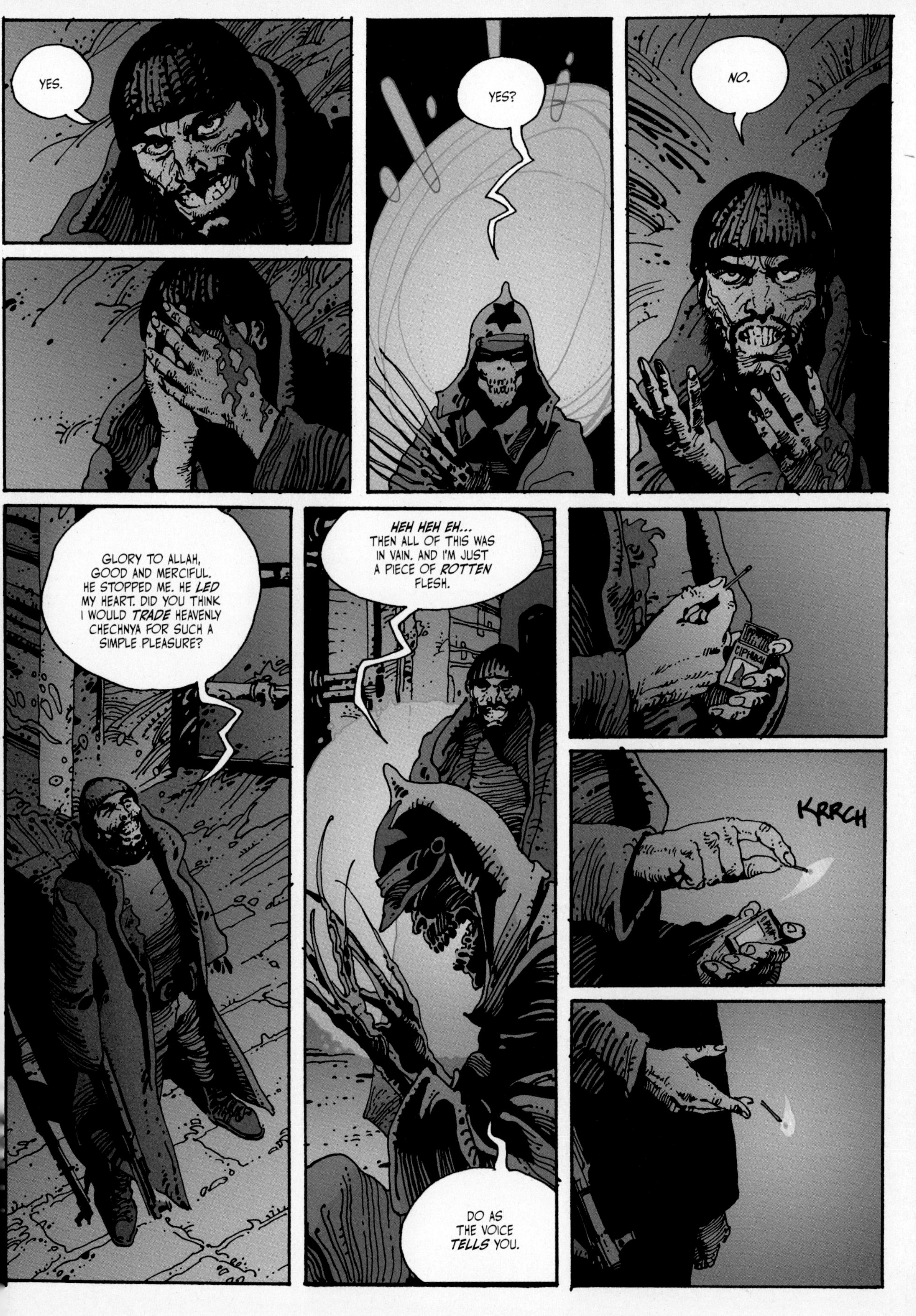
YES.
YES?
NO.
GLORY TO ALLAH, GOOD AND MERCIFUL. HE STOPPED ME. HE *LED* MY HEART. DID YOU THINK I WOULD *TRADE* HEAVENLY CHECHNYA FOR SUCH A SIMPLE PLEASURE?
HEH HEH EH... THEN ALL OF THIS WAS IN VAIN. AND I'M JUST A PIECE OF *ROTTEN* FLESH.
KRRCH
DO AS THE VOICE *TELLS* YOU.

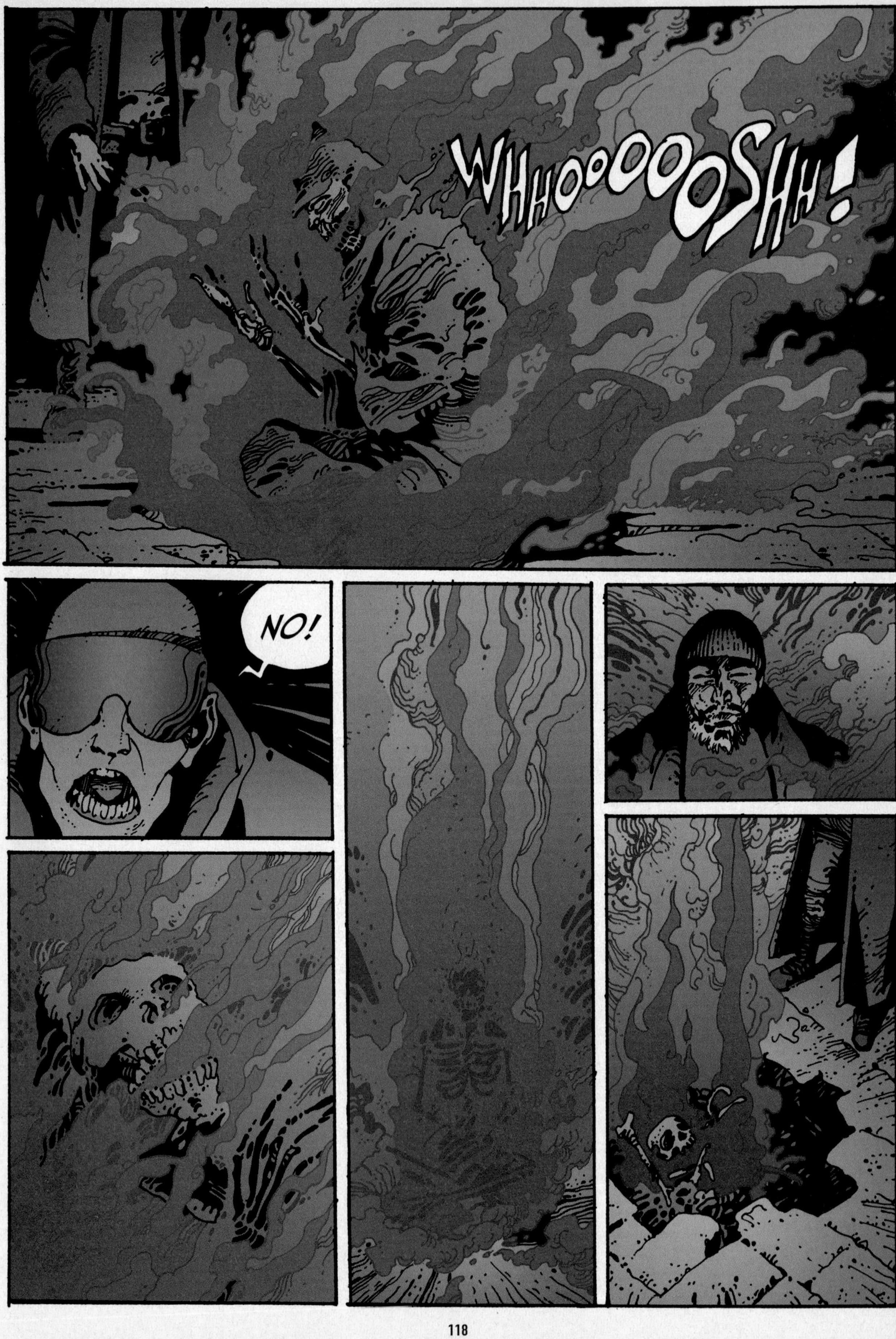
WHHOOOOOSHH!
NO!

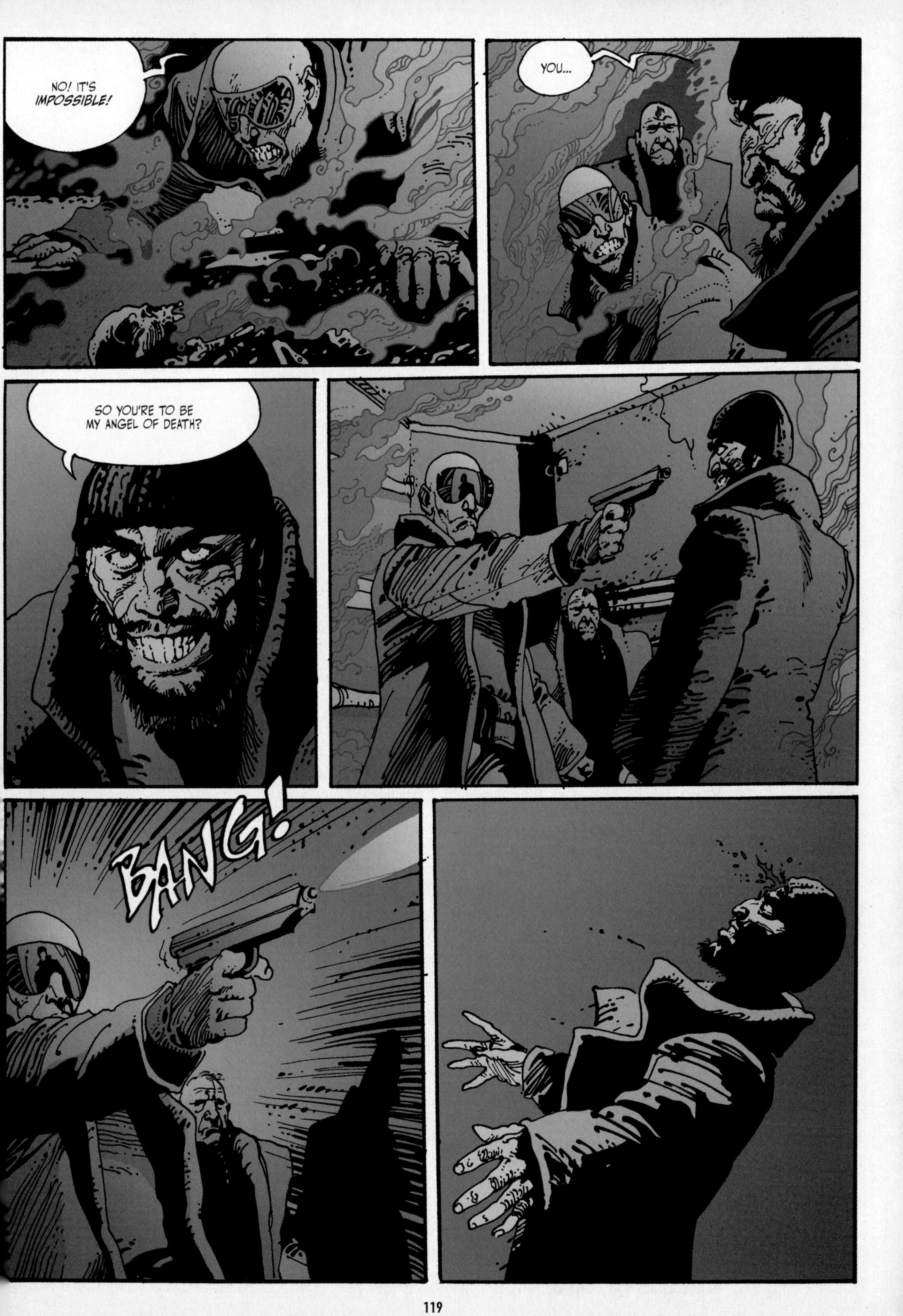
NO! IT'S IMPOSSIBLE!
YOU...
SO YOU'RE TO BE MY ANGEL OF DEATH?
BANG!

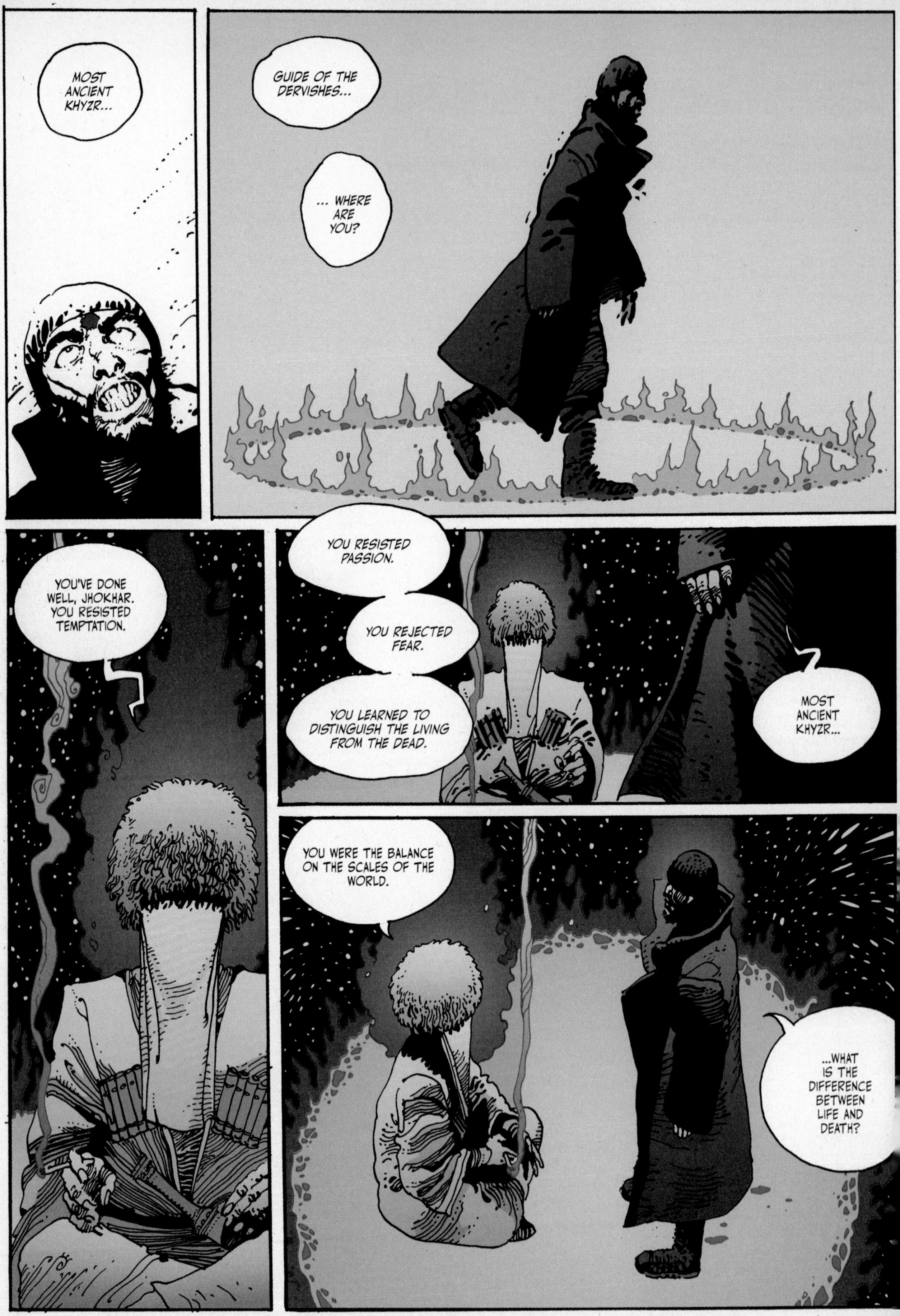
MOST ANCIENT KHYZR...
GUIDE OF THE DERVISHES...
... WHERE ARE YOU?
YOU'VE DONE WELL, JHOKHAR. YOU RESISTED TEMPTATION.
YOU RESISTED PASSION.
YOU REJECTED FEAR.
YOU LEARNED TO DISTINGUISH THE LIVING FROM THE DEAD.
MOST ANCIENT KHYZR...
YOU WERE THE BALANCE ON THE SCALES OF THE WORLD.
...WHAT IS THE DIFFERENCE BETWEEN LIFE AND DEATH?

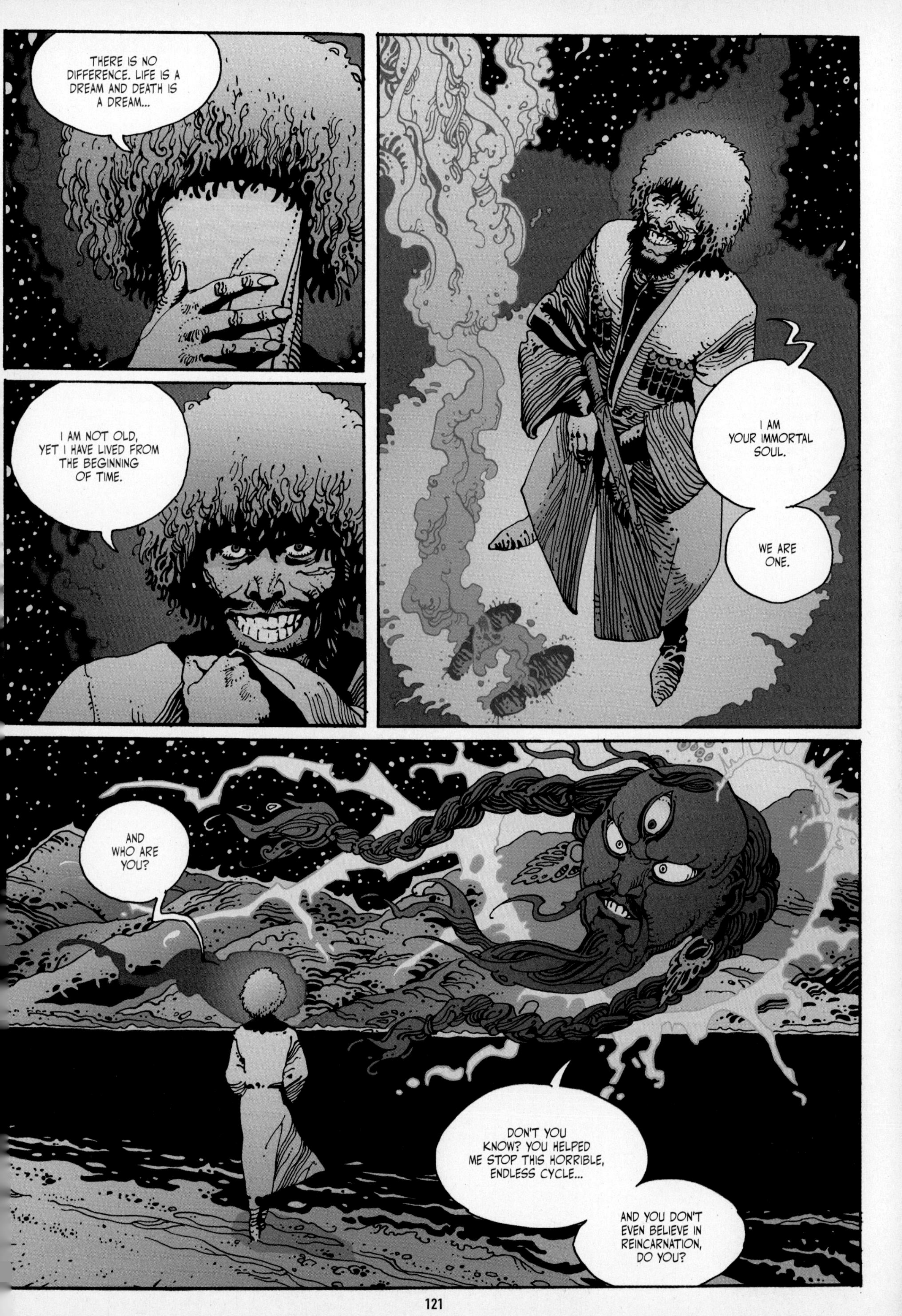

THERE IS NO DIFFERENCE. LIFE IS A DREAM AND DEATH IS A DREAM...
I AM NOT OLD, YET I HAVE LIVED FROM THE BEGINNING OF TIME.
I AM YOUR IMMORTAL SOUL.
WE ARE ONE.
AND WHO ARE YOU?
DON'T YOU KNOW? YOU HELPED ME STOP THIS HORRIBLE, ENDLESS CYCLE...
AND YOU DON'T EVEN BELIEVE IN REINCARNATION, DO YOU?

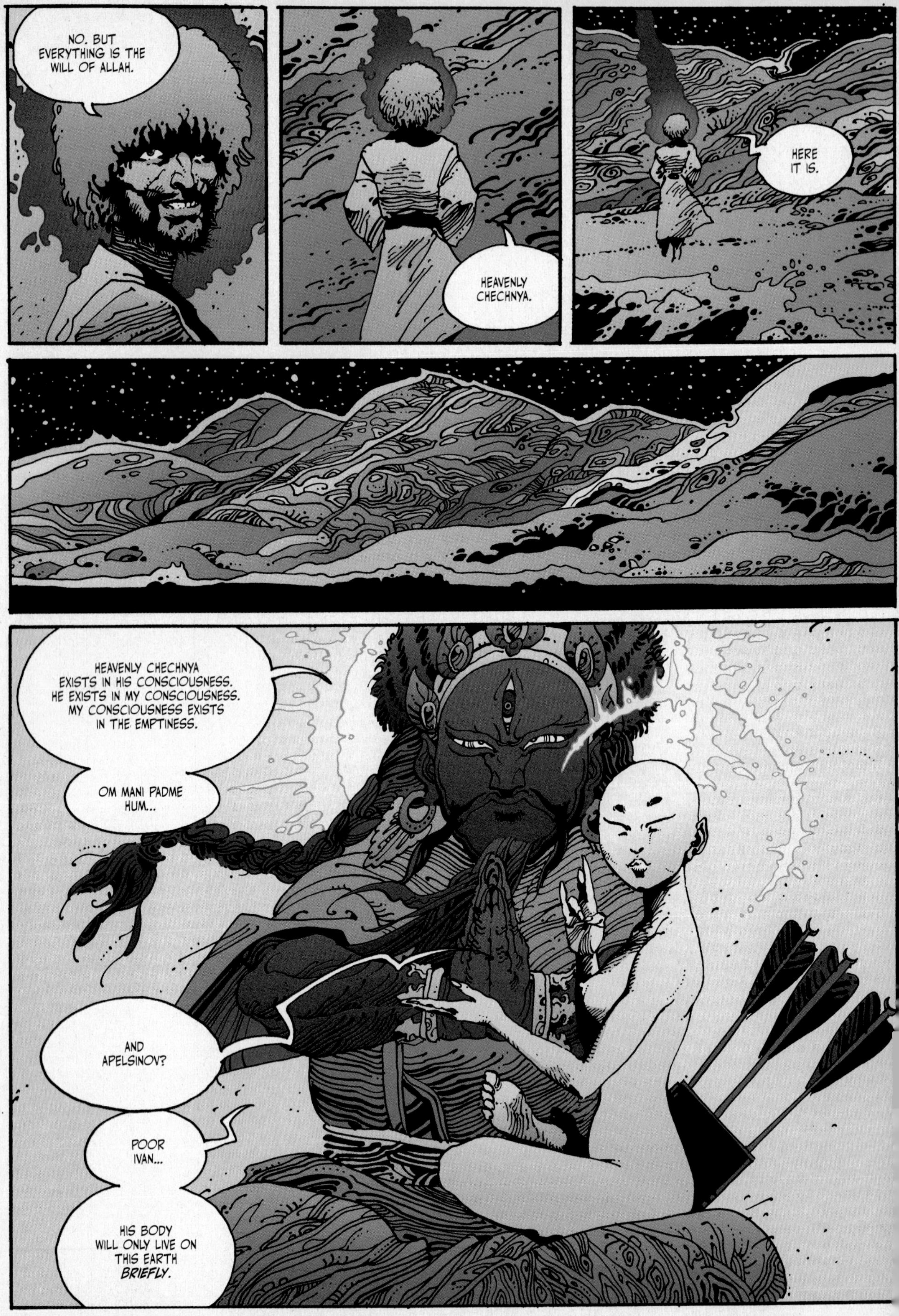

NO. BUT EVERYTHING IS THE WILL OF ALLAH.
HEAVENLY CHECHNYA.
HERE IT IS.
HEAVENLY CHECHNYA EXISTS IN HIS CONSCIOUSNESS. HE EXISTS IN MY CONSCIOUSNESS. MY CONSCIOUSNESS EXISTS IN THE EMPTINESS.
OM MANI PADME HUM...
AND APELSINOV?
POOR IVAN...
HIS BODY WILL ONLY LIVE ON THIS EARTH *BRIEFLY*.

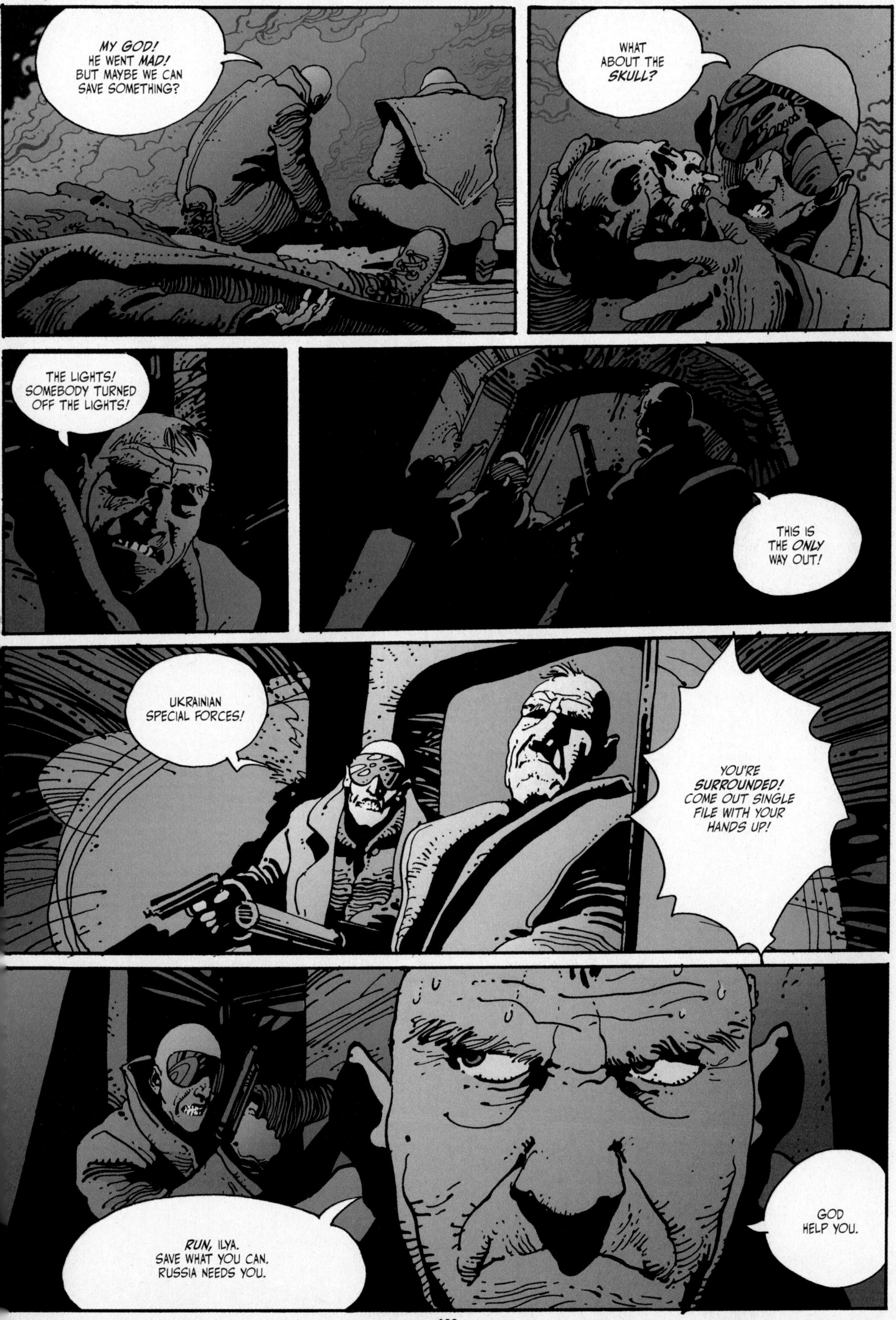

MY GOD! HE WENT MAD! BUT MAYBE WE CAN SAVE SOMETHING?
WHAT ABOUT THE SKULL?
THE LIGHTS! SOMEBODY TURNED OFF THE LIGHTS!
THIS IS THE ONLY WAY OUT!
UKRAINIAN SPECIAL FORCES!
YOU'RE SURROUNDED! COME OUT SINGLE FILE WITH YOUR HANDS UP!
RUN, ILYA. SAVE WHAT YOU CAN. RUSSIA NEEDS YOU.
GOD HELP YOU.

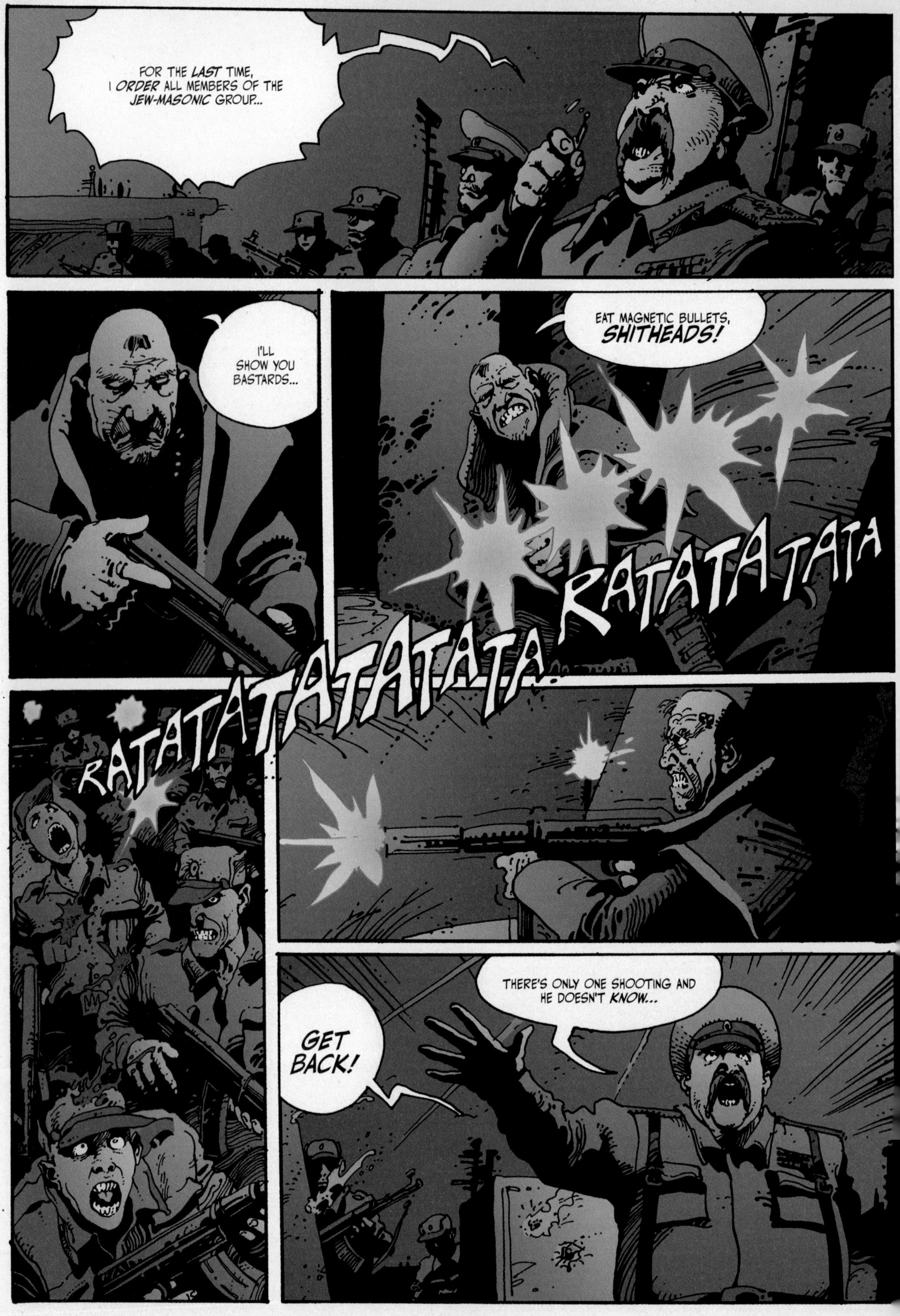

FOR THE LAST TIME, I ORDER ALL MEMBERS OF THE JEW-MASONIC GROUP...
I'LL SHOW YOU BASTARDS...
EAT MAGNETIC BULLETS, SHITHEADS!
RATATATATATATATA
RATATATATATA
THERE'S ONLY ONE SHOOTING AND HE DOESN'T KNOW...
GET BACK!

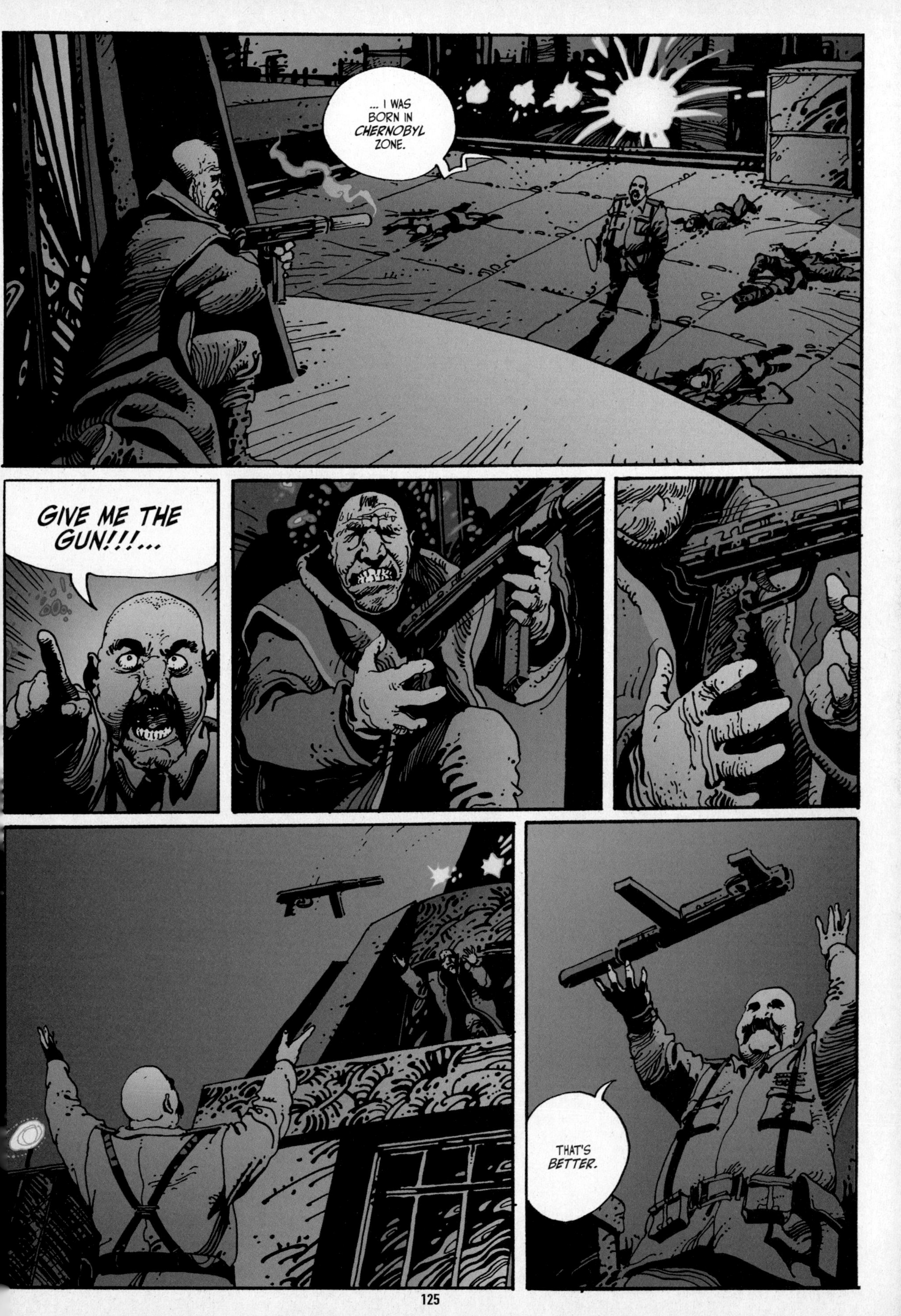

... I WAS BORN IN CHERNOBYL ZONE.
GIVE ME THE GUN!!!...
THAT'S BETTER.

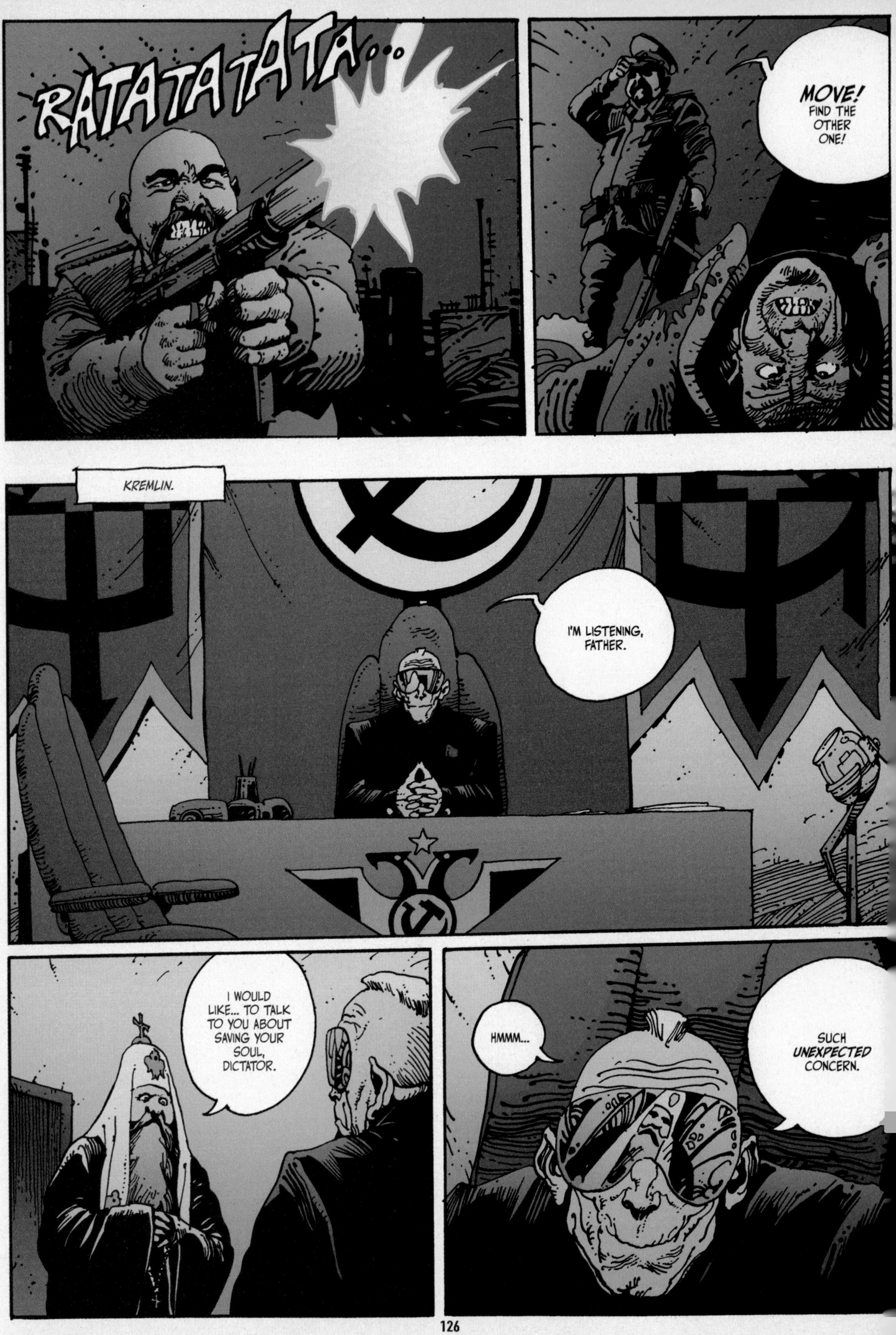
RATATATATA...
MOVE! FIND THE OTHER ONE!
KREMLIN.
I'M LISTENING, FATHER.
I WOULD LIKE... TO TALK TO YOU ABOUT SAVING YOUR SOUL, DICTATOR.
HMMM...
SUCH UNEXPECTED CONCERN.

DON'T YOU BELIEVE THAT YOU WILL GO TO HEAVEN WHEN YOU DIE? WOULDN'T YOU LIKE TO REPENT YOUR *SINS*?

AREN'T YOU AFRAID THAT THE FIRES OF HELL WILL SWALLOW YOU FOR YOUR TRANSGRESSIONS?

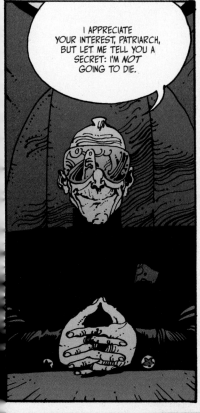

I APPRECIATE YOUR INTEREST, PATRIARCH, BUT LET ME TELL YOU A SECRET: I'M *NOT* GOING TO DIE.

AREN'T YOU *GLAD* TO HEAR THAT?

BLASPHEMY*!!!*

127

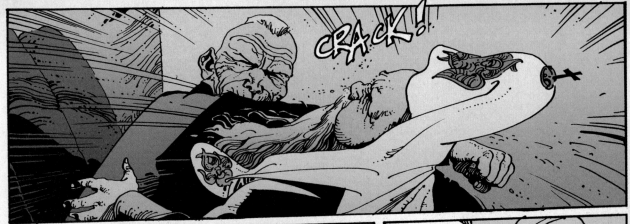

I KNEW IT. THE PATRIARCH IS AN *ASSASSIN.* HEH HEH...

I AM WEAK. I AM *WEAK.*

I THINK YOU'LL HAVE A *LONG* REST AHEAD OF YOU, DURING WHICH YOU CAN CONTEMPLATE THE WAY OF OUR LORD.

BUT I'LL HAVE EVEN MORE TIME, SINCE I'M IMMORTAL.

THE *EYES* OF THE DEVIL! YOU ARE THE *ANTI-CHRIST!*

OKAY, OKAY. IF YOU SAY SO.

DAMN. WHERE ARE MY GLASSES?

AH, THERE.

THE *PEN!*

THE WILL OF GOD!

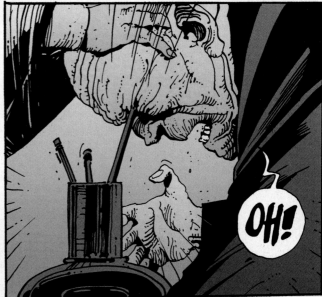

OH!

OOOKH!

AAAA...

OH LORD! GUARDS!

HELP! THE DICTATOR IS *DYING!!!*

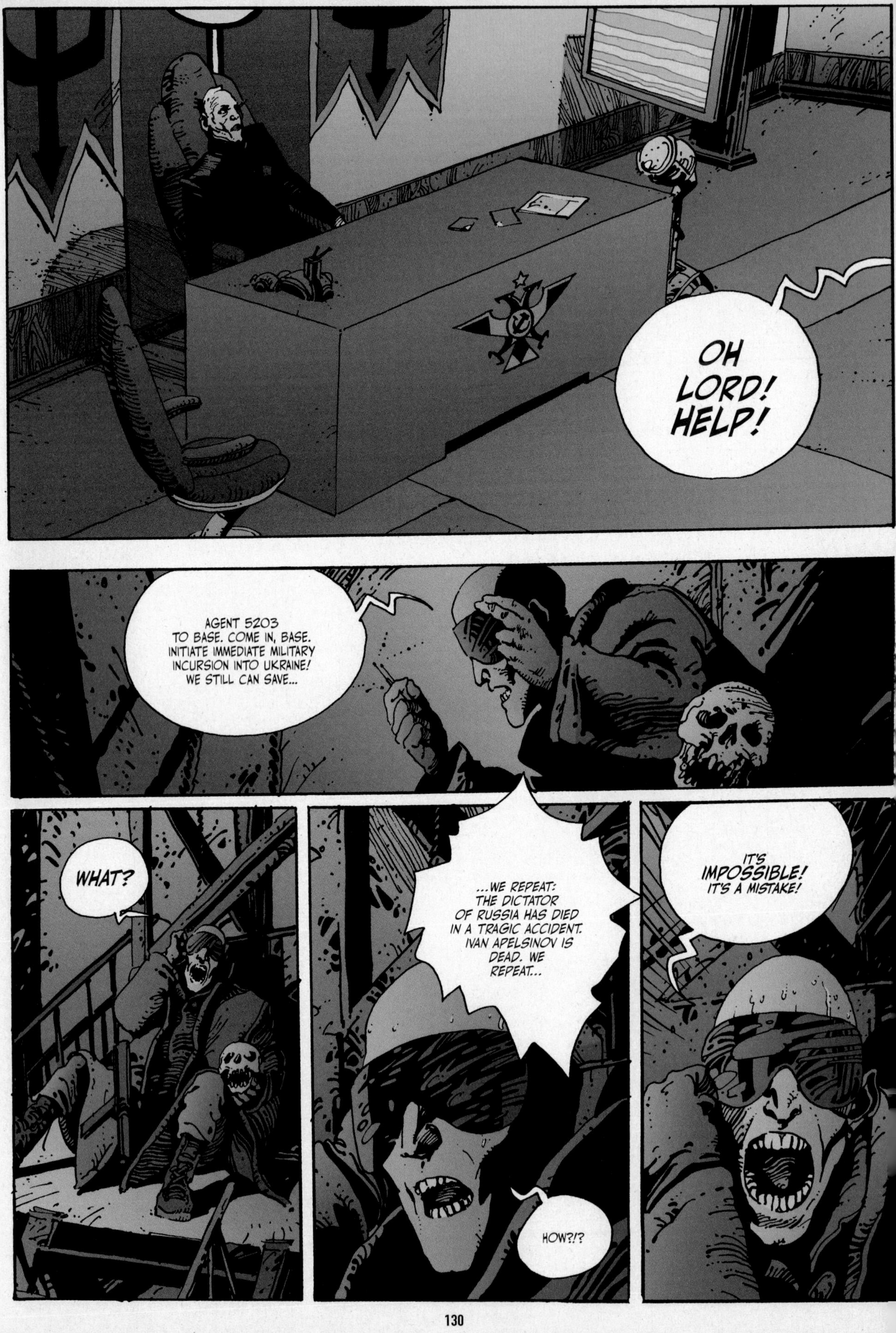
OH LORD! HELP!
AGENT 5203 TO BASE. COME IN, BASE. INITIATE IMMEDIATE MILITARY INCURSION INTO UKRAINE! WE STILL CAN SAVE...
WHAT?
...WE REPEAT: THE DICTATOR OF RUSSIA HAS DIED IN A TRAGIC ACCIDENT. IVAN APELSINOV IS DEAD. WE REPEAT...
HOW?!?
IT'S IMPOSSIBLE! IT'S A MISTAKE!

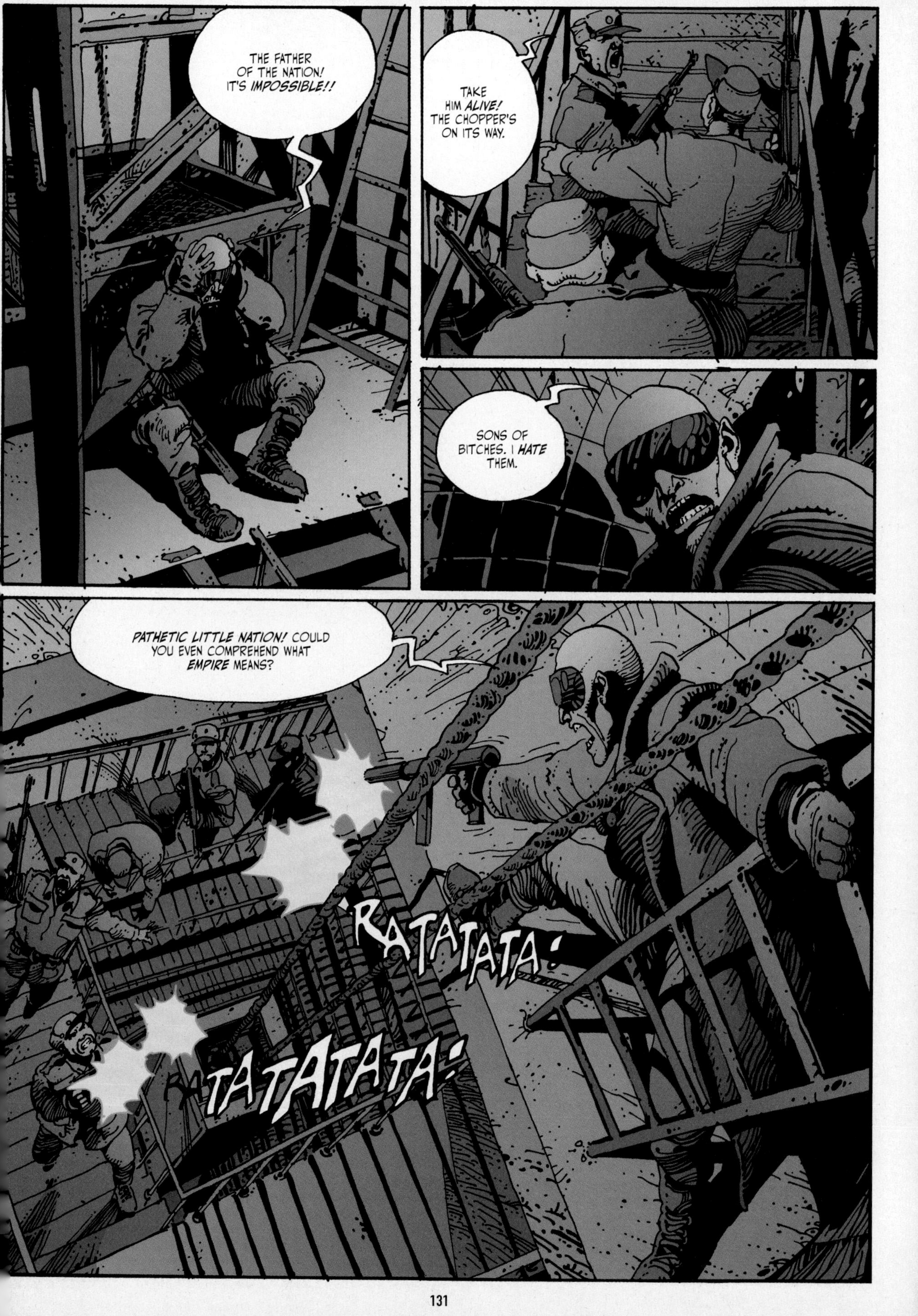
THE FATHER OF THE NATION! IT'S IMPOSSIBLE!!
TAKE HIM ALIVE! THE CHOPPER'S ON ITS WAY.
SONS OF BITCHES. I HATE THEM.
PATHETIC LITTLE NATION! COULD YOU EVEN COMPREHEND WHAT EMPIRE MEANS?
RATATATA!
RATATATATA!

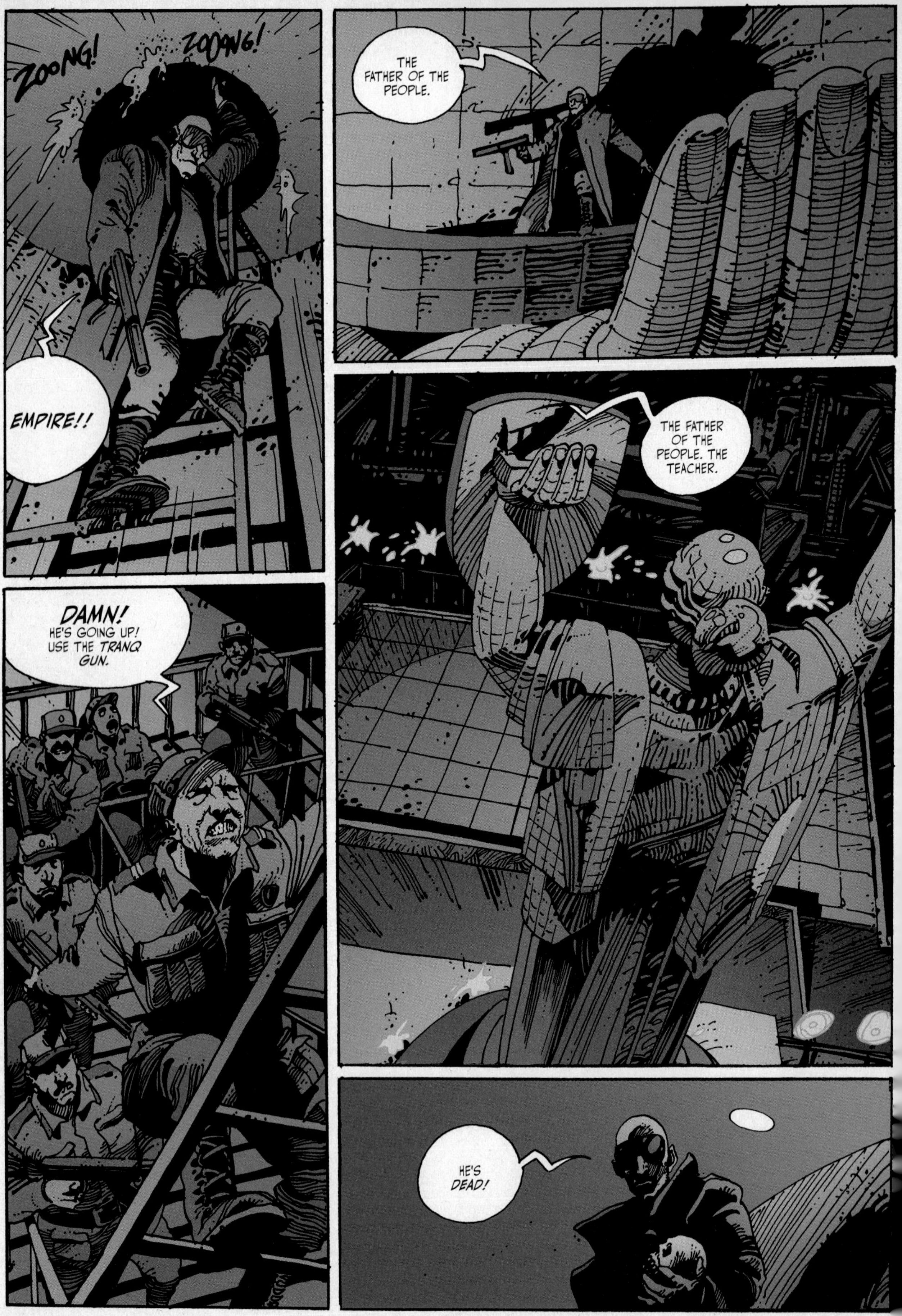
ZOONG!
ZOONG!
EMPIRE!!
THE FATHER OF THE PEOPLE.
THE FATHER OF THE PEOPLE. THE TEACHER.
DAMN! HE'S GOING UP! USE THE TRANQ GUN.
HE'S DEAD!

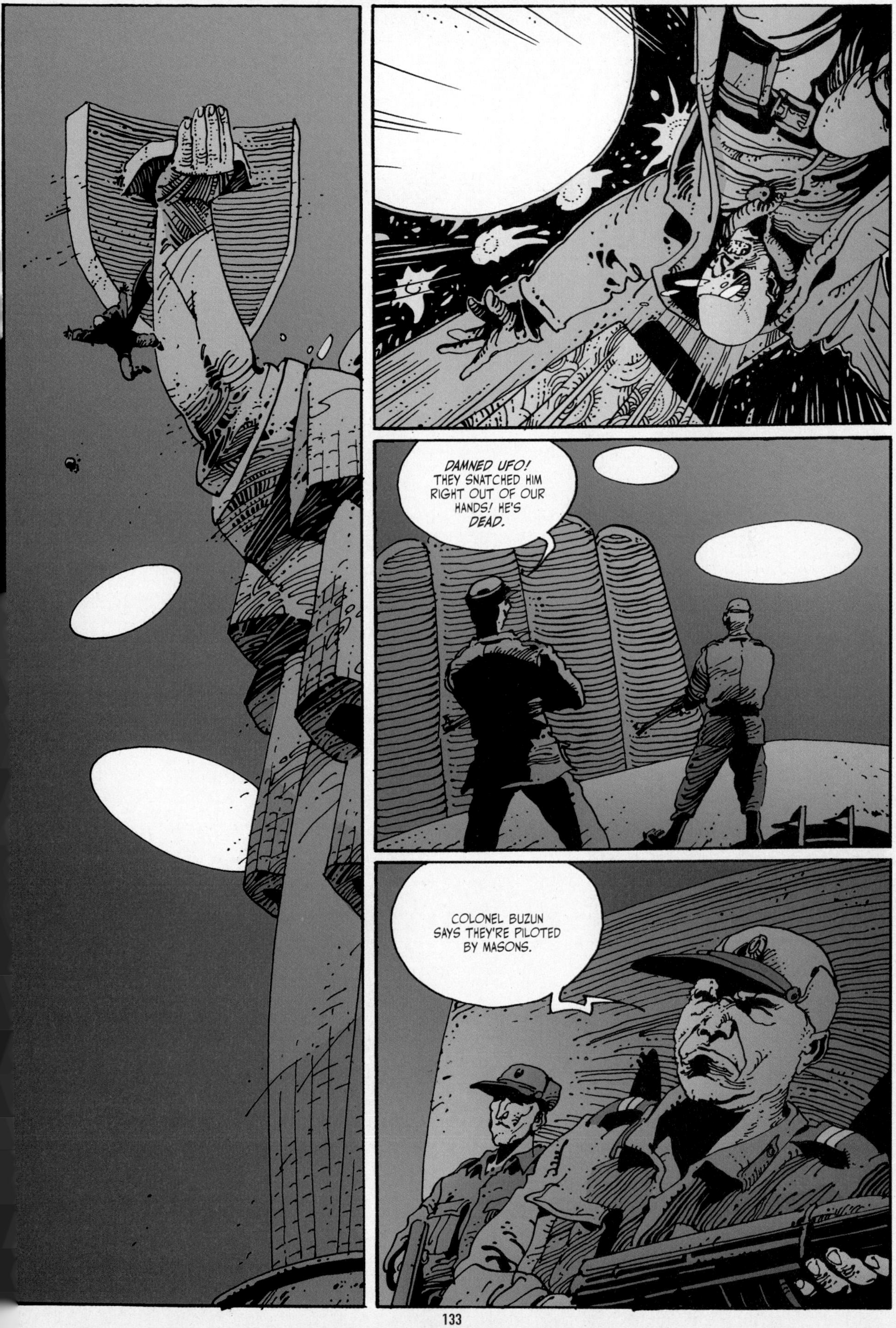
DAMNED UFO! THEY SNATCHED HIM RIGHT OUT OF OUR HANDS! HE'S *DEAD.*
COLONEL BUZUN SAYS THEY'RE PILOTED BY MASONS.

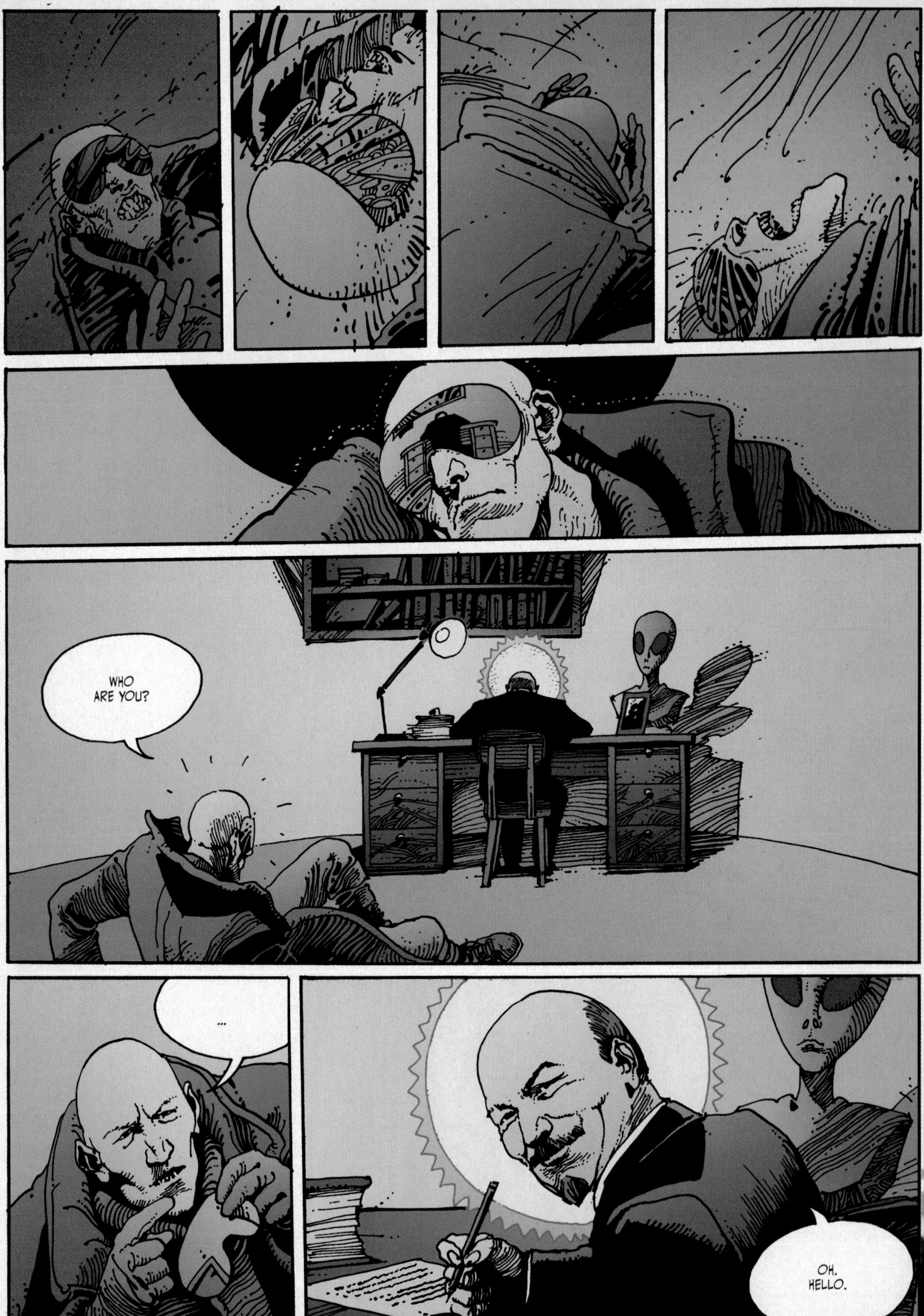
WHO ARE YOU?
...
OH. HELLO.

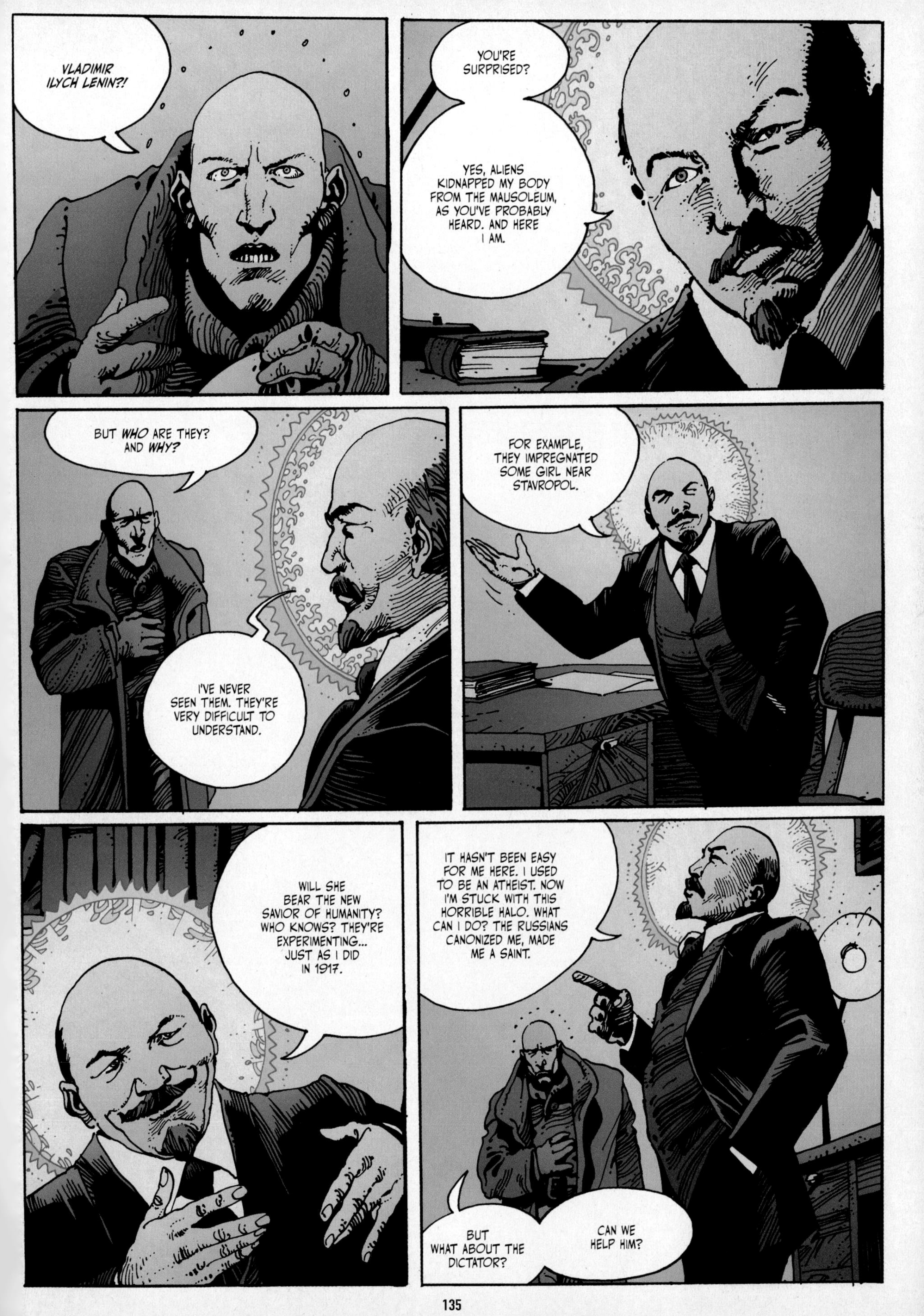

VLADIMIR ILYCH LENIN?!
YOU'RE SURPRISED?
YES, ALIENS KIDNAPPED MY BODY FROM THE MAUSOLEUM, AS YOU'VE PROBABLY HEARD. AND HERE I AM.
BUT WHO ARE THEY? AND WHY?
I'VE NEVER SEEN THEM. THEY'RE VERY DIFFICULT TO UNDERSTAND.
FOR EXAMPLE, THEY IMPREGNATED SOME GIRL NEAR STAVROPOL.
WILL SHE BEAR THE NEW SAVIOR OF HUMANITY? WHO KNOWS? THEY'RE EXPERIMENTING... JUST AS I DID IN 1917.
IT HASN'T BEEN EASY FOR ME HERE. I USED TO BE AN ATHEIST. NOW I'M STUCK WITH THIS HORRIBLE HALO. WHAT CAN I DO? THE RUSSIANS CANONIZED ME, MADE ME A SAINT.
BUT WHAT ABOUT THE DICTATOR?
CAN WE HELP HIM?

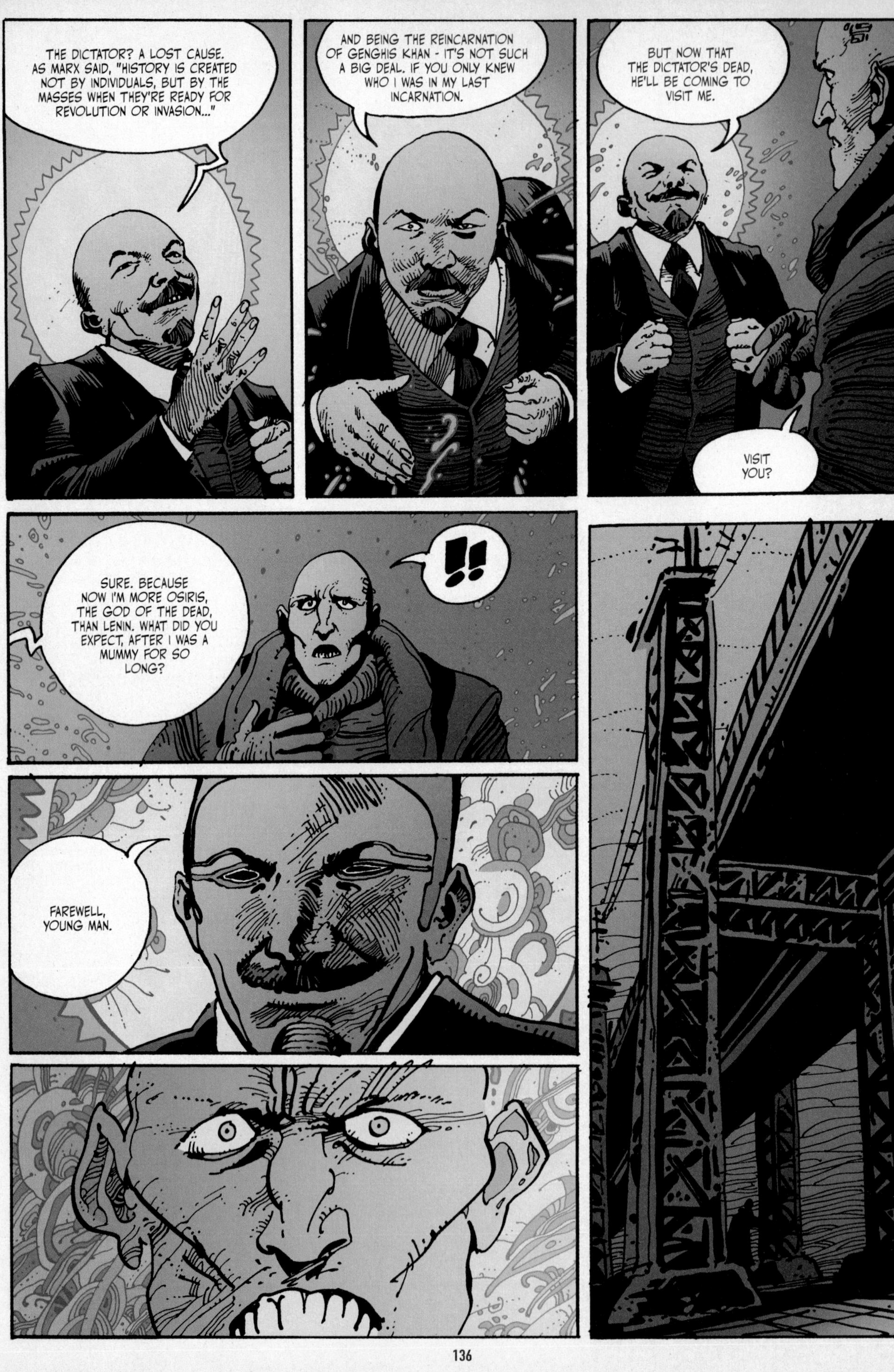
THE DICTATOR? A LOST CAUSE. AS MARX SAID, "HISTORY IS CREATED NOT BY INDIVIDUALS, BUT BY THE MASSES WHEN THEY'RE READY FOR REVOLUTION OR INVASION..."
AND BEING THE REINCARNATION OF GENGHIS KHAN - IT'S NOT SUCH A BIG DEAL. IF YOU ONLY KNEW WHO I WAS IN MY LAST INCARNATION.
BUT NOW THAT THE DICTATOR'S DEAD, HE'LL BE COMING TO VISIT ME.
VISIT YOU?
SURE. BECAUSE NOW I'M MORE OSIRIS, THE GOD OF THE DEAD, THAN LENIN. WHAT DID YOU EXPECT, AFTER I WAS A MUMMY FOR SO LONG?
!!
FAREWELL, YOUNG MAN.

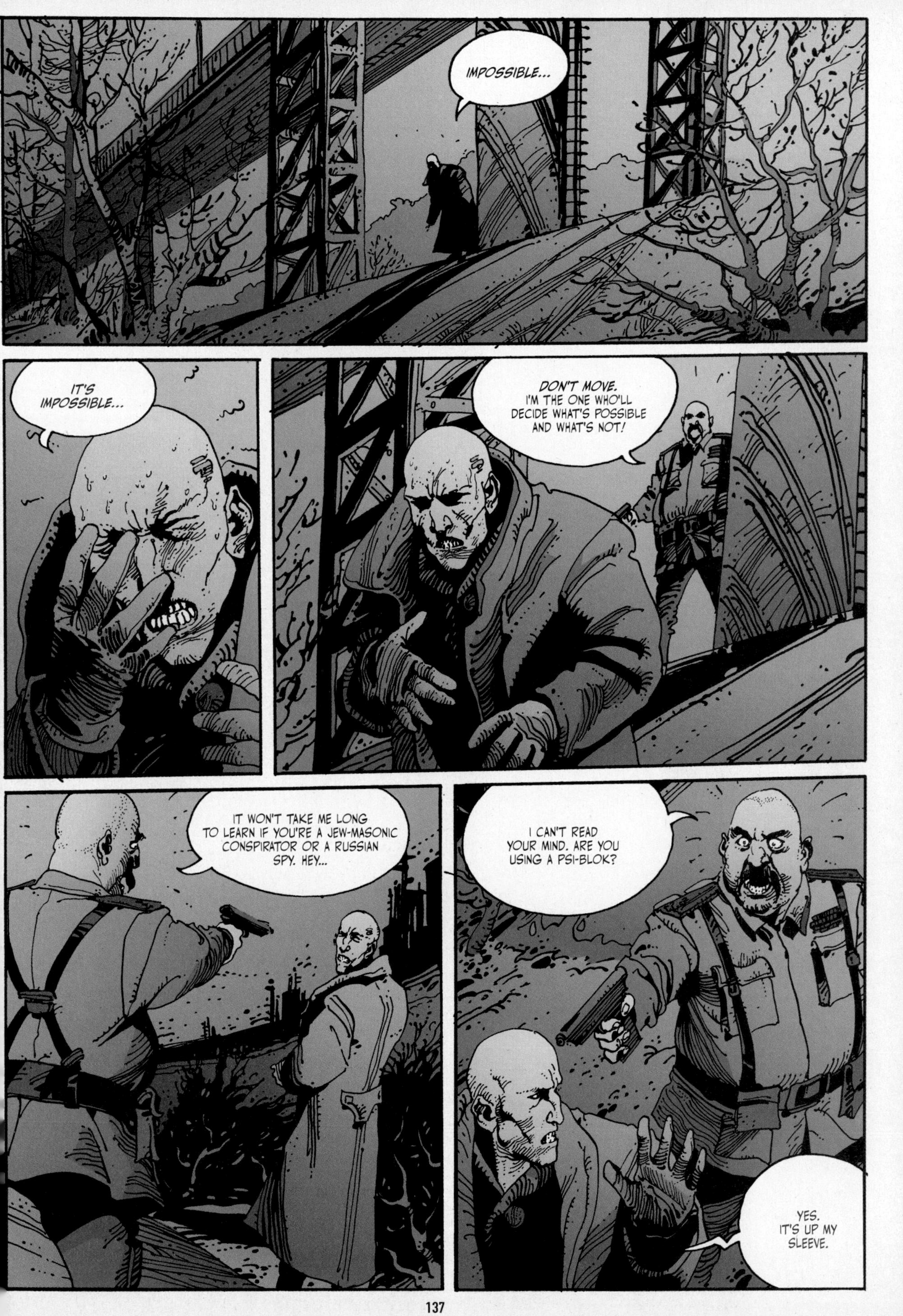
IMPOSSIBLE...
IT'S IMPOSSIBLE...
DON'T MOVE. I'M THE ONE WHO'LL DECIDE WHAT'S POSSIBLE AND WHAT'S NOT!
IT WON'T TAKE ME LONG TO LEARN IF YOU'RE A JEW-MASONIC CONSPIRATOR OR A RUSSIAN SPY. HEY...
I CAN'T READ YOUR MIND. ARE YOU USING A PSI-BLOK?
YES. IT'S UP MY SLEEVE.

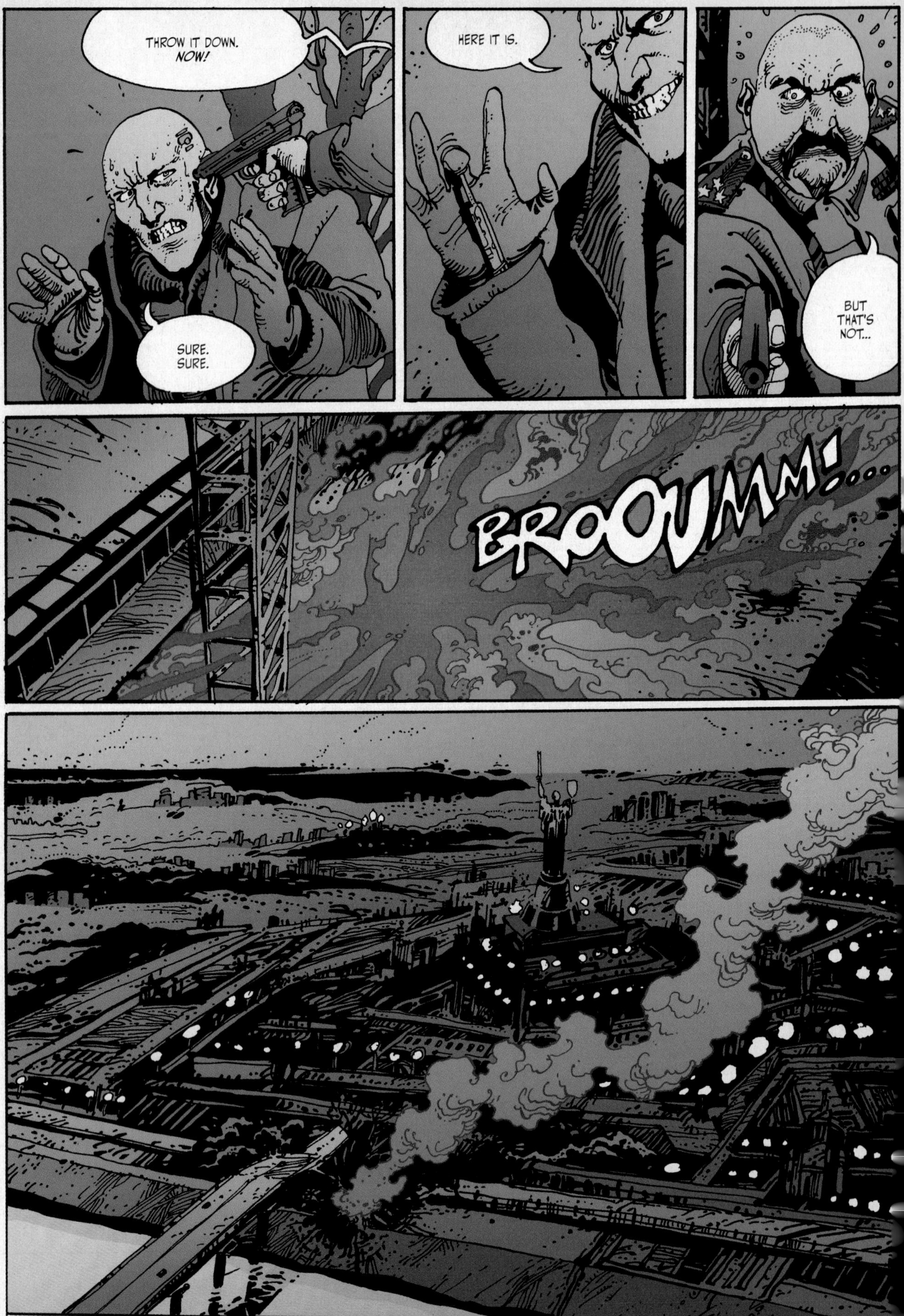
THROW IT DOWN. *NOW!*
SURE. SURE.
HERE IT IS.
BUT THAT'S NOT...
BROOUMM!...

KYZYL, TUVA REPUBLIC.

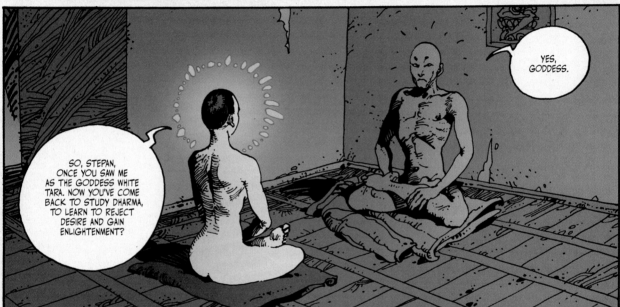

YES, GODDESS.

SO, STEPAN, ONCE YOU SAW ME AS THE GODDESS WHITE TARA. NOW YOU'VE COME BACK TO STUDY DHARMA, TO LEARN TO REJECT DESIRE AND GAIN ENLIGHTENMENT?

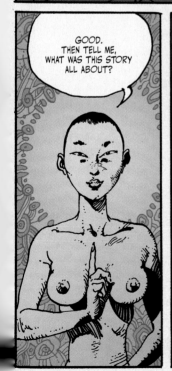

GOOD. THEN TELL ME, WHAT WAS THIS STORY ALL ABOUT?

HMMM. THAT EVERYTHING SHOULD BE IN BALANCE OR THE WORLD WILL FALL APART?

THINK HARDER.

MAYBE...HEH...TO SAVE YOUR SOUL YOU SHOULD FUCK THE GODDESS?

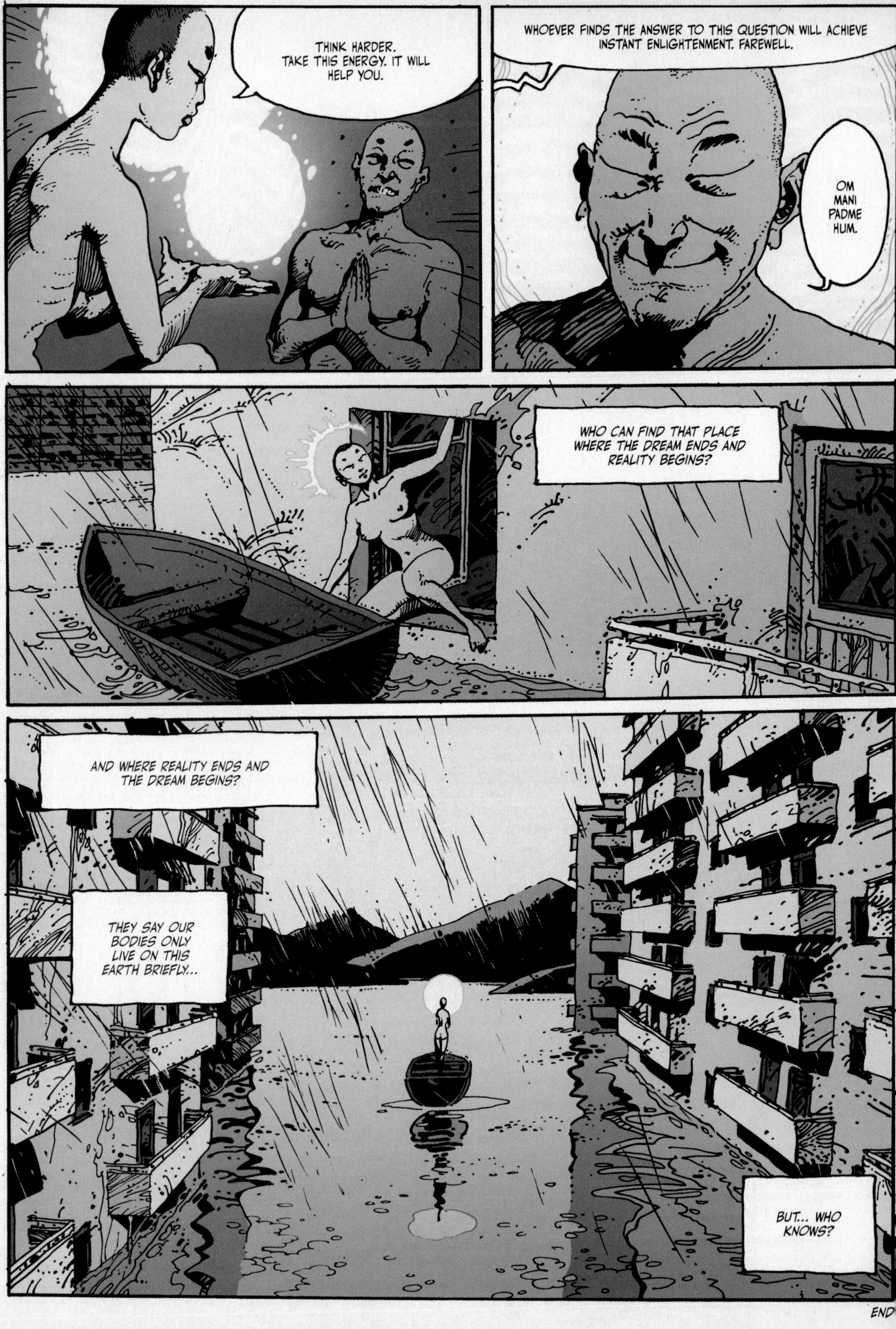
THINK HARDER.
TAKE THIS ENERGY. IT WILL HELP YOU.
WHOEVER FINDS THE ANSWER TO THIS QUESTION WILL ACHIEVE INSTANT ENLIGHTENMENT. FAREWELL.
OM MANI PADME HUM.
WHO CAN FIND THAT PLACE WHERE THE DREAM ENDS AND REALITY BEGINS?
AND WHERE REALITY ENDS AND THE DREAM BEGINS?
THEY SAY OUR BODIES ONLY LIVE ON THIS EARTH BRIEFLY...
BUT... WHO KNOWS?

END

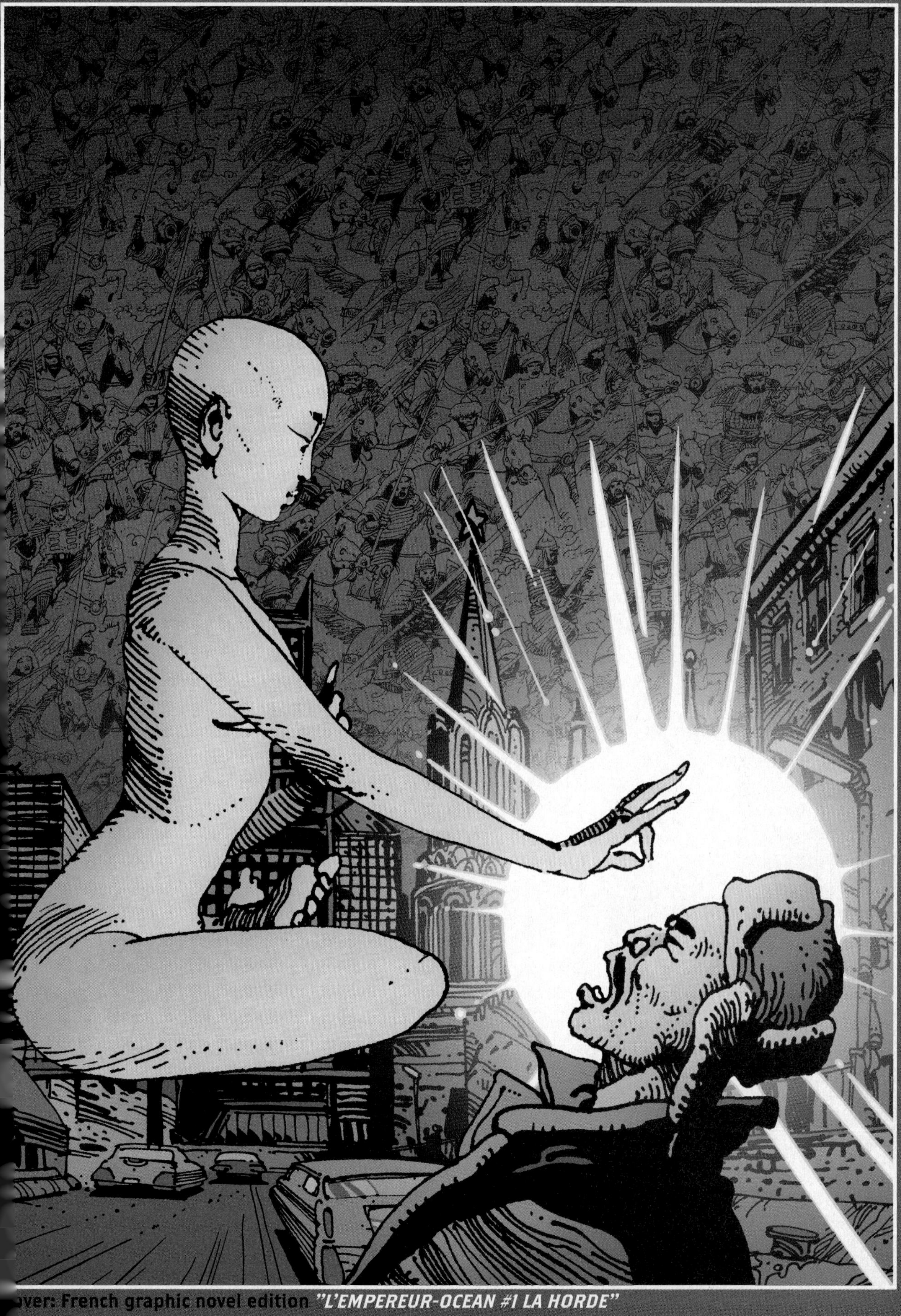

over: French graphic novel edition *"L'EMPEREUR-OCEAN #1 LA HORDE"*

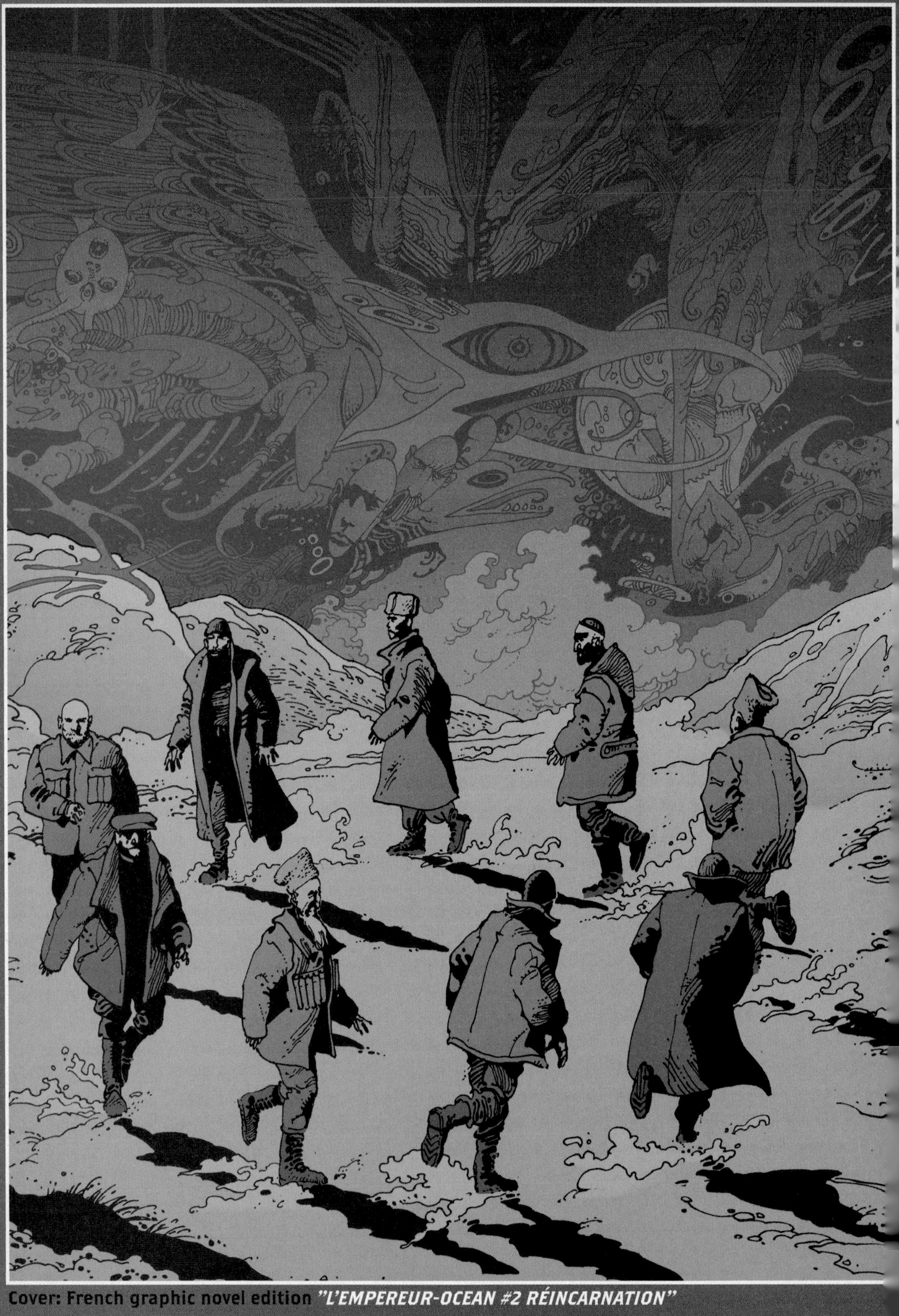

Cover: French graphic novel edition ***"L'EMPEREUR-OCEAN #2 RÉINCARNATION"***

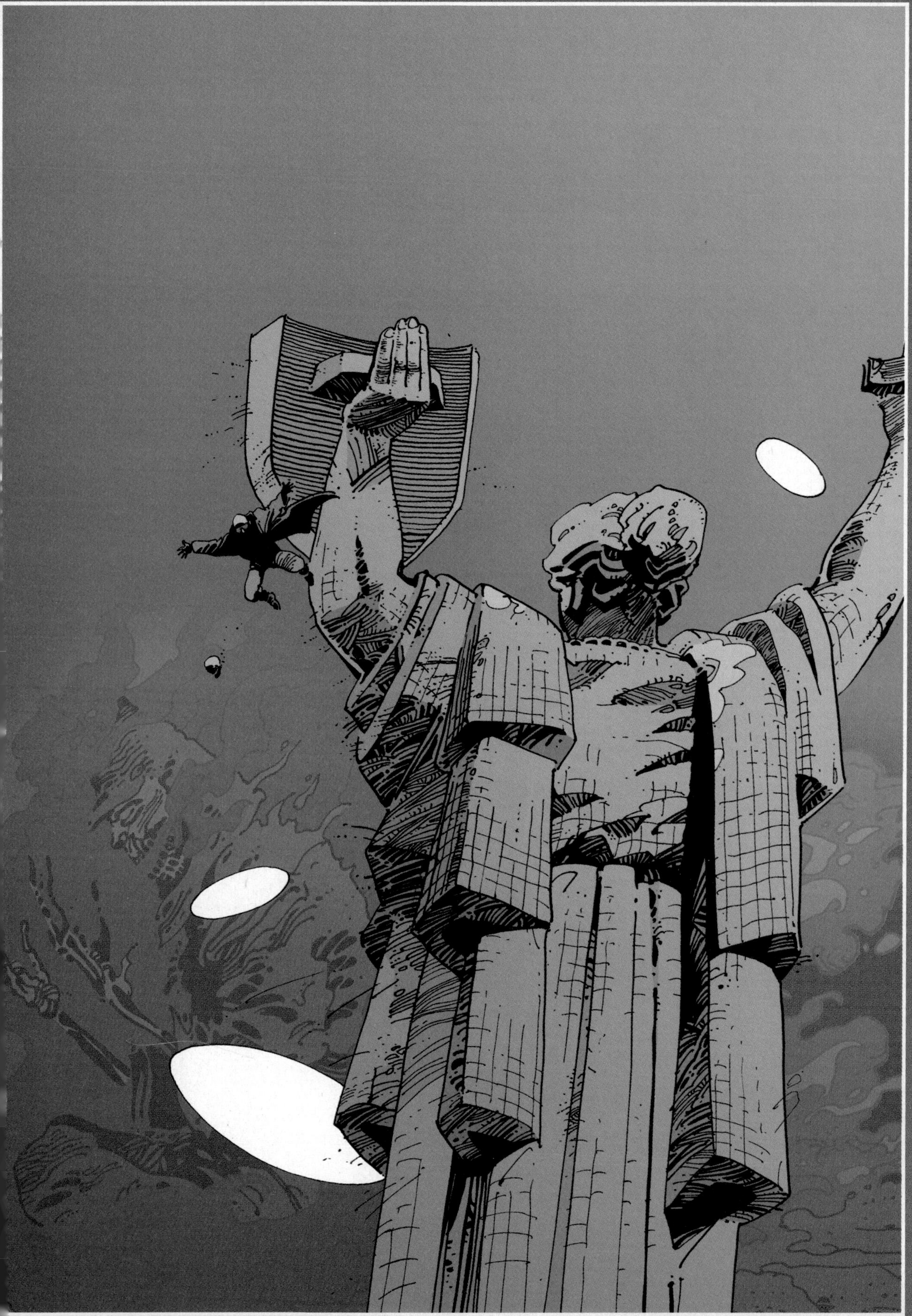

over: French graphic novel edition *"L'EMPEREUR-OCEAN #3 LE TOMBEAU"*

MORE BOOKS FROM HUMANOIDS / DC COMICS:

TOWNSCAPES

Softcover, 176 pages
Written by Pierre Christin and illustrated
by Enki Bilal with colors by Dan Brown

Part of the "Bilal Library," a collection of the works of one of the world's most talented graphic artists, Enki Bilal, whose best selling books are published in more than fifteen languages around the world.

In the TOWNSCAPES collection, Bilal collaborates with writer Pierre Christin to tell three tales of modern day towns caught up in fantastic circumstances. THE CRUISE OF LOST SOULS, SHIP OF STONE and THE TOWN THAT DIDN'T EXIST. Each story presents a timeless tale set in the trappings of the present, with a yearning towards the fables of yesterday.

"Bilal's drawings, as always, are impressively rendered..."
– *Publisher's Weekly* on *The Town That Didn't Exist*

THE TECHNOPRIESTS VOL. 1: INITIATION

Softcover, 160 pages
Written by Alexandro Jodorowsky
with art by Zoran Janjetov and Fred Beltran

The bastard son of a pirate, the young boy called Albino has only one goal, to become a member of the Technoguild and free the minds of every citizen in the galaxy, or die trying. And he just might!

"For those with the stomach for imagery that makes work by Tarantino and Peckinpah look like that of Disney and Don Bluth, Humanoids' series offer unique peeks into the mind of a mad genius at his unsettling peak."
--*The Austin Chronicle*

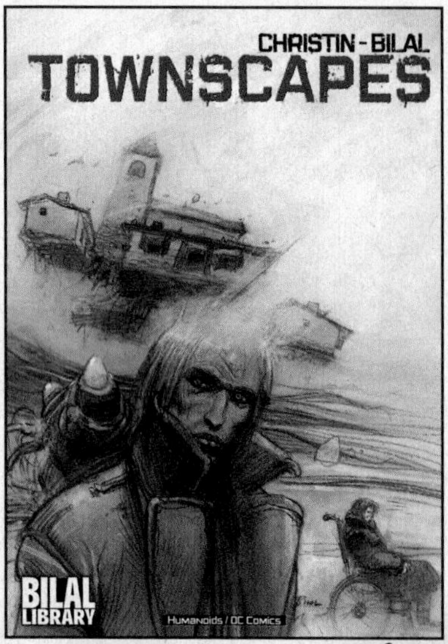
CHRISTIN - BILAL
TOWNSCAPES
BILAL LIBRARY
Humanoids / DC Comics

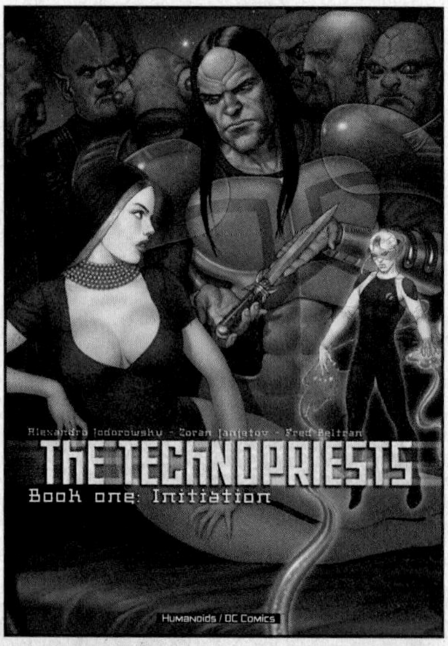
Alexandro Jodorowsky - Zoran Janjetov - Fred Beltran
THE TECHNOPRIESTS
Book one: Initiation
Humanoids / DC Comics

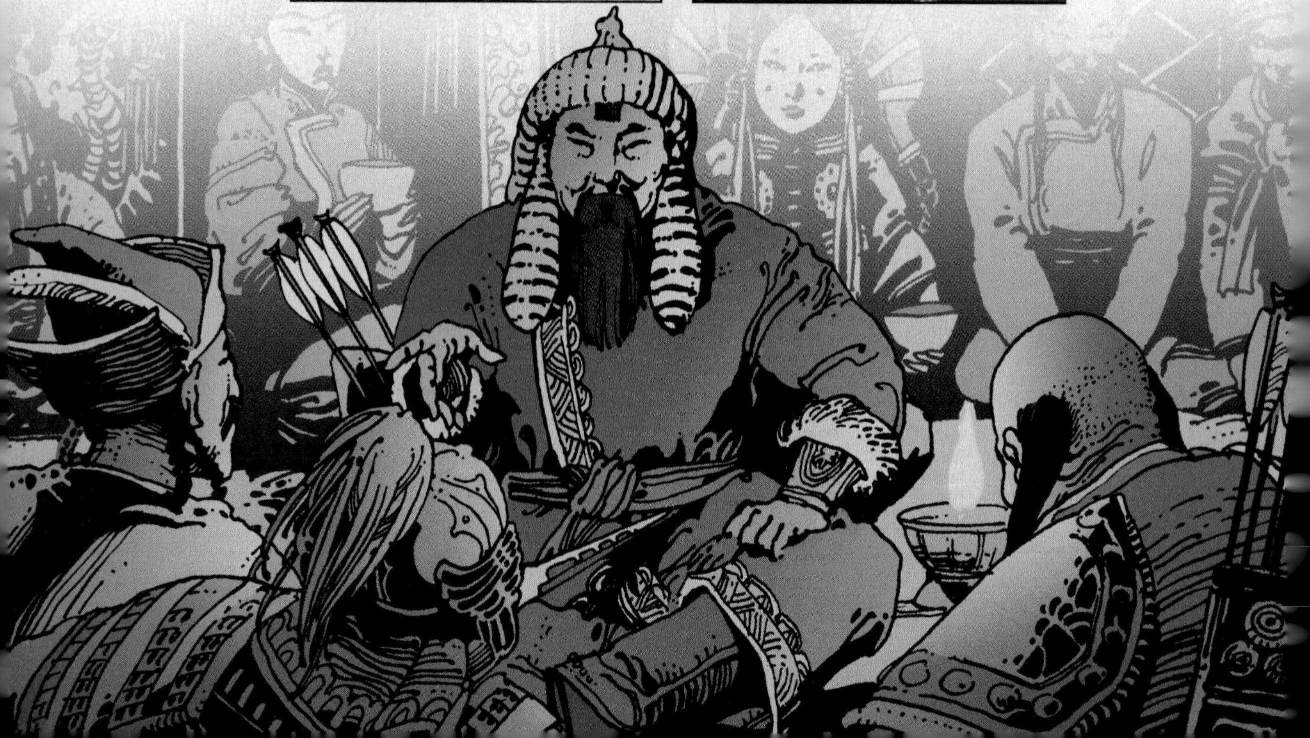